British South Asian Theatres
A Documented History

British South Asian companies have formed one of the most significant features of theatre throughout the world in the last thirty years. Despite their remarkable achievements, details of their activity have remained largely unrecorded. This book draws on archives and an extensive series of interviews to reverse that neglect of a vital element in the history of contemporary theatre.

The formation and development of many British Asian-led companies, including Tara Arts, Tamasha, Kali, Rasa and Rifco, are covered in detail. An accompanying DVD provides an album of items from theatre practitioners' private collections: historical documents, programmes, designs, photographs, and clips from recordings of rehearsals and productions.

The book is a companion volume to *Critical Essays on British South Asian Theatre* edited by Graham Ley and Sarah Dadswell, also published by University of Exeter Press.

Graham Ley is Professor of Drama and Theory at the University of Exeter. He has written and published widely, including *From Mimesis to Interculturalism: Readings of Theatrical Theory before and after 'Modernism'* (University of Exeter Press, 1999), *A Short Introduction to Ancient Greek Theater* (2nd revised edition University of Chicago Press, 2006) and *The Theatricality of Greek Tragedy* (University of Chicago Press, 2007).

Sarah Dadswell is a cultural historian specialising in performance and Honorary Research Fellow in the Department of Drama at the University of Exeter. She co-edited *Victory over the Sun: The World's First Futurist Opera* (University of Exeter Press, 2011) with Rosamund Bartlett.

Exeter Performance Studies

Series editors: Peter Thomson, Professor of Drama at the University of Exeter; Graham Ley, Professor of Drama and Theory at the University of Exeter; Steve Nicholson, Reader in Twentieth-Century Contemporary Theatre at the University of Sheffield.

From Mimesis to Interculturalism: Readings of Theatrical Theory Before and After 'Modernism'
Graham Ley (1999)

British Theatre and the Red Peril: The Portrayal of Communism 1917–1945
Steve Nicholson (1999)

On Actors and Acting
Peter Thomson (2000)

Grand-Guignol: The French Theatre of Horror
Richard J. Hand and Michael Wilson (2002)

The Censorship of British Drama 1900–1968: Volume One 1900–1932
Steve Nicholson (2003)

The Censorship of British Drama 1900–1968: Volume Two 1933–1952
Steve Nicholson (2005)

Freedom's Pioneer: John McGrath's Work in Theatre, Film and Television
edited by David Bradby and Susanna Capon (2005)

John McGrath: Plays for England
selected and introduced by Nadine Holdsworth (2005)

Theatre Workshop: Joan Littlewood and the Making of Modern British Theatre
Robert Leach (2006)

Making Theatre in Northern Ireland: Through and Beyond the Troubles
Tom Maguire (2006)

"In Comes I": Performance, Memory and Landscape
Mike Pearson (2006)

London's Grand Guignol and the Theatre of Horror
Richard J. Hand and Michael Wilson (2007)

Theatres of the Troubles: Theatre, Resistance and Liberation in Ireland
Bill McDonnell (2008)

The Censorship of British Drama, 1900–1968: Volume Three, The Fifties
Steve Nicholson (2011)

Victory over the Sun: The World's First Futurist Opera
edited by Rosamund Bartlett and Sarah Dadswell (2011)

Critical Essays on British South Asian Theatre
edited by Graham Ley and Sarah Dadswell (2012)

British South Asian Theatres

A Documented History

edited by

Graham Ley and Sarah Dadswell

UNIVERSITY
of
EXETER
PRESS

Cover image: Tara Arts flier for *This Story's Not for Telling* reproduced with kind permission.

First published in 2011 by
University of Exeter Press
Reed Hall, Streatham Drive
Exeter EX4 4QR
UK
www.exeterpress.co.uk

British Library Cataloguing in Publication Data
A catalogue record for this book is available from the British Library.

Paperback ISBN 978 0 85989 833 1
Hardback ISBN 978 0 85989 832 4

Typeset in Sabon, 10 on 12 by
Carnegie Book Production, Lancaster
Printed in Great Britain by
Short Run Press Ltd, Exeter

Contents

The accompanying DVD (see inside back cover) contains clips from recordings of rehearsals and productions, photographs, documents and programmes. The DVD is arranged in 14 sections corresponding to the contents list above. The book includes cross-references to the DVD numbered according to the items within each section on the DVD.

Acknowledgements

The work collated in this book and the wider AHRC project has been wholly reliant on the enthusiasm, cooperation and goodwill of those who constitute the book's subject: Asian theatre practitioners. Our thanks are extended to all of those who shared their memories and insights into this performance history and afforded us access to personal archives and contacts; to practitioners and administrators of all the theatre companies and initiatives recorded in this book; and to those who have participated in community arts. Consultation was taken at specific points with Rozina Visram, Naseem Khan, Susan Croft, Alan Tweedie, Reginald and Jamila Massey. Special thanks also to Rukhsana Ahmad, Dhirendra, Saeed and Jennifer Jaffrey, Ravi Jain, Harmage Singh Kalirai, Shelley King, Amrit Kotak, Peter Lane, Zohra Seghal, Madhav Sharma, Janet Steel, Harbhajan Virdi and Rita Wolf. The researchers were able to piece together a valuable and regionally specific picture of activity through a series of interviews which were conducted in Scotland, Manchester, Bradford, Southall and Tower Hamlets. We therefore thank those who facilitated these interviews: Champak Kumar Limbachia, Dominic Rai and Aziz Zeria, and the interviewees as follows: Scotland—Harminder Berman, Femi Foloronso, Faroque Khan, Farid Mallick, Gurmeet Mattu, Sheela Mukherjee and Lalitha Rajan; Manchester—Abdul Malik Ahad, Tajinder Singh Hayer, Jim Johnson, Basir Kazmi, Shamshad Khan, Anjum Malik, John McGrath, Shashi Mohandas, Sazzadur Rahman and Nigel Soni; Bradford—Arshad Aziz, Paramjit Bassra, Kantilal Champaneria, Mr and Mrs Chauhan, Dhiru and Illa Chevda, Javad Iqbal, Najam Javed, Mohammad Hafeez Johar, Raja Tariq Mehmood, Ludi Miah, Ronchodbhai Mistry, Harjab Singh Pooni, Mohammad Rafique, Gurpaul Sandhu, Mehmood Sultan, Yousef Sultan and Zaffer Tanweer; Southall—Kuljit and Mohinder Bhamra, Perminder Chadha, Darhsan Singh Giani, Rajinder Joshi, Ajit and Amarjit Khera, Satnam Lully, Kailash Puri, Sataya Saberwal, Rifat Shamim and Channi Singh; and Tower Hamlets—Shamsuddin Agha, Norman Goodman, Kazi Abdul Khan, Ashraf Mahmud Neswar and Ansar Ullah.

The editors would like to thank their families and friends for the support they have given during the research period: Graham Ley to Teresa and Kiri, Anthony and Donna Linda and Richard and Kate; and Sarah Dadswell to Dave, Kiran, and Tashi Miller, Sally Bayley, Rachel Coward, Susan Grant, Margaret Glover and Julia Slater.

Preface

The aims of this book are to recognise the achievements of the Asian-led companies that comprise British South Asian theatre and to provide a resource for the study of them. The collective term of the title is indicative of the heterogeneity of cultures, histories and, in many cases, journeys to the UK of the people who established the theatre companies and the British-based South Asian audiences who regularly attend the performances. The emphasis in this documented history is on those producing initiatives that in one way or another have embraced the idea of what is commonly referred to as 'Asian' theatre in Britain, made by those who found themselves identified historically and culturally as Asians, and who themselves acknowledged a South Asian heritage. Those Asian-led producing initiatives created new companies, which over the last thirty years have negotiated diverse relationships with funding bodies and with audiences, creating a widespread pattern of live theatrical activity that forms a significant part of the history of contemporary British theatre and culture.

British South Asian theatre companies have until recent years been denied the recognition in academic studies that would be proportionate to their achievements. Prominence has over time delivered a fair degree of journalistic attention at least to some companies; the work of Tara Arts, Tamasha and Kali, to take three examples, has been reviewed relatively widely in newspapers and other media. What has been lacking is the kind of academic study that would track the history of these initiatives in British South Asian theatre systematically, so allowing this performance phenomenon to assume its rightful place in considerations of national and international theatre history. Accordingly, what we are presenting here is a series of separate historical accounts of a number of producing initiatives and Asian-led theatre companies. Our guiding principle for inclusion has been to cover the formative period of British Asian theatre companies with a national profile, unless those companies were relatively short-lived, in which case we have been able to include the individual history in its entirety. They are not subjected to a binding narrative, but taken together they do amount to what in many respects may be described as 'a history'. The background to the emergence of these companies from the 1970s forwards is complex, stretching over many centuries, and it is traced in some detail in an essay by Colin Chambers in the companion volume to this documented history.[1]

The accounts that form the documented history make extensive use of original sources and, as such, they demonstrate the patterns of fullness or inadequacy that we found in the available sources. In collating the information we have relied heavily on oral histories gathered through interviews, notably for activities for which there is little documentary evidence.[2] The documentation that has been retained—formally archived or not—by companies and individual practitioners, varies greatly in extent and accessibility. Our accounts vary accordingly, offering and supporting different kinds of insight into the processes and policies of individual companies. Our strict remit has been to review live theatre, and we have had to pass by other Asian performance arts, including dance, music, poetry and storytelling. This limitation also applies to those British South Asian practitioners—directors, playwrights, actors and designers—who have pursued careers that were not primarily realised through the Asian-led companies. Just as it is impossible to compress complete histories of all British South Asian theatre companies into one volume, so it is to attempt a survey of the breadth and heterogeneity of all community initiatives involving drama. The opening section of this book on British-based South Asian language theatres is indicative of a complex social and cultural history of performers and the communities to which they belong.

The book is organised in sections in what is approximately a chronological sequence, although initiatives inevitably overlapped in time. It begins with a survey of theatrical activity by British groups and communities in the South Asian languages. The second section tracks the formative years of Tara Arts from its foundation in the 1970s as it explored a range of aesthetics and obtained its own dedicated building by the mid-1980s. As that group developed into a company in the 1980s, other groups came into being in London (Actors Unlimited, Hounslow Arts Cooperative, British Asian Theatre and Asian Cooperative Theatre) in a series of developments that was to a degree stimulated by the presence of Tara Arts. The subsequent sections provide the only documented history of these companies that exists to date.

---

1 Colin Chambers, 'Images on Stage: A Historical Survey of South Asians in British Theatre before 1975', in *Critical Essays on British South Asian Theatre*, eds Graham Ley and Sarah Dadswell (Exeter: University of Exeter Press, 2012); see in addition the earlier chapters of Colin Chambers, *Black and Asian Theatre in Britain: A History* (London: Routledge, 2011). For a specialist study of one aspect of this earlier history, see Sarah Dadswell, 'Jugglers, Fakires, and *Jaduwallahs*: Indian Magicians and the British Stage', *New Theatre Quarterly*, 23.1 (2007), pp. 3–24.

2 A copy of the interviews carried out by the research team in the course of the wider AHRC project, and on which these accounts draw, is housed in Exeter Digital Archives, University of Exeter.

At the end of the 1980s and the turn of the new decade, two companies led by women were established: Tamasha and Kali. The accounts of them here consider their foundation and development in the first period of their activity. During the 1990s two other initiatives were pursued which engaged with the Asian communities in very different ways: Man Mela, based in south London, and an innovative pattern of production at the Watermans Arts Centre, in Brentford, west London. Also in the 1990s, Asian communities in Oldham and Bradford saw the emergence of two community groups, respectively Peshkar and the Asian Theatre School, whose emphasis was on developing Asian participation in the arts and professionalism within the sector. The most recently formed companies that are represented here are Rifco (the Reduced Indian Film Company) and Rasa Theatre; while Rifco's history illustrates a pattern of professional development encouraged by earlier Asian-led theatre, Rasa's history points to alternative patterns of migration and modes of performance.

Our decision to attach a DVD of research materials to this history was relatively simple, since the number of illustrations a book may publish alongside text was far too small for our purposes. So the accompanying DVD provides an album of representative documents and illustrative images and clips from recordings, audio and audio-visual, organised in the same sections and in the same order as in this book.[3] These images also include documents, but on the same indicative and illustrative principles, since we could not aim to publish even all those documents to which the accounts allude.

The primary documentation presented in this book is complemented by the separately published collection *Critical Essays on British South Asian Theatre*, which addresses some of the materials and issues which are absent from this volume.[4] The publication of both books is the outcome of a research project funded by the Arts and Humanities Research Council and conducted (October 2004–March 2009) by a research team at the University of Exeter. The research team was led by Graham Ley, with Sarah Dadswell as the full-time Research Fellow, Chandrika Patel as the associated doctoral student, and Stephen Hodge, Jerri Daboo and Phillip Zarrilli, who was unfortunately unable to contribute to the project as he would have wished. Technical support in the Drama Department came from Jon Primrose, Chris Mearing and Peter Hulton, and administrative support from Nela Kapelan. The contributors are marked by their initials at the close of each section (Chandrika Patel—CP, Graham Ley—GL, Sarah Dadswell—SJD), while the DVD was constructed by Peter Hulton from the materials selected by

---

3 They are noted in the text in bold type and in brackets by a simple reference (**DVD 1, 2, 3 etc.**) to the numbered images in the corresponding section of the DVD itself.

4 See footnote 1 above.

the contributors. References to interviews conducted with practitioners by the contributors are given in full in a footnote in the first instance, and thereafter abbreviated in the main text.

When the Exeter research project started, it is fair to say that documentation in this field was extremely limited. Encouragingly, that has now changed, and there can be little doubt that the range of resources will continue to grow for those wishing to reflect upon and extend the research on this remarkable history. We should note here, in this connection, the specialist collections edited by Dimple Godiwala and by Geoffrey Davis and Anne Fuchs in particular; a study by Dominic Hingorani offers a critical introduction to selected plays and productions, supported by documentation, while Colin Chambers has combined Black and Asian in a theatre history.[5] Websites are subject to change, but some currently carry brief histories and good images of programmes and productions. SALIDAA (South Asian Diaspora and Literature Arts Archive) is the foremost such online resource, although the Theatre Collections of the Victoria and Albert Museum and other metropolitan archives (e.g. London Metropolitan Archive, Birmingham City Archive and 'Moving Here' archive), and increasingly individual British Asian theatre companies, provide online images and information related to theatre activity.

---

5 *Alternatives within the Mainstream: British Black and Asian Theatres*, ed. Dimple Godiwala (Newcastle: Cambridge Scholars Press, 2006); *Staging New Britain: Aspects of Black and South Asian British Theatre Practice*, eds Geoffrey Davis and Anne Fuchs (Brussels: Peter Lang, 2006); Dominic Hingorani, *British Asian Theatre: Dramaturgy, Process and Performance* (Basingstoke: Palgrave, 2010). For Chambers, see footnote 1 above.

Abbreviations

ACE	Arts Council of England
ACGB	Arts Council of Great Britain
ACT	Asian Cooperative Theatre
AWWC	Asian Women's Writing Collective
BATC	British Asian Theatre Company
BHASEL	Black HIV and Aids South East London
BP	British Petroleum
CRE	Commission for Racial Equality
FOH	front-of-house
GLAA	Greater London Arts Association
GLC	Greater London Council
HAC	Hounslow Arts Cooperative
HAVAC	Hounslow Asian Visual Artists Collective
ICA	Institute of Contemporary Arts
IPTA	Indo Pak Theatre Association
ITC	Independent Theatre Company
LAB	London Arts Board
Latte	Local Asian Theatre Touring Enterprise
LBGU	London Borough Grant Unit
MAAS	Minority Arts Advisory Service
MAC	Midlands Arts Centre
NAAY	National Association for Asian Youth
RADA	the Royal Academy of Dramatic Art
Rifco	the Reduced Indian Film Company
SBS	Southall Black Sisters
TIE	theatre in education
YMCA	Young Men's Christian Association
YPT	Young People's Theatre

Web addresses were correct as the book went to press, except where a date in parentheses indicates the last time a page was accessed.

1

British-based South Asian Language Theatres

> Asian language theatre is distinctive—the use of vernacular allows it to explore a character more rooted in the community, which Asian drama in English language often struggles with.[1]

As this section illustrates, theatre performed in South Asian languages has a rich and long-standing history in the UK. This section offers a survey of contemporary theatre activity by predominantly British-based South Asians in a number of South Asian languages, frequently referred to as 'language theatre'. The picture presented here focuses on language theatre activity in the London area, but should be seen as indicative of a broader national phenomenon.

Early reports: Naseem Khan and Dr Elizabeth-Clarke

In 1976 Naseem Khan produced a groundbreaking report commissioned by the Arts Council and Community Relations Commission, *The Arts that Britain Ignores: the Arts of Ethnic Minorities in Britain*.[2] This report was the first to record the activities of South Asian language theatres in the UK. It highlighted the artistic activities of diverse 'ethnic' communities in Britain and included chapters on three South Asian communities: Indians, Pakistanis and Bangladeshis. The report sought to expose the 'natures of cultures developed and supported by particular communities' and 'the extent to which the host-community is aware of, supports and offers facilities to ethnic minority cultural activities'.[3] In her chapter on Bangladeshis, Khan records a variety of initiatives including the drama activities of the Oriental Artists led by Shah Rehman, the Bengali Artistes Association and its production of *Tipoo Sultan*, and the drama classes at

---

1 'The Seerfr Project Business Plan 2005–2008', Zero Culture (August 2004), p. 1.

2 Naseem Khan, *The Arts Britain Ignores: The Arts of Ethnic Minorities in Britain* (London: Commission for Racial Equality, 1976).

3 Khan, *The Arts Britain Ignores*, p. 125.

Bethnal Green Adult Education Institute. These initiatives were all created for and run by the local Bangladeshi communities of East London and, according to Khan, were 'sensitive to both the needs and the character of the community'.[4]

Khan's chapter on Indians includes the activities of 'ad hoc' community theatre groups such as Birmingham's L and P Enterprises (run by Vasant Badiani) and the London-based Indian National Theatre (run by Amrit Kotak), set up in 1974. It reveals the initiatives of individuals who created Gujarati plays for the mainly East-African Gujarati audiences, 'offer[ing] live entertainment in an acceptably filmic traditional mould—in which none of the social proprieties are essentially offended'. The Derby-based Jugnu group created its own 'socio-drama' in playlets that explored contemporary social conflicts. This aspect suggests the shoots of what would now be called 'British Asian' themes, which featured alongside India-based themes.[5] Khan's report also gives an indication of the cost of the productions. These ranged from £300 for the Bengali Artistes Association's *Tipoo Sultan* (raised by the Bengali communities) to the £1,000 budget of Kotak's *Kadam Milake Chalo* (*Let's Pull Together*). This performance was produced by the Indian National Theatre and, having taken into account the cost of touring, made a loss of £80.[6] Khan also pointed out that the language theatre companies needed to associate with community groups in order to attract British Asian audiences to plays. The report concluded that these uncategorised 'ethnic' theatres were 'hole and corner affairs', unsupported owing to a 'lack of effective contact between new-British and native-British'. In addition, they did not always have access to the spaces used by 'white' funded theatre companies.[7]

The Minority Arts Advisory Service (MAAS) was a body set up in the wake of Khan's report. It produced a monthly supplement, *Echo—Living Arts in Ethnic Communities*, that reviewed the activities of South Asian language theatres.[8] In 1982 the MAAS compiled a register of theatre-practising communities, which included Gujaratis, Bengalis, Marathis, Muslims, Sikhs, Tamils and Bangladeshis. The theatre activity operated under various community-led organisations and reflected their respective South Asian demographics. Thus, Slough Asian Arts, established in 1980 and producing work in Punjabi, was located in a predominantly Sikh area; the Belgrave Drama Society, which produced work in Gujarati, was based in Leicester with a large Gujarati-speaking community and, according to

---

4 Khan, *The Arts Britain Ignores*, p. 19.

5 Khan, *The Arts Britain Ignores*, p. 71.

6 Khan, *The Arts Britain Ignores*, pp. 21 and 70 respectively.

7 Khan, *The Arts Britain Ignores*, pp. 125–27.

8 *Echo* supplements (1976–1996) are archived in the Minority Arts Archive at the University of Warwick's Central Campus library and catalogued as MAAS/4/1.

Echo, in 1982 was active in both stage and local-radio plays. The register also included the London Kalai Kuzhu (London Arts Group), based in Kent and established in 1979, which had produced four Tamil plays by 1982. In 1978 *Echo* had reviewed two Marathi plays, *Sundar Me Honar* (*I Will Become Beautiful*) and *When Raigarh Wakes*, by the North London-based organisation Maharashtra Mandal (group), established in 1932.[9] Founded in 1969, the Asian Artistes Association's first Urdu play *Baat Ek Raat Ki* (*It Happened One Night*), produced by the director S.I. Agha, was shown at the Waltham Forest Centre in June 1980.[10] A dance drama, *Anarkali*, was produced by the same company and shown at the Commonwealth Institute in March.[11] Overall, the collected reviews of South Asian language productions in *Echo* supplements suggest a thriving and diverse South Asian arts scene in the period from the late 1970s to the 1990s.

In 1990 the Arts Council published a report they had commissioned from Dr B. Elizabeth-Clarke, *Black Theatre in England*.[12] It revealed the need for funding in order that organisations which had operated during the 1980s, such as the Hounslow Arts Cooperative (HAC) and Asian Cooperative Theatre (ACT), could survive and develop.[13] To support this argument, Elizabeth-Clarke's detailed report listed the artistic portfolios, strengths and weaknesses, and financial needs of individual Asian organisations, concluding with a list of recommendations. Although both Elizabeth-Clarke's and Khan's reports highlighted the valuable artistic contribution of South Asians to British society and the lack of funding opportunities available to them, neither functioned as a catalyst for funding opportunities for South Asian language theatre. The emergence of the first English-language South Asian theatre company in 1977, Tara Arts, marked a new era unforeseen in Khan's report. Not wishing to be associated with any one specific South Asian community or South Asian language, Tara chose to perform in English, thereby addressing the wider British public. While this move revealed the desire to explore the Asian experience in English present in strands of earlier South Asian artistic activities, it also shifted attention away from the marginalised and unfunded South Asian language theatre companies and in so doing, reinforced their predominantly 'ignored' status. But despite the increasing flow of central funds to the activities of other professional British Asian theatre companies, the South Asian language theatres have survived and continued to function in non-professional structures.

---

[9] *Echo*, no. 20 (November 1978) and no. 12 (March 1978).

[10] *Echo*, no. 80 (July 1980).

[11] *Echo*, no. 13 (April 1978).

[12] B. Elizabeth-Clarke, *Black Theatre in England* (Arts Council, 1990). The report is housed in the MAAS Archive, University of Warwick.

[13] See the later sections in this book on these companies.

Community aesthetic

The element of community participation in terms of volunteers and amateurs is a significant characteristic of South Asian language theatres. In Khan's report, the case studies of Amrit Kotak's Gujarati play *Kadam Milake Chalo* (*Let's Pull Together*—Nehru's old slogan), involving amateur performers who came from different parts of London and rehearsed at weekends, continues to ring true for many existing South Asian language companies.[14] For example, Amiya Bhattacharjee, the club secretary of The Dramatists Club in Hayes, observed that '[t]here are more actors than spectators willing to participate in Bengali productions'. The club, which has been running for over three decades to promote Bengali culture, regularly produces Bengali drama performed by amateur Bengali enthusiasts for the greater part.[15] By contrast, in April 2005, at the rehearsal of the Gujarati play *Sambandho Ni Pele Paar* (*Beyond Relationships*), a family saga about widowhood written by director-in residence Tushar Trivedi, at the Bharatiya Vidya Bhavan in London the process was less interactive and more director-driven.[16] Trivedi had a clear idea of how he wanted his words delivered, and the amateur actors observed his gestures and then 'acted' them in their dialogues. This rehearsal practice is not uncommon in the touring drama companies from India, which are very popular with South Asian audiences in Britain.

Professional touring dramas

Productions by South Asian language theatres are usually marketed by fliers distributed through a community contact, word of mouth or a vernacular newspaper. Alongside the community-based productions, the fliers for professional touring dramas can also be found. These are often sponsored by private individuals or UK-based community-based organisations that take responsibility for the marketing and touring. These imported productions can attract large audiences, particularly if they contain 'Bollywood' stars, examples of whom here would be Shabana Azmi and Farooq Sheikh in *Tumhari Amrita* (*Your Amrita*, based on Guerney's *Love Letters*), directed by Feroz Khan (1994), and Poonam Dhilon and Sooraj Thaper in *The Perfect Husband*, staged at Watermans and Fairfield Hall (2005) in Croydon respectively (**DVD 1–2**). The Tagoreans form 'an organisation that believes in Rabindranath Tagore's philosophy of life and draws its inspiration from his creativity in various fields'. In addition to its British-based activities,

---

14 Khan, *The Arts Britain Ignores*, p. 70.

15 Telephone conversation between Amiya Bhattacharjee and Chandrika Patel, 26 June 2005.

16 I attended the rehearsal of the Gujarati play *Sambandho Ni Pele Paar* on 9 April 2005 and spoke to the director Tushar Trivedi afterwards about the play.

The Tagoreans also invites touring dramas from India that are popular with Bengali communities in the UK.[17] Naseem Khan refers to such touring productions as 'Indian imports' of a 'drawing room comedy' genre that tend to reach conclusions 'accommodating to existing values'.[18] In language-based newspapers such as *Gujarat Samachar*, one of the Gujarati weeklies published in Britain, one can also see advertisements for the 'imported' Gujarati dramas from India, which are extremely popular with Gujarati communities (DVD 3).

The Bharatiya Vidya Bhavan: imported versus local

What emerges from Khan's report and the reviews in *Echo* is a strong and continuing presence of talented UK-based South Asian artists who are responsible for the creation of South Asian language theatres. In that context, the idea of an 'imported' director-in-residence at an 'Indian' cultural institute such as the Bharatiya Vidya Bhavan in West Kensington, employed on a fixed contract from India to write and produce Gujarati plays for the British Asian audiences, might seem contentious, raising many issues about the 'cultural' identity of South Asian language theatres. Since its humble beginnings above a shop in 1972 the Bhavan describes itself as 'ha[ving] performed the role of sponsoring, research, dissemination, appreciation and patronage of Gujarati drama' in the UK. Its first Gujarati play *Ame Barfna Pankhi* (*We Are Birds of Ice*) was performed at the Commonwealth Institute in 1978. Although the Bhavan is also used for staging Bengali dramas and other Indian classical music and dance activities, its almost exclusive focus on Gujarati plays is striking, having produced over thirty-five, the 'majority of which [have] toured extensively throughout the UK and Europe'.[19] There is a remit to produce two plays a year but, according to Trivedi, the resident director (2003–2006), that does not always happen [Trivedi 2005]. In compliance with the 'cultural objectives' of the Bhavan, the script is subject to the approval of the drama committee, some members of which also participate in the productions. Most of the plays produced at the Bhavan are traditional stories set in India, revolving around extended families with a certain amount of comedy. The sets for the plays are sometimes imported from India. Trivedi talked of a set portraying a Kathiawadi village (Kathiawad is a region of Gujarat) imported from India that went down well with the Gujarati-speaking audience, who loved to see such 'authentic' scenery reproduced in the UK context. Although audience members have

---

[17] http://www.tagoreans.org.uk.

[18] Naseem Khan, 'The Public-going Theatre Community and Ethnic Theatre', in *Dreams and Deconstructions: Alternative Theatre in Britain*, ed. S. Craig (London: Amber Lane Press, 1980), p. 74.

[19] http://www.bhavan.net.

tended to be mostly first-generation South Asians, over the last three decades the Bhavan has sustained a loyal Gujarati-speaking audience, with the second generation also participating.

The Bhavan also caters to requests from particular South Asian communities to perform plays in their chosen venues for a variety of purposes. Trivedi mentioned his production of *Chandrabala*, which was performed for the Jain community in Colchester. The play was well received, although some of the audience had never seen a Gujarati play before [Trivedi 2005]. One of Trivedi's Gujarati plays *Mane Parnavo Ek Chokari* (*Marry Me a Girl*) was shown at the Watermans Arts Centre in Brentford, London, as part of the celebrations for a wedding in 2004. The activity at the Bhavan provides a striking example of the nurturing of an 'imported' identity more widely associated with the South Asian language theatres in the late 1970s and 1980s, in which the form acquires a 'cultural' identity through its association with a cultural institute such as the Bhavan. In community settings it is not unusual to see a mention of a dinner combined with the 'show' (play), with the additional purpose of marketing the show to other community groups such as the Lions Club, the Patel Samaj and the Brahmin Society.[20] The community groups who purchase these shows may have other agendas, such as fund raising, which are then carried out as part of the 'show'. Theatre therefore becomes a catalyst to fundraising and the promotion of social interaction, in addition to its function as entertainment. Language-based dramas are frequently incorporated into the festival celebrations such as Diwali and Onam, and often include children and adults from a particular South Asian community. Thus, in community, cultural and social settings, South Asian language theatres can play a variety of roles. Firstly, they contribute towards nurturing and maintaining caste-/religion-based linguistic identities through the use of South Asian languages and social themes. Secondly, they function as a catalyst bringing together particular social groups to promote social interaction and raise funds for their respective organisations. Finally, they may be regarded as instruments for maintaining an imaginary relationship with one's 'homeland', an outcome that 'imported' dramas can often create through the sounds of languages and materiality.

---

20 Kiran Purohit, a writer/actor/director based in the UK who has also worked at the Bhavan, mentioned these groups in our conversation on 31 October 2005. Such community groups, which can be caste-/language-based, continue to thrive in the UK, providing a social framework for the diverse South Asian communities through the organisation of a variety of events.

British Asian spaces: the Watermans Arts Centre and sites of contemporary language theatre

By contrast, in the mid 1990s the initiatives taken by Hardial Rai at Watermans Arts Centre aimed to focus on exploring British Asian themes rather than Indian-based themes. Rai wished to explore these themes by using the existing South Asian vernacular structure, rather than by turning to the 'western-style' of theatre-making established in the 1980s by British Asian theatre companies such as Tara Arts and HAC. His goal was to make the 'Asian Vernacular' theatre visible to the wider audience by taking it out of ill-equipped venues into professional theatre spaces, thereby bringing it into the infrastructure of English-language British Asian theatre. As part of this initiative, the West London-based KalaMunch and Shivam Theatre companies, working in Punjabi, Gujarati and Hindi, were launched and their members offered the possibility of professional development.[21]

Watermans continues to provide a mainstream platform for South Asian language theatres in Gujarati, Hindi and Punjabi, some of which are mentioned here in language order. For example, in 2005, the Slough-based Jayjayvanti Theatre Company staged Punjabi adaptations of Gujarati plays written by the late Jayant Bhatt, which included *Beta Mast Kalander* (*Vagabond Son*), about an immigrant family from East Africa, and *Jawai Raja: A Suitable Suitor*, a play 'set in futuristic India [2050] that lambast[ed] arranged marriages and dowry system in India and among the South Asians across the diaspora'.[22] (DVD 4–5). Founded in 1991 by the late writer and producer Jayant Bhatt and Hina Baxi, 'Jayjayvanti has staged over four hundred shows in a repertoire of eleven plays at venues in UK, USA, Canada and Portugal.'[23] Snehlata Verma is the artistic director of United Theatre, established in 2004; her Punjabi play *Ik Chader Malli Si*, based on a literary classic by the late Rajinder Singh, was staged in 2006.[24] The husband-and-wife team Gurdip Kaur Chaudhry and Jitender Singh marked the launch of their Matribhoomi Theatre Company in January 2007 with their inaugural production of *Paiso Ki Hera Pheri* (*Everyone's after the Money*), a 'Bollywood style comedy' in Punjabi that returned for more performances in June 2007 and October 2007.[25] In 2008, the company's other Punjabi plays include *Patiala Junction*, 'a comedy with Punjabi songs and Bhangra dances', and *Pendu Peo London Wich*, set in London, about a Punjabi man who comes to live in London.[26]

---

21 See the section on Watermans in this book.
22 http://www.the-drum.org.uk/event/beta-mast-kalandar.
23 http://www.middxpremier.com/entertainment/theatre/jawai_raja.htm [accessed 21 January 2009].
24 http://www.redhotcurry.com/entertainment/theatre/badde_aadmi.htm.
25 http://www.redhotcurry.com/entertainment/theatre/paison.htm.
26 www.the-drum.org.uk/event/pendu-peo-london-wich.

The Bhavan remains a key venue for current South Asian language theatre activity and continues to produce Gujarati plays.[27] In recent times, the Bengali communities remain committed to producing dramas with companies such as The Mukush (Mask) in Essex, The Bengali Artistic Group in London and the Dramatists in Hayes [Bhattacharjee 2005]. The Dramatists have been producing Bengali dramas since their first play *Noti Binodini*, which was performed at the Manning Hall and the Commonwealth Institute in 1982, and restaged twelve years later at the Intimate Theatre in 1994.[28] Like the Gujaratis and the Bengalis, the Punjabi communities also remain active, with Southall-based groups such as The Punjabi Theatre Academy (UK), established for over a decade, producing plays such as *Suraj Dha Grahain* (*Eclipse of the Sun*), *Soni Mehiwal* (a traditional Punjabi love story), *Bebe Cilayet Wich* (*Mother-in-Law in London*), *Shaheed* (*Martyr*), *Udham Singh, Sirhand Di Dewar* (a Sikh historic drama set in AD 1710), *Massacre 1919: Jallianwala Bagh to Caxton Hall*, *Puwara Bottle Da* (*Beat the Bottle*), *Lohri Night* (*Traditional Punjabi Night*), *Phansi-Toun-Phelan* (*Before the Hanging*), *Nickkian Zindah-Wadha Sakha* (a Sikh historic drama set in AD 1703) and *Lion of Punjab, Maharajah Ranjit Singh*, the last staged at Watermans in July 2006.[29]

IPTA, the Indo Pak Theatre Association, established by Rifat Shamim in 1978, was previously called the International People's Theatre Association, before changing its name in 1981.[30] IPTA's contemporary productions include *Shishe Ke Khilone* (*Toys of Glass*) in 2006, based on Tennessee William's *The Glass Menagerie*, and *Darwaza Khula Hai* (*The Door Is Open*), also in 2006, which was set in a council flat in North London and explored sexuality within the Asian community.[31] According to its publicity flier, IPTA was:

> affiliated to the Indian People's Theatre Association—an arts movement founded in 1943 by progressive writers, playwrights and film-makers to explore contemporary social issues through arts.

[27] According to the current director of the Bhavan, Dr Nanadakumara, from 2006 the Bhavan has ceased to employ a director-in-resident from India. Telephone conversation between Dr Nanadakumara and Chandrika Patel, 20 January 2009.

[28] This information was found on the back of the programme of the Bengali play *Aami Montree Habo* (*I Want to Become MLA*—MLA is similar to MP, a Member of Parliament) by Dramatists, staged at the Intimate Theatre in North London on 26 June 2005.

[29] The titles of all these productions were listed in a brochure at the fund-raising event for the production of *Lion of Punjab* organised by Punjabi Theatre Academy, which took place in Southall on 13 March 2005.

[30] Contact details are available at http://www.brent.gov.uk/cdirectory.nsf/pages/lbb-1?opendocument&id=CG-557.

[31] http://www.redhotcurry.com/entertainment/theatre/kanyadaan.htm.

> Since its inception, IPTA has produced over twenty ground breaking plays, reflecting the changing nature of the UK's Asian population ... [and] has translated and transposed modern western classics for Asian audiences by well-known playwrights, including Arthur Miller, Samuel Beckett and John Osborne.[32]

IPTA's Gujarati plays include *Toonj Mari Ganga, Toonj Mari Kaashi* (*You Are My Ganga, You Are My Kaashi*, a title that reflects the river *Ganga* and the place of pilgrimage *Kaashi*, both holy landmarks for the Hindus), a comedy set in India about the generation gap and changing values within Asian community, in 2005; and *Kanyadaan* (the term used to describe the moment when a girl is given away at a wedding), set against the background of the caste system with a plot about a daughter marrying an 'unsuitable' boy, staged in 2008.[33]

Pervaiz Alam's London-based Desi Canvas's Hindi/Urdu plays include *Safar* (*The Journey*), staged in London, Leicester, Birmingham, Edinburgh's Fringe Festival and the Royal Opera House in the West End in 2002, and, in 2005, *Zahoor ka Hotal* (*Zahoor's Hotel*), set in India—both parts of his Nostalgia trilogy.[34] United Theatre's Hindi comedy *Baade Aadmi* (*Big People*), a satire on high society with a cast of twelve including Bollywood and television personalities, was staged in 2006.[35] In 2007 Krishan Tandon's Sakshi Theatre Co presented a Hindi play, *Talaash* (*The Mirage*), a family drama set in London and based on the theme of marriage for convenience. In addition, language theatre is also created in the lesser-known South Asian languages, such as Sindhi (language of the Sindh region of Pakistan) and Pothwari (spoken in Northern Pakistan), with the purpose of promoting their distinct language-based identities. In 2005 an English/Sindhi play, *A Very Sindhi Wedding*, was sold out at the Bharatiya Vidya Bhavan.[36] In 2008, a Pothwari play, *Mein Ve Khuker Kha Saan*, was staged at The Drum in Birmingham, directed and produced by Tahir Chaudhry.[37]

New directions: the future of British-based South Asian language theatre?

A closer analysis of the Gujarati play *Lottery, Lottery* will provide an interesting example of a contemporary production that explored the British Gujarati community's preoccupation with material wealth (**DVD 6**).

---

32 This extract is taken from the publicity flier of *Shishe Ke Khilone*, a Hindi/Urdu play, staged at Watermans, 28–31 July 2005.

33 http://www.redhotcurry.com/entertainment/theatre/kanyadaan.htm.

34 http://www.doollee.com/PlaywrightsA/alam-pervaiz.html.

35 http://www.redhotcurry.com/entertainment/theatre/badde_aadmi.htm.

36 Tamasha's production *House of the Sun* featured the Sindhi community.

37 A production based on the tele-drama directed by Tahir Choudhury.

Lottery, Lottery came about as part of the Hardial Rai's Zeroculture initiative to professionalise language-based South Asian theatres in UK. Produced by the Shivam Theatre, the play was first staged in Gujarati at the Arts Depot, London, in 2005, and was then adapted in both English and Gujarati and staged at the Lyric Theatre, Hammersmith, in 2006. The production that I shall be exploring, performed at the Bharatiya Vidya Bhavan in November 2006, was mainly in Gujarati and partly in Hindi and English.[38]

Kiran Purohit, the actor/writer/director of the play, introduced *Lottery Lottery* live on that occasion as follows: 'It is a new experiment. Away from Bollywood, away from Hollywood, no set, no *bhapko* (glamour or pomp). I have tried to present your favourite sweets on a simple plate.' The aroma of a Gujarati *jaman* (meal/dinner) greeted the audience as they entered the foyer of Bhavan on a cold winter's evening. In his introduction Purohit stressed the importance of supporting such a home-based production written about the issues concerning the British Gujarati communities, which had to compete with the more popular 'imported' comedy dramas from India. He announced this to be an 'interactive play', suggesting that it invited an active participation and response to the actors from the audience. Unlike the elaborate set often associated with 'traditional' South Asian language theatres, *Lottery, Lottery* opened with a minimalist set containing a small three- tiered 'home-made' temple, a single-seater sofa and a table-chair with a laptop. The play is about a *Vania* family,[39] which consists of Atisukh (meaning *very happy*), Santosh (*contentment*), and their two children Chaiya and Chabil, who dream of being rich and successful. The play opens with a *puja* (offering to God) ritual offered by Santosh, who is traditionally dressed in a Gujarati-style cotton sari. Each cast member makes a wish: Santosh wants to win the lottery, Chaiya wants to become a 'Bollywood' star and Chabil wants to become a successful businessman, while the neighbour, Mrs Jani, wishes that the in-laws, who are planning a visit from India, are not granted a visa. The 'Bollywood' song 'Paisa he Kaisa' ('See, This Is How Money Is') playing in the background sets the relevant tone.

In the second act of *Lottery Lottery*, the transformation of Santosh to Sue after the lottery win is comically portrayed (DVD 7). The image of Santosh sitting on a floor preparing vegetables for an evening meal portrayed a strong sense of Gujarati life at home. The appearance of *Prabhu* (the Hindu god Vishnu) as a character, to the sound of 'Bollywood' song *Kiska Hai Intezar Mai Hu Na* (*Who Are You Waiting for while I Am Here?*), adds a contemporary tone to the 'traditional' imagery of a Hindu god (clad in *Pitamber* (saffron) *dhoti* and glittering *Mughat* (crown)), borrowed

---

38 *Lottery Lottery*, Bharatiya Vidya Bhavan, 25 November 2006.

39 *Vania* is a sub-caste.

directly from the popular Indian TV serial *Mahabharata*. The musicality of the 'Bollywood' song taken from *Main Hoo Na*, the film produced by and starring Shahrukh Khan, inadvertently highlights the God-like status of the 'Bollywood' star Khan, whose song is played as an anthem to the 'real' god. Despite the promise of 'No Bollywood' made by Purohit at the start of the play, the narrative of *Lottery Lottery* is infused with 'Bollywood' sensibilities of Hindi songs and glamour.

Prabhu's presence, with his sermon-like speech, dominates the second act of the play. He discusses global as well as Gujarati community issues with Atisukh, including *moh* (attachment) for money, status and the virtues of humanity (DVD 8). There are some amusing moments when Santosh recites lyrics from a *garba*[40] mixed with British references: '*Hu To Lucky Dip Bhari Bhari Ne Thaki, Oh Kanuda Tara ...*' ('Oh Krishna, I am so tired of filling in Lucky Dips'). The cast's Gujarati names are also linked to global references. For example, Chabil's name is linked to Bill (Clinton) and the full name Chabildas to *Häagen Dazs*. What drives the play is this kind of dialogue, in which the Gujarati language is lyrically interwoven with Hindi and English global words and references. The play, with its multi-lingual character, was well-received by the Bhavan audience on the night.

Purohit's hybrid Gujarati dialogues, containing British, global and 'home' references portraying the British Asian experience, may be contrasted with the 'imported' production of *Paiso Maro Parmeswar* (*Money Is My God*). This Gujarati play, set in India, was produced at the Y Theatre, Leicester, in May 2005 by the locally based Desi Stage.[41] The verbatim performance was enthusiastically delivered by the second-generation Gujarati youth from Leicester who had diligently attended six weeks of rehearsals of this 'package' production, imported from India by J. Kalyani, a Mumbai-based director, on invitation from the UK producer Vinod Kotecha. In what is a standard practice, the performers conscientiously mimed the gestures to the recorded script, containing the *shuddha* (pure) Gujarati language of 'home' taught by the Indian director. The youngest member of the cast, fourteen-year-old Poorvi Kotecha, commented that 'it was difficult as there is no improvising', although she felt the use of recorded dialogues 'helped with the projection' of sound.[42] The imported pre-recorded dialogues reflected the ideal/traditional language of a 'traditional' Gujarati *natak* (drama) one might see in India, rather than the cast's British Gujarati idiom. While

---

40 *Garba* is a form of folk dance with claps practised during the annual *Navratri* (nine nights) festival celebrated in community and school halls throughout the UK.

41 Desi Stage's first dance-drama *Kalja No Katko* (*A Piece of Heart*) was performed in 2004.

42 Personal conversation with Poorvi Kotecha, 6 May 2005, at the Y Theatre in Leicester.

the hybridity of Purohit's dialogues might suggest an integrated identity for British Gujaratis, the 'imported' recorded dialogue of *Paiso Maro Parmeswar* in *shuddha* Gujarati might suggest a desire to associate with 'back home', an element still central to the 'integrated' British Asian identity.

The diverse South Asian language theatres are distinctive, and continue to exist outside the 'sector'[43] umbrella that funds the predominantly English-language, British South Asian theatres. The language theatres fulfil different functions in cultural, community and social settings. They provide a platform to nurture and maintain caste- and faith-based identities through participation, and thus promote social interactions within diverse South Asian groups in the UK.

[CP]

43 'The Sector' is an interim term used in the *Whose Theatre ...?* (2006) report by Baroness Lola Young to refer to Black Minority Ethnic theatre groups. It was produced as a result of a series of 'Sustained Theatre' consultation meetings concerned with the infrastructure and development needs of the Black and minority ethnic theatre sector over a projected ten-year period. The meetings were organised by the Arts Council in London and other cities in 2005.

2

Tara Arts

from 1977 to 1985

Foundation and the earliest productions

The motivation for the foundation of Tara Arts, the earliest and longest-running British Asian theatre company, came from the murder of Gurdeep Singh Chaggar, a Sikh teenager, in Southall in June 1976. The founding members were themselves young men, most of them then studying in higher education, none of them in drama. They were unsure of what form their response should take, but they were looking for cultural expression rather than direct political action. Their main choice eventually fell on theatre-making. They could initiate and steer this themselves, at least at a rudimentary level, and they were convinced of the need to advance the visibility of young Asians in acts of cultural self-representation.

The founding members were not theatrically skilled, although Sunil Saggar and Ovais Kadri had seen fringe theatre productions. The immediate community for the founding group was predominantly in the Clapham area. Both Saggar's and Jatinder Verma's families were involved with the Hindu Society there, and they had talked about perhaps creating some theatre work that was more contemporary in appeal than the traditional short Diwali festival performances relating to Rama. In nurturing this idea, Verma got support from his former drama teacher at the Spencer Park school, Terry Furlong, and the accent on the contemporary united Saggar, Kadri, Verma, Praveen Bahl and Vijay Shaunak, who were politically left-wing and also culturally attuned to the contemporary scene in music. All were just finishing their continuing and higher education: Saggar and Kadri went on with their legal training, Bahl got his first job, and Verma committed to an MA in history at Sussex, which was to provide him with material for later productions.

The choice of Rabindranath Tagore's *Sacrifice* (*Balidaan*) for a first production offered a humanist, potentially allegorical or symbolical text from the most dignified name in modern South Asian dramatic literature, one that was already well acclimatised to Britain and to respectable, community performance in Britain, and which could be seen to resonate with the anxieties that followed the murder of Chaggar. Yet Saggar and Kadri had to be talked into it, since their bias was firmly to the contemporary.[1]

Sacrifice was given three performances at the Battersea Arts Centre in August 1977, after rehearsals at a church hall in Streatham, with a cast of sixteen, including a musician, Atul Patel.[2] The set consisted of an arc of three painted flats, between which entrances and exits were made; the action of Tagore's play was set in the eighteenth century, and the production was given historical costume. Manuscript notes by Verma exist, which lay out the pragmatics for the production:

1. Examine carefully preliminary designs—are they possible? e.g. can we afford silk?!
2. Start with assumption of cheapest and most easily available materials—e.g. those that can be got at home.
3. Then detailed designs of each piece of main costume—i.e. the dresses/tunics that are to be made.
4. For the designs, of course, one needs measurements.
5. Having decided upon final designs, see (i) what is available from people in the group, (ii) what can be used after alterations, and (iii) what will have to be made.

In Verma's manuscript draft of a synopsis to the play, he summarises the moral that he sees arising from the action:

> that our adherence to and practice of customs, traditions which are conceived of as our 'religion', our 'culture', cannot be distinguished from our lack of appreciation of each other beyond the roles in which we are placed—father, son, elder, young priest, layman; Hindu, Muslim; Gujurati, Punjabi—cannot be distinguished from our inability to rise up united to the challenge posed by life in Britain—of which racism is the obvious, and all-encompassing feature.

Tagore's own English translation was adapted and abbreviated, with the substitution of a plain, prosaic diction for poetic elaboration. So, for example, a passage such as 'Then why has the Goddess, who weaves the web of this

---

1 Ovais Kadri, Praveen Bahl and Sunil Saggar interviewed by Graham Ley at the Tara Arts Centre, Earlsfield London, 17 May 2008.

2 The Tara website contains a bare record of past productions, listing cast, writer, director and designer. The archive itself, held at the Tara Centre in Earlsfield, was organised in box files by the name of the production, with some few additional boxes. Papers and documents cited or quoted here were contained in those box files, by production, unless otherwise referenced or noted. The video archive is currently at the same location, and there is also a separate photographic archive held there, organised by production.

world-illusion, assigned my place in the barren waste of childlessness?' from the original becomes 'Then why has the all-powerful Goddess denied me a child?' in the Tara version.[3] As a breach of tradition in itself, this modernisation had to be justified from the principles enshrined in Tagore's play. So, in the production programme, there is a page dedicated to the issue of adaptation which ends with these paragraphs:

> The theme—of the fetters of tradition—seemed to us to be sufficiently important and relevant to us today, to take liberties with the original text.
>
> It goes without saying that we have great respect and admiration for Tagore; and we feel sure that he would have sympathised with our motto: to interpret anew, with a different relevance, old sayings. In other words, to use our heritage, not be drowned by it.

It is doubtful whether the symbolic quality of Tagore's play—questioning adherence in a traditional kingdom to the rite of blood sacrifice to the goddess Kali, and exploring the psychology of loyalty and rebellion—would have communicated a specific purchase on the contemporary to its audience. The programme has two pages devoted to introducing the Tara group, 'who have got together to examine aspects of our culture, especially in so far as it is relevant to our lives here ... In other words, we seek to express the young coloured experience in Britain.'

> For us, 'culture' is the prime medium of expression. To truly appreciate our position here in British society is to give life to our cultural heritage. This means reacting to the National Front and others like them; and not dismissing but rather feeling for Lewisham, Notting Hill, Southall: what happens to them happens to us.

After quoting the *Bhagavad Gita*, the primacy of culture is ambitiously asserted, leaving an exciting but rather vague impression:

> No Raam, no Mohammed, no Christ is going to fill in the gaps in our lives. Our culture has resource enough for us to meet the challenges of living in Britain ...
>
> Each generation has the duty to express anew, a different relevance, old sayings.
>
> It must be stressed once more that these are the views of the Arts

---

3 Rabindranath Tagore, *Sacrifice and Other Plays* (London: Macmillan 1923), p. 106; Tara script from the archive.

> Group, who have produced the play; not all the Players necessarily hold the same general views.

The programme concludes with a quotation on the soul from the *Brihad-Aranyaka Upanishad* (**DVD 1–10**).

The group by this point has a profile. The five founding members are involved in the artistic activity (the 'Arts Group'), but are now part of a wider grouping (who may also become 'Players'), which itself draws on wider support, not all of it from within the Asian community: the set for *Sacrifice* was designed by Furlong. The production was seen by two young sisters, Rekha and Arti Prashar, who came as part of the community interest from families associated with the Clapham Hindu Society, and were not initially keen to get involved, but found themselves impressed by the production.[4] It was then Rekha who made the link with the Millan Centre in Tooting Bec and the community worker there, Geeta Amin, who made the Centre's hall available to the group. So the sphere of activity was in inner south-west London, with some meetings held at Saggar's house, and subsequently weekly meetings at the Millan Centre in Trinity Road. As such, it was located away from current areas of conflict in south and west London, to which reference was made in the programme notes to *Sacrifice*, and it was conscious not only of its youth and the generational issues within the Asian community but also of its own diversity of backgrounds, affiliations and beliefs. It is in this setting that the accent falls firmly on culture, rather than direct action, and a xeroxed handout which dates from early 1978 spells out a number of significant and operative principles that had begun to form (**DVD 11**).[5] In this document, the formation of Tara is ascribed to a 'group of young Asians in Wandsworth', and its aim is 'to express and make popular various aspects of our cultural and literary heritage, but to do this always in English', primarily to make it relevant to the young Asian experience in Britain.

> We also do our work in English because we are concerned by the fact that there are many different organisations catering for Asians but no organisation that caters for all Asians, regardless of whether they are Muslim, Hindu or Sikh, or speak in Gujurati, Punjabi, Urdu, Bengali, etc.
>
> We feel that for us all, in Britain, it is vital to begin to think of ourselves as Asians; this is particularly important today, with lunatics such as the National Front around.
>
> We are not a political organisation, but we feel that it is not

4 Rekha Prashar interviewed by Graham Ley at the Tara Arts Centre, Earlsfield London, 15 May 2008; Arti Prashar interviewed by Graham Ley at the Tara Arts Centre, Earlsfield London, 16 May 2008.

5 Contained in the *Fuse* production box-file.

> healthy to totally ignore the larger political scene, if only because politics here will not forget us.

Some of the language clearly shows deference to the parental apprehensions of the older generation:

> We are an expanding group; we want more and more youngsters who feel like us, or feel we can be useful in helping them to express themselves, to join us in our activities. We have much to offer in terms of Asian culture, and feel that we can work with the young with enthusiasm and respect, given the chance.

By February 1978 a report in *Echo*, the journal of the Minority Arts Advisory Service, reveals that plans were in place at Tara 'to develop a play based on some of the pre-occupations of Asian youth living here', and that weekly drama classes were being offered at the Millan Centre in preparation.[6] The play was to be produced 'with the help of a professional director', and it became part of the Youth Programme of the Young Peoples Theatre scheme at the Royal Court in London, directed by Gerald Chapman after improvisations led by him. Arti Prashar found herself persuaded by Verma and her sister Rekha to take up the leading role in the play, after 'the girl had pulled out because her parents wouldn't allow her to do theatre'. She recalls that it was Chapman who inspired her, with his assured process of preparing a cast for a production [Arti Prashar 2008]. Other activities during this period had been poetry recitals and minor dramatisations of poetry, and a film showing of *Garmhava* to raise money and interest in the group. But this play allowed the group to work together on a shared youth theme drawn from personal experience and 'express it' in contemporary language, scripted by Verma, so hopefully encouraging others to join. The subject was the Asian experience at school in Britain, to be performed for schools and community audiences. *Fuse* had a cast of twelve, and the resultant script after devising contrasted the feelings and responses of two newly arrived young Asians with those of Asians already at the school who have grown up in Britain. In this respect, new member Yogesh Bhatt was able to contribute his experiences, since he had come to the UK relatively

---

6 *Echo*, no. 11 (February 1978), p. 3: MAAS/4/1, Minority Arts Archive, Modern Records Centre, University of Warwick. The Minority Arts Advisory Service (MAAS) was set up after the publication of Naseem Khan's *The Arts Britain Ignores: The Arts of Ethnic Minorities in Britain* (London: Commission for Racial Equality, 1976), a report commissioned by the Arts Council of Great Britain, the Calouste Gulbenkian Foundation and the Community Relations Commission. The MAAS was funded by the first two of these and Marks and Spencer, publishing a listings guide called *Black Arts* and two consecutive periodicals: *Echo: Living Arts in Britain's Ethnic Communities*, 1977–82, and *Artrage: Intercultural Arts Magazine*, from 1982.

recently [Kadri, Bahl and Saggar 2008]. There are tensions and banter between white and Asian kids, which are demonstratively shot through with racism, but the true dilemma lies in the incompatibility of a received culture and the British environment, most tersely expressed (in the version of the script on file) in 'How do you put together English eyes and an Asian heart?' The performed play was 'very short and should, I think, be described as "work in progress"', as Clive Tempest witnessed in a review for *Echo*, observing that the play shows Asian adolescents who are all 'confused about what values and traditions should guide their lives'.[7]

In the summer of 1977, in an interview for *Echo*, the director of the Annual Asian Youth Festival, the distinguished actor Roshan Seth, had reflected on the festival performances that year, and expressed 'doubts and queries about the work that groups themselves presented'.[8] The work consistently tried to reproduce Indian art-forms, but Seth stated his belief that

> art created here should use the techniques of Indian culture, but to express the situation here ... Why not something about Indian women working in Macvities Biscuits, or whatever, instead of about village women on a building site in India?

In a review for the same journal by a member of Tara Arts early in 1978, an Urdu-language production at the Commonwealth Institute of a comedy set in Lahore comes in for related criticism, not for its dramaturgy or production values, but for its questionable relevance:

> The Tara Arts Group does not criticise the play: on its own terms it worked very well indeed ... But the regret, for us, is because the play brought to the surface again the question Why? and For Whom?
>
> What possible justification, in terms of the Asian community in Britain (40% of whom are born here), is there for presenting a play set in Lahore, spoken in Urdu, and staged in London? In particular, what relevance for the young? Surely it's time that we as Asians stop shirking the reality of living here, in Britain, by deadening our sense with imported titillation? Home is *here*.

In the programme note to *Fuse* the concern for relevance was extremely strong: 'Although based on very personal and local experiences, we feel the play is sufficiently general to afford an insight into the experiences of Asians growing up in this country.' (DVD 12–13).

By this point, and with the production of *Fuse*, Tara had laid out and enacted a definition of a contemporary British Asian theatre. It continued,

---

7 *Echo*, nos 21, 22 (December 1978/January 1979): photocopied in *Fuse* file.

8 *Echo*, no. 3 (June 1977), p. 1: MAAS/4/1, Warwick.

under the same principles and basic practical arrangements, into 1979 with the preparation and performance of *Playing the Flame*, scripted by Verma and directed again by Chapman. It is clear from notes in the archive file that Amrit Wilson's study *Finding a Voice: Asian Women in Britain*, published late in 1978 by Virago, the feminist press, became a major source in developing the script, in which pre-marital sex between a Hindu girl, Jyoti, and a Muslim youth, Omar, led eventually to the suicide of Jyoti. The presence of young Asian women in the Tara Arts Group, with its accent on performing, was a potentially sensitive issue in personal and family terms and in relation to attitudes in the local and wider Asian community. The position of young women within the thematic scope of British Asian theatre being developed by Tara was also bound to be an issue dramaturgically. None of the founding members of Tara had been female, but the group had rapidly come to include both Arti and Rekha Prashar, with both performing in *Fuse* and Rekha again performing in *Playing the Flame*. Both were to play significant roles in the evolution of Tara over its first decade, and while Rekha insists that she felt that there was no come-back at her as a woman involved in the group, Arti holds a completely different memory of her first five years.

> My impression of all those years actually was that I ended up being the only woman travelling with a load of men. That was very tough at the time. Certainly going deep into the community, into the Asian community venues, they just regarded you as a prostitute, full stop. There was no other option in a way. Why else would this young girl be travelling around with these men? And that was quite hard to deal with.
>
> [Arti Prashar 2008]

The play had a narrative that tracked the relationship between Jyoti and Omar from its beginnings in discos to pregnancy, an abortion, a subsequently arranged marriage which Jyoti leaves, and her suicide in a London tube station, with barely indicated naturalistic settings indoors and in the street. An unattributed review of *Playing the Flame* in *Echo* noted that Tara had moved from 'a concept of ethnic art as an external representation of some imperfectly remembered distant past to the use of art as a medium for expressing and interpreting our experience here'.[9] The review went on to observe that although the issues the play raised were 'too complex and huge', the questions were important:

> The conflict between parents and children, Muslim/Hindu, between men and women, are seen to operate in a society far-removed

[9] *Echo*, no. 26 (May 1979), p. 1: MAAS/4/1, Warwick.

> from that which gave rise to such conflicts originally. The parents' traditional view of society, racism and the women's movement are all glimpsed.

The reviewer drew attention to some inadequacies in the construction of the play, which gave 'insufficient explanation for many of the steps taken by the central characters':

> In particular the ending though neat as a device to end the play was a pessimistic one, in so far as Jyoti was given no possibility for survival. After all the experiences she goes through it would have been heartening to have had a glimmer of hope for girls in her position at the end. Instead we were given her dramatic and ill-explained suicide.

Playing the Flame was performed at the Jackson's Lane Arts Centre, Bethnal Green Institute, the Carlton Centre, Battersea Arts Centre, Bruce Grove Community Centre, the Indian YMCA and Greenford Community Centre from 3 to 14 April 1979. The Bruce Grove venue was the centre for the Asian Action Group Haringey, with whom Tara had begun to link constructively, with Reynu Sethi, who played Jyoti (alongside Paul Bhattarcharjee's Omar), and other performers coming now from Haringey (**DVD 14**).

Outline for a future

The intricacies of personal motivation through multiple spoken exchanges over these first years are impossible to trace with any great accuracy, but two sheets of a handwritten draft proposal by Verma reveal his firm grasp of a future for Tara. The proposal was for 'the establishment of a full-time Asian drama group, which over time will be expected to extend into an Arts centre', and, as Verma recalls, dates from April 1979.[10] The document is divided into 'Justifications', 'Aims', 'Reasons for above aims' and 'Finance and Personnel'. Under 'Justifications', Verma writes of the increasing 'alienation of young and successive generations of Asians from the traditions of their parents', with cultural expressions cast predominantly in a 'frozen mould', and not interpreted 'in terms of life in Britain'. His particular target is 'multi-cultural education', which 'disseminates an idyllic view' of South Asian religions and has its focus on 'social life in the sub-continent'. The contrasting 'Aims' of the group would be 'To express aspects of Asian life in Britain (including relations with the wider community as well as relations within the Asian community)' and 'To <u>reinterpret</u> Asian traditions in light of Asian experience in Britain'; and Verma notes in parentheses 'I feel that the two are naturally linked, but this need not necessarily be so.'

---

10 Undated document contained in the *Playing the Flame* production box-file.

The 'Reasons for the above aims' include the group's relevance and its role as a 'fillip to the effective articulation of Asian presence in Britain'.

> Most importantly, it will activate educational/cultural/creative work—the re-interpretation of aspects of Asian tradition will necessarily behove the participants to make a study of the traditions. Their interpretation in light of Asians in Britain will be a creative activity. The expression of this tradition will be of great educative import—not only insofar as Asian participants and audiences, but, equally crucially, insofar as English audiences are concerned, whether in schools, etc or public at large.
>
> This will be a by far more constructive, positive, contribution to genuine multicultural life in Britain today.

The proposal envisages seeking funding from 'the major arts-funding bodies and charitable institutions', and national and local government, not just for running costs 'but also for a centre, a base for the group—even if this means a derelict house'. Each member of the group would be paid a yearly salary, ensuring at least a twelve-month commitment, and the group would tour its work. It would be chaired by an Artistic Director and an Assistant, who would combine administrative and artistic work, and there would be a publicity officer. Members might be either professional or amateur actors.

> Given such a composition, it shall obviously be in flux: professionals will go to 'better' things, amateurs perhaps turn professional: drop-outs may be found in either case. That does not matter, except insofar as at least a 12-month commitment will be expected from everyone, except the Artistic Director and Assistant, who will commit themselves for a period of 2–3 years.

There was, at this time, very little sign in Tara's theatre work of the attention to traditional culture that Verma outlines here. But the structural profile for the group would remain remarkably constant, even if all that was gained in September 1979 was funding from the Commission for Racial Equality for one year for an administrator. Verma took this post, and it was his vision of a central figure (or figures) that remained constant, initially as much through the exercise of dramaturgy and script-making as through administrative persistence and basic competence. There can be no doubt that this determination and the firm development of a vision were fostered by the unwavering support of 'the boys', as the Prashar sisters term the founding members. Kadri explains their position:

> Can we make it clear that none of us [Kadri, Bahl, Saggar and Vijay Shaunak] was interested in making a professional career out of it? We

> honestly did this because we believed in it. To this day we believe in it. It was an article of faith for us that we're going to support Jatinder through this, through thick and thin. Because we saw, through other Asian organisations, that what always happens is that people break up and divide: it was an article of faith that criticism would be internal, and on the external front we would always support him. And to this day we have, because he's got great talent.
>
> [Kadri, Bahl and Saggar 2008]

Satirical and historical performances

An update on Tara in the journal *Echo* records that from April 1979 'a series of pithy sketches ... toured to Leicester, Hatfield, Lambeth, Battersea and the City of London Poly';[11] and in a later report for *Echo* Verma's summary includes reference to the 'development of a "Revue" format—in which various pertinent and topical themes could be tackled through a series of short sketches'.[12] Bahl and Kadri recall that the election of the Conservative government under Thatcher was the stimulus, but it was not the theme, with material ranging through class and the position of women to sexuality in the community. So a show would last about forty-five minutes, and be composed of about seven or eight sketches. Bahl recalls that they were jointly conceived, were often about sexuality and 'the hypocrisy around religion', and that he joined Verma in the writing [Kadri, Bahl and Saggar 2008]. Kadri and Bahl recall that they were physically attacked for disrespecting their culture and religion when they took the show to the conference of the National Association of Asian Youth at a venue in Warwick. The negative reaction was broader than that one incident, and was founded on the belief that problems in the Asian community such as religious bigotry should not be 'aired publicly'. Unfortunately, there is no further documentation of this initiative, which is interesting in reaching out beyond London to Leicester and Bradford, and to Newcastle and Glasgow; it ran from May 1979 until April 1980. Documentation is also lacking on *The Third Step*, identified as Tara's third 'original production' in the August update in *Echo*, which 'tackles the theme of the relationship between the Home and the World, as seen through the development of a father and his daughter'. The October issue of *Echo* writes of 'work in progress' on *The Third Step*, which featured a 19-year old Priya:

> She leaves school to work in an industrial laundry, in order to ease the financial burden on her brother, since their father retired

---

11 *Echo*, no. 29 (August 1979), p. 3: MAAS/4/1, Warwick.

12 *Echo*, no. 37 (April 1980), p. 6: MAAS/4/1, Warwick.

> three months ago. Her close relationship with her father and the conditions of work in the laundry lead her to walk out—in which she is supported by other women workers. The walk-out occurs at a particularly sensitive moment as her sister-in-law has already begun negotiations for her marriage.

This synopsis suggests clear connections with *Playing the Flame*, and also has a resonance with the stand taken by the Asian women workers at Grunwick.[13] Yet in December 1979 a different play, *Yes, Memsahib!* was presented at the Midland Arts Centre in Birmingham; *The Third Step* was performed two years later.[14]

In the draft proposal for an Asian drama group of April 1979, Verma had identified education as a major concern, and had emphasised the need to interpret cultural traditions in the light of the experience of (young) Asians in Britain. Yet the significant departure from the model of British Asian theatre set up in *Fuse*, *Playing the Flame* and the subsequent development of *The Third Step* was a new emphasis on history rather than cultural tradition. Verma's own higher education and teaching activity was in history, and the programme for *Yes, Memsahib!* acknowledged that 'This production is based on the thesis, "The Uganda Railway and Migrant Labour, 1895–1905", by J. Verma' (side 6), referring to his MA dissertation at the University of Sussex. The programme was itself a small educational pamphlet of twelve sides, containing a background essay with photographs from the time, other images, quotations from leading British figures and historical records, cited precisely (**DVD 15–20**). The show had been considered a historical revue by Verma, and it was composed and performed in nine sketches and an epilogue, following the journey of Munoo from the Punjab to Nairobi. He is summarily dismissed from his post as a Memsahib's cook and enrols to work on the East African railway, where he organises a labour protest, is bound after coming into conflict with the overseer, but escapes to be a shop-owner in Nairobi.

In his report for *Echo* in April 1980, Verma offered a short but revealing commentary on this departure under the sub-heading 'Historical Perspective':

> Of late, Tara has looked to history to provide insights into contemporary Asia life in Britain. The first of these productions, 'YES, MEMSAHIB', analogised directly the experiences of Indians who were taken to East Africa to establish the British colony, with

---

13 *Echo*, no. 31 (October 1979), p. 2: MAAS/4/1, Warwick.

14 Earlier in 1979 Parminder Vir, who would later be instrumental in the Greater London Council (GLC)'s approach to ethnic arts, and Verma had become officers for the MAAS for the midlands and south, and the north, respectively.

that of Asians in Britain today, living under the shadow of the anti-immigration lobby.[15]

That the issues of exploitation, summary justice backed by the threat of violence, labour resistance, enforced migration and the ability to escape and survive would communicate themselves readily to an audience is clear, but with the force of a relevant and continuing history rather than substantially by analogy. Dramaturgically, this is a distinct and separate line from that created with *Fuse*, and it is apparent in the approach to language. Here Munoo and Amir are talking:

AMIR: Didn't you hear beasts roar last night? Patterson-sahib walks out of tent. I see with my own eyes, walks out and stands, looking at noise!
MUNOO: He not standing if noise show its face! I tell you truly, brother, these lions only for white sahibs—they spirits of chiefs killed by sahibs. Not liking railway going through land. Come to warn sahibs go back.
AMIR: I don't know, brother, they eat my two wives. Not liking Indians.
MUNOO: That to punish you for taking their women.
AMIR: What I to do? Let Africa women starve? Famine here bad as India famine. I have a heart, brother. That why I take four women for wife.

[*Yes, Memsahib!* from sketch 6, 'A railhead camp in East Africa']

The satirical form parodies the contrast between this colonial 'Asian' language and the dominant received English of the colonising sahibs, but it also fails to move things forward. In *Fuse*, the contemporary idiom belongs equally to the Asian and non-Asian youths, and so operates strongly as a medium for the expression of lived experience. The integrity of the subordinate, subaltern experience might demand a more radical bilingualism or other discursive or linguistic tactics if it were to pose that ready analogy that Verma intended—the leap across to lived experience in contemporary Britain (DVD 21–22).

Related problems arise with *Jhansi*, which is cast in similar language to Verma's version of Tagore's *Sacrifice* (DVD 23–24). Performed in April 1980, the play was summarised by Verma in his report on Tara for *Echo* in April 1980 in these terms: 'JHANSI used the story of the Rani of Jhansi, during the Indian "Mutiny" of 1857, to consider the position of a woman in a conventionally male-dominated society.' The Rani, Lakshmi Bai, is the

---

[15] *Echo*, no. 37 (April 1980), p. 6: MAAS/4/1, Warwick.

regent for her young son Damodar Rao, and the play tracks her diplomacy to the point where she aligns with the sepoys of the 'Mutiny' after the British have threatened to annex her kingdom. The language is 'stage courtly':

> ADVISER: Still no reply from Captain Skene-sahib, your Majesty.
> RANI: (testily) Have his much-vaunted virtues of punctuality melted in India's heat!
> ADVISER: Perhaps more pressing matters occupy him now …
> RANI: (interrupting) The sepoy mutiny? (Dismissively) With Delhi and Lucknow re-taken, it can hardly be a matter of days now before the mutiny is suppressed. No—he must still be awaiting an answer from the Governor-General in Calcutta. (Firmly) The succession must be approved.
> ADVISER: (concurring) Uncertainty of authority at times like these would lead to problems.
>
> [*Jhansi*: p. 3, scene II]

Inkalaab, 1919, which followed in the summer and autumn of 1980, addressed a colonial atrocity directly, with a frame that explicitly related the oppression to forms in the present day. The subject was the massacre in the Jallianwala Bagh at Amritsar by forces under the command of British General Dyer, and it was written and directed by Verma. The large-scale historic context and events were experienced through the figure of Sarfraz, who became a servant to General Dyer. The direct analogy to the contemporary experience of Asians in Britain was prompted by the Prologue, in which a young Asian talked to his parents about his arrest by the police, and the analogy was confirmed in the final scene with General Dyer transforming into a contemporary police officer. The programme notes included a summary of events surrounding the massacre, and in conclusion insisted on its historical significance in the path towards independence:

> The consequences of the massacre at Jallianwala were such as to make 1919 stand out like 'the Mutiny' of 1857.
>
> Racial tensions were intensified on the sides of both whites and Indians …
>
> [Programme to *Inkalaab, 1919*] (DVD 25–36)

Funding, personnel and plans for a building

In addition to the grant for an administrative figure from the Commission for Racial Equality (CRE), Tara had by this time also gained a small grant from the Greater London Arts Association (GLAA), and £600 from the Arts Council of Great Britain (ACGB) for the purchase of equipment. The British

Council of Churches had begun to be supportive, and was to increase its funding substantially to cover payment of a single administrative salary for 1980–81. Funding records for Tara in these early years are patchy, and the recall of the timing of awards and their delivery does not always match the records that do exist.[16] A Balance Sheet dated 2 October 1980 shows the total CRE grant at £7,070, the British Council of Churches at £1,000, the ACGB equipment grant at £600, and the GLAA award for workshops at £100. Tara also won an award for £275 at the Minority Rights Group ceremony at the Institute of Contemporary Arts (ICA) in London that year. To give an impression of production expenses from this Balance Sheet, the total income from *Yes, Memsahib!* was £917; the expenses on lighting hire, slides and equipment, sound, costumes, props and make-up, publicity, programmes and touring came out at £514, of which touring amounted to £234.[17]

In an article titled 'Funding Focus' in *Echo*, Verma wrote of the freezing of grant applications by the CRE in April 1980, and that since then there had been 'no revenue support for the group whatsoever; it has been existing, primarily, by its own efforts and unpaid full-time work of two of the members'.[18] This second figure was Rekha Prashar, and they had rented an office above a shop in Tooting Broadway:

> Phoning venues, making bookings ... Let's try the libraries, let's try the community centres, take the shows around. And then we would also organise posters and see how we could get it done cheaply. We managed to find a really good Asian printer in Tooting. I formed a really good relationship with him, and he would do our printing really cheaply.
>
> [Rekha Prashar 2008]

A subsequent grant from the British Council of Churches for 1982 provided for Rekha's salary in addition, and she later undertook an arts administration training course on a bursary from the Arts Council. But in his article for *Echo*, 'Funding Focus', Verma complained that applications to the ACGB and the GLAA had been frustrated by attempts to categorise Tara as a professional, amateur or community arts group, none of which was truly applicable.

The pattern of extremely bare funding is revealed in a (draft) statement for the year ending 31 March 1982, which records the ACGB at £4,500, the CRE at £3,313, the GLAA at £1,050, Wandsworth Borough Council at £1,000 and West Midlands Arts Association at £400, with a grand total of

---

16 These few early financial documents are contained in the box-file 'Funding'.

17 These leading figures also appear in a statement of accounts confirmed by Counter Tax Accountants for the year ended 31 August 1980.

18 *Echo*, no. 45 (Spring 1981), p. 3: MAAS/4/1, Warwick.

grants at £10,313; expenses in this sheet included a salary at £3,800 and vehicle purchase (on HP) at £1,896. But, from a year later, in a statement of accounts for the year ended 31 March 1983, there is a marked increase, with the ACGB grant rising to £21,118 and the Greater London Council (GLC) providing £6,500, the GLAA £1,100, Wandsworth Borough Council £1,750, the British Council of Churches £2,500, the City Parochial Foundation £2,500, and Regional Arts Associations £600, giving a grand total of awards of £36,068. Box office contributed £7,943, and total income was £45,515; from this, expenses on productions were £6,577 and wages and salaries came to £23,500. These increased amounts accompany the change to professional status for the touring company in the autumn of 1982, and are the beginning of what was to prove the financial consolidation of the Tara Arts Group.

The membership of the group in these early years is regularly stated to be between twenty and twenty-five, and this broad span of commitment, supported by the figures at the centre, proved itself to be an extremely effective survival mechanism in very difficult times. With the election of the monetarist Conservative government in 1979 funding bodies went through a period of uncertainty, stasis and retrenchment, and in London the principal initiative in supporting ethnic arts came from the GLC under Ken Livingstone. Following a GLC conference in May 1982, an Ethnic Arts Sub-Committee (of the GLC's Arts and Recreation Committee) was created and given a budget of £300,000 in 1982–83.[19] This not only led to the appearance of the GLC in Tara's production funding, but also to negotiations for the establishment of a centre for the group, as envisaged in Verma's early proposal for an Asian drama group. Parminder Vir had worked for the Minority Arts Advisory Service until 1980, when she left to work at the Commonwealth Institute and subsequently became Ethnic Arts Advisor to the GLC. Rekha Prashar recalls that Vir had come to see a few Tara shows and that, once they felt that Vir was interested in the idea of a centre, she and Verma started looking for a building. There was a distinct context for this new determination:

> It had to do with what was going on at that time with organisations. People were saying that they wanted to be building-based because that would secure their future. So we were in that cycle as well. We were saying if we get a building it's highly likely we'll get recognised, we'll get money from the Arts Council, we can up the ante in terms of not just doing small-scale touring, we can go on to middle-scale. Maybe we can find a place where we can actually do our own

---

19 Material on the conference held on 28 May 1982, and on subsequent consultation with ethnic minority organisations, is held in the library of the London Metropolitan Archives, with the call-mark S.20.16 GLC.

> productions … And also it had to do with the fact that a lot of black organisations were saying 'building base, building base'. We knew that the GLC would fund this, and it would actually secure our future. That was the driver.
>
> [Rekha Prashar 2008]

History and symbolism: the British Asian subject

For Tara, as a touring drama group, continued existence and progress with funding depended on the generation of material that would sufficiently define its place in the broad category of ethnic arts. Verma had implanted a firm historical dimension in productions that he had both scripted and directed, and in early 1980 in the review of Tara for *Echo* he had anticipated 'dislodging the myth that the Asian presence in Britain is essentially a post-1960 phenomenon'.[20] In that same review he went on to observe that 'substantial evidence has been uncovered of Asian domestics, seamen, petty traders, soldiers in Britain from the Eighteenth Century onwards', and this list parallels the research field on which the historian Rozina Visram was to publish her book later in the decade, although Verma was unaware of Visram or her work.[21] In the event, *Vilayat: England Your England* was a play in three acts which were set, in sequence, in 1974–76, 1978 and 1981, bringing the action into the present time of the production, which ran in May and July 1981 at venues in London (North London Polytechnic, Merton Hall, Theatro Technis, Fellowship House in East Ham, Fleet Community Education Centre in Belsize Park, Battersea Arts Centre, The Commonwealth Institute, Anson Hall in Brent and the Croydon Warehouse) (DVD 37–45). So, instead of looking for analogies to be drawn to the contemporary from a portrayal of colonial history, the play—as a flier explained—adopted a different dramaturgical tactic, examining

> the inter-connections between Asian life today and its colonial past, through the life of Ashwin: an immigrant from India who strives to 'make something' of himself in Britain. This life becomes the source of constant reminiscence and assessment for three 'ghosts' of Asians past in this country: an Ayah, a Lascar (seaman) and a Member of Parliament.
>
> (DVD 38)

In notes about the structure of the play, dated 16 December 1980, Verma had been concerned about the balance between an apparent naturalism 'which

---

20 *Echo*, no. 37 (Spring 1980), p. 6: MAAS/4/1, Warwick.

21 Rozina Visram, *Ayahs, Lascars and Princes: Indians in Britain 1700–1947* (London: Pluto, 1986) and *Indians in Britain* (London: Batsford, 1987).

is increasingly interrupted by the Chorus, thus breaking into stylisation of song and movement'; an addition in red pen has 'No, can't be done: naturalism exerts its own dynamic—of narration, of credible follow-ons, of dialogue.' The leading character was to arrive in Britain in the 1960s, find his qualifications not recognised, and so study for banking exams while working on the railway. Verma continued in his notes:

> The story is really about the abiding, deep-rooted faith in the British of the Banker (the other side of this faith is, of course, his own sense of inferiority and colonialism): how, though disappointed by British at every turn, the Banker nevertheless bounces back with faith ...

In these notes, the Banker (later Ashwin) was to join the Tory party and end up 'killing daughter for going out with man of own choice'; but in the resultant script (dated February 1980 in the archive) Ashwin becomes a Labour councillor in Tooting, and is defeated in the 1979 election. Instead of Ashwin killing his daughter, he himself is beaten up by National Front thugs who break into his home, and joins the three ghosts who have been visiting him and his wife, Salina. Ashwin's aspirations to a political career are glossed in the programme by noting that 'the most prominent of the early Asians were the politicians—especially the 3 Members of Parliament'. History also features explicitly and strongly in a series of statements about Tara, in the conclusion to the 'Historical Background' given in the programme and in answers to the questions 'What is Tara?' and 'Why Tara?':

> What is TARA?
>
> An Asian community theatre group, presenting original plays, in English, about Asian life in Britain today and through history ...
>
> Why TARA?
>
> TARA exists for people who are interested in drama and seek to express their interests in the company of other Asians. It exists also to learn about, and teach, Asian history and culture, and about how we live in Britain today ...
>
> (Programme to *Vilayat: England Your England*) (**DVD 42**)

The insistence that history might be theatrically teased into a revealing relationship with the contemporary British Asian experience subsequently carried Verma's dramaturgy into an exploration of the iconic figure of Gandhi in *Lion's Raj*, in Tara's professional launch at the Edinburgh Festival in September 1982. Verma describes the shift to a desire for professional status as an 'organic' development in the group, recognising the ambitions of a core of committed members; Rekha Prashar emphasises the drive for recognition and funding that surfaced in the early 1980s, in association with the bid to be 'building-based'.[22] To direct *Lion's Raj* for the Edinburgh professional launch, Tara turned to Anthony Clark, leaving Verma to concentrate as a writer on the essence of his chosen figure. This was the year of the Richard Attenborough film *Gandhi*, with Ben Kingsley in the title role, which premiered in Delhi in November; but Verma was developing ideas for his script from a year earlier, recorded in a notebook started in December 1981. In an entry from 26 January 1982, Verma notes that

> *Lion's Raj* should attempt, vigorously, the explication of the 'ambiguous culture' thesis—viz. 'original Asian in Britain'.
>
> Gandhi in himself becomes quite a different subject. So, bearing this in mind, find those situations which betray the ambiguity.

Clearly history here is not just a dramatic narrative of events that may stimulate an awareness of colonialism while hopefully providing some kind of analogy to a contemporary situation, as it had been diversely in *Yes, Memsahib!* and *Jhansi*. Verma's dramatic negotiations with history have here fixed upon the idea of a symbolic figure who will contain the essence of the ambiguity of the Indian or Asian in Britain. The choice of Gandhi represents a step behind Ashwin in *Vilayat* to find a more powerful theatrical tool, as a later entry from the notebook (March 1982) spells out:

> THE ATTEMPT is to locate Gandhi in a phenomenon of which he is the foremost exemplar—that of the creation of a new being, consequent upon the Raj. A being that desperately sought (seeks) to hold on to the 'Indian' in himself whenever the 'English' becomes nauseating; yet, every contact with the 'Indian' leads to a recoil against the 'Indian'.

In *Lion's Raj*, the symbolic stature of Gandhi is mediated through exposure to the divergent views of contemporary young British Asians, with all roles in the play taken by the cast of three, Rita Wolf, Paul Bhattacharjee and Mohammed Naim Khan (**DVD 46–52**). Yet in this case, and in contrast to *Vilayat*, the chorus of the play does not constitute history impinging on the experience of the modern British Asian, but a set of diversely opinionated contemporary Youths reflecting exclusively on Gandhi's symbolic stature from a standpoint in the present. The language of the play is caught in this exploration of the 'ambiguous culture', in the contrasting tones of the colloquial rhetoric of the Youths of the chorus, the caricature of Gandhi's

---

[22] On the 'organic' shift to professional status, see Verma's concise summary in Graham Ley, 'Theatre of Migration and the Search for a Multicultural Aesthetic: Twenty Years of Tara Arts', *New Theatre Quarterly*, 52 (1997), pp. 349–71, p. 351.

English in the play's opening scene in England and the voice of the sahib that Gandhi assumes when in India.

The production that accompanied the professional *Lion's Raj* to Edinburgh, *Scenes in the Life of ...*, was developed by the wider group over five months of improvisation. It was directed by David Sulkin from the Royal Court Young People's Theatre, with additional performances at the Commonwealth Institute and the Croydon Warehouse in November 1982. As the flier advertised, it expressed 'A young woman's view of what it is to be an Asian in Britain' (**DVD** 53). The programme (**DVD** 54–57) provides the scenario:

> A 28-year old Asian woman is interviewed by a white playwright, who is seeking material for his next play. The information she offers—and that which she withholds—form the subject of this play.
>
> The woman, Sumita Karnath, recounts key experiences in her life—school in East Africa, her work as a community centre director, home life, her relationship with a group of Asian activists ...—in an effort to articulate what it means for her to be an 'Asian'.
>
> (**DVD** 55)

The relationship with the lines of exploration laid down by Amrit Wilson in her interviews with Asian women in Britain in *Finding a Voice* is very strong, and implicitly there is a statement—made alongside a professional launch in an international festival—that British Asian experience can only be fully represented by a British Asian theatrical apparatus (**DVD** 58). Verma also wrote this script, and it would be misleading to suggest that there is a total division between the two. *Scenes in the Life of* ... offered a much less fraught discursive world, with a place for Punjabi, Hindi and Urdu. A preview by Katy Best in *The Stage* (19 August 1982) records the forward planning that drew on this potential in languages.

> This autumn, Tara is to use 'Scenes in the Life of ...' for a joint project with Croydon English Language Scheme and Croydon Warehouse Theatre. Asian women who are learning English will study the text of parts of the play which Tara will later perform for them, leading to subsequent discussions on the issues. As the play features the life of an Asian woman and examines what it means to be 'Asian', it is intended to spark off contributions from the English students about their own experience.
>
> These are to be incorporated into the original play and the new expanded version will be put on at Croydon Warehouse Theatre in late November.

The original cast for *Scenes in the Life of* ... numbered twelve; for the production of *Sapno Kay Ruup* (*The Shape of Dreams*), which was loosely derived from it, it came down to three women: Sudha Bhuchar, Naushaba Khan and Rekha Prashar (**DVD 59–60**). For *Sapno Kay Ruup*, Verma came in as both writer and director, and this is actually the first Tara production of which there is audio-visual documentation, in a substantially unedited, single-camera video recording, like many of those that follow.[23] The first thirty-five to forty minutes of the recording show a rehearsal, which is followed by a performance and then a post-show discussion, much of which is inaudible or barely audible. In earlier productions Tara's Asian actors had played all characters, Asian and white, and here the women actors play men as well as women. The play incorporates some familiar Hindi songs and simple dance sequences, and it is the leading character's situation that is explored or presented, in a manner that suggests its generic status. In that respect Tara's bare mise-en-scène—of a painted flat with a half-face and large eye, geometrically designed painted floor and three folding chairs—readily sustains a generic interpretation and response. The English language is experienced as an instrument of bullying and abuse, its lack being a guarantee of subjection and automatic disfranchisement. Each short scene is written to give a 'sketch' of a typical moment in the emigration–immigration from East Africa of a young woman, Sumita, to a husband in the UK. This form of construction lends itself well to demonstrative parallels: so the oppressive verbal assault from the Immigration Officer on Sumita links with a similar verbal assault by her husband on her. The recording provides a good indication of the bare style that Tara had adopted, matching extremely limited resources to a core address to the experience, or imaginative responses, of its audiences (**DVD 61–63**).

The post-show discussion is frustrating listening, even on maximum volume, but like others on record it reveals the insistent presence of Verma, who is keen to take up issues and broaden the discussion. In particular, in this discussion and in relation to the *Sapno Kay Ruup* script, he speaks of 'a continuing challenge to provide some kind of shape, some kind of form which is absolutely relevant, absolutely right, not only for ourselves but also for our audience …'. It is revealing that at this time he goes on to say that 'the one area I would find more important to explore would be traditional drama from the subcontinent, which has a context which to me is extremely alien', with the problem of how it might be extended to audiences here. Those are the twin challenges identified, and it is striking that the traditional occupies the prominent position it had in his early proposal for an Asian drama group, and that the resource of history which had been a major impulse since *Yes, Memsahib!* until *Lion's Raj* finds no mention.

---

23 Catalogued as VHSTARA 0116, and dated December 1982.

Two strands of development

The subsequent productions in 1983, through to *Chilli in Yor Eyes* of June 1984, continued to emphasise Tara's community involvement and direct engagement with the social and political aspects of the experience of Asians in Britain, with youth as a path into family life and generic, generational tensions. But alongside these came two productions that looked to the Sanskrit epic, the *Mahabharata*, as a source: *Shikari the Bowman* of November 1983 and the collaboration with the Cardiff-based Theatr Taliesin, *Mahahbharata/Mabinogion*, in September 1984. The climax of this development was undoubtedly the ambitious production of *Miti Ki Gadi* (*The Little Clay Cart*), a Sanskrit drama possibly from the fifth century CE traditionally ascribed to Sudraka, in December 1984.

That this line of development from traditional sources, unlike the dialogue with colonial history, might pose problems to the group is foreshadowed in Verma's scripting of the earliest manifestation of the impulse, *Diwali* of October 1981. The production was directed by Paul Bhattacharjee, and the scenario is the staging of a version of the *Ramayana* with a reluctant cast, in conflict with a director who urges them to recognise their own culture (DVD 64–65). But the principal thread in the play is that of the objection of the actress playing Sita to the submissive role of her character in the epic story, and of the blurred borders between the performers and the characters. Initially reluctant to play the characters, the performers gradually assume the roles to an alarming degree that sidelines the authority of the director. As Sudha Bhuchar recalls, this take on the traditional storyline offered 'something quite provocative', and in 'performing at the Diwali functions, part of the job was to provoke people to think differently', an aim that was consistent with Tara's view of its function as a group.

> There was this whole thing of who was Rama to question Sita, and that used to make people uncomfortable in the audience, certainly the Hindus, because Jatinder would make that parallel with the honour of women now, and who are you to question honour.[24]

Despite Verma's growing conviction about an engagement with traditional forms, the two subsequent productions that drew on traditional story-patterns had little in common and did not represent the development of a distinct line in performance. *Shikari the Bowman* was the product of five months of improvisations and was performed by an amateur cast directed by Yogesh Bhatt in Wandsworth, Brixton, Southall and Hillingdon for just over a week in November 1983 (DVD 66–68). This community project centred on concerns about the Police Bill proposed by

[24] Sudha Bhuchar interviewed by Graham Ley, London, 31 October 2007.

the Conservative government in the run-up to the general election of June 1983. Yet the form it took had its young protagonist, Amrish, joining a drama group which chose to enact the story of Bhil, the untouchable who pays for his training with the Pandavas with the sacrifice of his right hand. So, in another 'direct analogue', Amrish pays for help for the production from the Police Community fund with a promise to clean up the community, notably the squats to which he himself belongs. Verma scripted the play, and it is hard not to detect his influence here. The subsequent collaboration with Theatr Taliesin in Cardiff (in September 1984, funded by South Wales Ethnic Arts) was a more curious mixture of skills and predispositions, drafting Welsh and Sanskrit story-patterns around the figures of Taliesin and Krishna into the service of a performance that centred on the conversion of a British MP to a greater awareness of his constituents (DVD 69).

The three other productions of 1983 besides *Shikari* came immediately after the professional launch, and were all the product of extended periods of research. For *Ancestral Voices* (*Awaaz Puraani*), a five-week period of research and workshops explored a response to elderly Asians, whom the Group had encountered over the years in their meetings and rehearsals at the Millan Centre in Tooting Bec; thirteen community centres catering for the elderly were visited in London and the Midlands (DVD 70–74). The scenario of the resulting script by Verma had four young Asians waiting to be transformed by machinery into white people, and lapsing into party-mode while waiting for the machinery to be mended. Their motivation to conform is interrupted, in this metaphoric scenario, by visitations from ancestral voices which the cast of four acts out. A video recording of the production exists [VHSTARA0001, dated 14 April 1983], revealing close continuity in design with *Sapno Kay Ruup*: a square, abstract-painted floor defining the acting area, two screens moved by the performers, plastic chairs and a costume rail at the back. The production was again directed by Anthony Clark (after *Lion's Raj*), and displays the technical challenge for newly professional performers of stepping into the portrayal of the old in Tara's established, sketch-based dramaturgy. A note dated 7 January 1983 by Verma states that this project and production had a £10,000 guarantee against loss from the ACGB, and that £600 was expected from the ACGB Theatre Writing Scheme (DVD 75).

The Passage came from a residency in Loughborough throughout May 1983, the aim of which was the dramatisation of the Asian experience of that community. The play by Verma was an episodic but naturalistic story of Kashuji and his family, who comes from India to work in factories and reaches the point where he owns six houses in a street. Ultimately, the theme is that of British Asian youth experience and generational conflict, with the son challenging what his father sees as his *izzat* (honour) through his desire for independence in the choice of work and relationships, and so unintentionally threatening his sister's weaker hopes of self-determination. The production was in this instance directed by Verma and performed at the Battersea Arts Centre, Croydon Warehouse and outdoors in the Covent Garden Piazza in July 1983 (**DVD 76–78**). There was a change of cast once the show left Loughborough, with Sudha Bhuchar and Naushaba Shaheen Khan coming in for the first time to the professional company, which prompted objections from one of the professional male actors. The result was, as Khan recalls, that the women were paid at a lower rate.[25] The review in the *Asian Times* (15 July 1983) is full and appreciative, as if the Tara group has, for the unnamed reviewer, thoroughly proved its worth in providing a convincing picture of the Asian experience, both in script and performance:

> 'The Passage' is a definite must for one and all, not just to observe their very truthful portrayal of Asian life but also to understand and identify with the intricate web which holds the Asian community together in Britain.

Like that of *Ancestral Voices*, the script of *The Passage* shows Verma at ease in composing a contemporary vernacular adjusted to generations, with an admixture of languages, largely as interjection or short, pithy statement. Construction by episodic scenes or sketches provides a narrative framework that accommodates the recurrent theme of generational conflict and misunderstanding, and the dramaturgy is settled if unadventurous. This is the form of British Asian theatre that Tara had created, and which is welcomed in its polished form by the reviewer. It carried through into *Chilli in Yor Eyes* in the following year, with a diversion at the end of 1983 into a confusing study in *Meet Me* of a relationship between a young Hindu photographer Kama and a Muslim model Shaheen, which was the product of three weeks' research on mental illness in Asian communities in London, Birmingham, Coventry, Sheffield and Bradford. The research was also conducted in hospitals, meeting psychiatrists and watching videos, but both Bhuchar and Khan remember feeling that the play itself actually drifted from a direct relation with what they had found [Bhuchar and Khan 2007]. The programme for *Meet Me* (**DVD 79–87**) lists elements from the research, such as schizophrenia and Electro-Convulsive Therapy, and imbalances in the attention and treatment delivered to Asian patients by psychiatric services, before introducing the scenario of the play itself, which was 'to evaluate "sane" humanity's visions of mental health': 'In arriving at this viewpoint, an equivalence was perceived between certain states of Love and certain types of mental illness' (**DVD 82**).

---

[25] Sudha Bhuchar and Naushaba Shaheen Khan interviewed by Graham Ley, London, 14 December 2007.

The story itself repeats the theme of a young relationship resulting in pregnancy and motherhood, with attendant conflicts from close family and a breakdown into despairing violence. Yet the script operates with a curiously dislocated dialogue from the beginning, in the disorientating context of photography.

(KAMA is conducting SHAHEEN in a photo session, in the PARK)

KAMA: Up a bit Shaheen—the right eyebrow!—hold it! Hold it! That's my bubble-yubble!
SHAHEEN: Your what?
KAMA: Chewing gum! Next pose—on the grass—sitting waiting for the Knight-rider to whistle you into—
SHAHEEN: To what?
KAMA: What do you fancy?
SHAHEEN: A bath full of rose petals!
KAMA: Noor Jehan here we come!—wait for it—wait—wait—hold it—hold it—fantastic!
SHAHEEN: Come Kama—let us embrace the destiny of pilgrims!
KAMA: Had your sister for breakfast again?
SHAHEEN: Scruff bag!
KAMA: Now the head-over-heels look!

(SHAHEEN poses an infatuated look)

KAMA: Too poetic Shaheen—we're ethnicals—the roots trip!
SHAHEEN: How?
KAMA: Graphic! The realism of dreams!
SHAHEEN: Show me.

(KAMA goes over to SHAHEEN and picks up her legs, helping her to do a hand-stand)

Meet Me, scene 2

Anjali Ewing, reviewing for the *Asian Post* (Vol. 2, no. 8, 31 December 1983) was understandably puzzled both by simplistic elements of the direction (by Yogesh Bhatt) and the script itself, mingling a portrayal of fraught family life and generational conflict with mental illness, psychiatry and songs, leaving the titles—*Meet Me*, or *Pyaar Kiya To Dharna Kya* (*Love just happens so why fear it?*)—as an enigma. Rakesh Bhanot for *Artrage* was also critical, calling the equation of the fear of love with the fear of madness a 'dubious parallel', and noting that the scenario had 'all the ingredients of yer actual Hindi movie' (DVD 88).[26] He found the doubling of parts 'without any

[26] *Artrage*, no. 6 (Spring 1984), pp. 4–5: MAAS/4/2, Warwick.

costume changes', the 'pseudo-Stoppardian dialogue', and the fact that 'one of the actors spoke only in Hindi/Urdu' confusing for the audience, and criticised the relation of script to theme:

> The programme notes are perhaps a clearer and more cogent statement of the problem than the actual theatrical performance. Many of the points mentioned in the notes are neither brought out in the text nor in the production.

The Earlsfield building

Undoubtedly, the most significant development of these years was the purchase, by means of funding from the GLC, of a house in the Earlsfield district of the London borough of Wandsworth to serve as an arts centre. It is significant from a number of perspectives, since it remains the only centre or permanent base that Asian theatre in the UK has, or has had, limited in scope though it may be. Tara Arts had been a touring theatre group, and a building would pose questions about a programme of arts activities to be located in Wandsworth.

The idea of such a centre had appeared very early, in Verma's outline for an Asian drama group from April 1979 discussed above, in which he wrote that the 'initial aims will not only be for running funds but <u>also</u> for a centre, a base for the group—even if this means a derelict house'. The formation of the GLC's Ethnic Arts Sub-committee in 1982, with a substantial budget for 1982–83, provided the first serious opportunity to lobby for this purpose, and the earliest documentation is a memo 'For the attention of Tony Banks, Chairman, Arts and Recreation Committee, G.L.C.', the body to which the Sub-committee was attached, dated 7 February 1983 under Verma's name.[27]

The memo specifies the house in Garratt Lane, and reveals that an offer of £50,000 made by Tara Arts on 3 February was accepted. The justification ('Why need it?', p. 1) mentions the use of the Millan Centre in Tooting Bec and 'private halls hired from Wandsworth Corporation' for current activity, and that the Tara administration 'is located in the private residence of one of the full-time workers'. The formation of the professional touring company is also noted as something which makes more acute 'the demands for a central focus of all the Group's work'. But firm emphasis is laid on 'ethnic arts provision', and the acquisition of the building 'will be a positive step forward for the development of arts activity in general in Wandsworth, and of Black Arts in particular'. Projected use would be for all activities other than public performances,

---

[27] All documents cited or quoted here below are contained in the box-file marked 'Centre'.

> viz., rehearsals, training workshops, supplementary classes, set construction, offices, storage, as well as forums on the nature of Asian politics and other aspects of life in Britain …
>
> It will, in sum, enable TARA to begin to fulfil its potential as a community arts group.

The memo moves on to suggest three choices for the Committee and Tony Banks to consider. The first would be the use of the existing £6,500 grant from the GLC as a deposit to secure the building, with further funds to be sought for maintenance in 1983–84. The second option would be for the GLC to buy the freehold, and lease it to Tara; the final option would be 'for Tara to be given a capital grant of £50,000 to buy the whole property; as an investment towards the establishment of the first Asian Arts centre in London.'

A document attached to the memo, entitled 'Report on Activities to date', provides details of workshops already held by Tara in the previous autumn:

> Between July and November 1982, TARA held a series of skills training workshops with outside tutors. The workshops were in movement and voice, and classical Indian vocal music. Another series of skills training workshops are being held in the period January–March 1983. These will develop upon the first series and also include Indian classical dance.

The report also has notes on 'supplementary classes':

> A year-long course in Asian history is currently being offered to members of the community. In addition, a class is also under-way on Asian literature. These classes are seen as integral parts of TARA activity. On a more informal level, TARA is undertaking regular discussions—open to the public—in an effort to define the nature and role of Asian politics in Britain.

Both the report and an additional document titled 'Activities Planned, 1983/4' emphasise the need for a third full-time worker, who would be an appointment in Publicity. Other funding requests outlined in these documents related to the purchase of a van and of 'basic' video equipment to facilitate video projects, and to the possibility of an 'Asian Arts conference', as well as to revenue costs (productions, administrator's salary, workshops and classes).

In the event, the building was purchased in June 1983 with a capital grant from the GLC. A short (undated and possibly draft) summary entitled 'Tara Arts Centre', written apparently in the summer of 1985, provides a useful account of progress in the intervening period.

> When the Centre was acquired in June 1983, the building consisted of a shop-front with a hall attached to its back, and two floors (originally as maisonette accommodation).
>
> In order to function as an effective Arts Centre, with proper facilities in the hall to host visiting dance, music and theatre companies, as well as seat an audience of 50–75, an architectural study was commissioned ... The major proportion of funding was secured from the GLC ...
>
> The major renovations involved in this phase included a structural overhaul of a flanking wall, bricking up windows in the studio (hall) space, reconstructing toilet blocks on the ground floor with a new access from the Front-of-House (FOH) area, and re-designing the FOH space to create a single entrance lobby. Central heating and new floors were also laid, with dance-lino covering in the studio and FOH spaces. This phase over-ran by approximately 10 weeks due to additional structural works.
>
> This [The first—**handwritten correction**] phase finished in late February 1985. After a brief period during which the Centre was open in March 1985, Phase II of renovations was begun, to undertake necessary cosmetic finishes; a suspended ceiling in the FOH area, overhauling of the main roof, a soundproof exit and partition doors to the studio, other Means-of-Escape improvements, and a new shop-front. These works ... finish in July 1985; and the Centre is due to open finally in September with a regular programme of activities.
>
> Despite more than half the year being given over to renovations, administration continued from the upper floors of the Centre, and projects and other activities were located in rented spaces in the vicinity of the Centre.

The programme of renovations was also funded by the GLC, who maintained and increased their revenue funding in the same period (**DVD 89–90**). Accounts by Churchill's for the year ended 31 March 1984 show the ACGB grant at £25,441 and the GLC's at £16,500, a figure that does not include the capital grant for the purchase of the building. A typed Profit and Loss sheet for the year ended 31 March 1985 shows the ACGB at £25,700, with the GLC at £57,948, while a projected income sheet for 1985–86 (dated 30 August 1985) shows the ACGB to date at £9,995, with the GLC revenue grant estimated at £86,708, the GLC capital grant at £14,439 and the GLC renovation grant at £49,000. The timing of both the proposal for the Centre and the execution of the project fell precisely within the unique period that made it possible, since the GLC was abolished by the government in 1986.

The summary of progress on the Centre quoted at length above concluded with the observation that 'The Community Arts programme was the most seriously affected activity as a result of the renovations', but noted that the Community Theatre team (distinct from the professional touring company) had produced *A Cabaret for All Seasons*, 'an anti-racist cabaret, as part of the GLC's Anti-Racist year initiative' (DVD 91–93). Revue sketches had formed part of Tara's incidental activity before, but this was the first major performance that had advanced them. There is a video recording of a performance, but unfortunately the sound has perished.[28] The label is marked Nottingham, and the tape shows a cast in black costume, two with white half-masks, in an open performance space with a raised stage behind it, on which sits a figure in a white full-mask wearing a pith helmet, who clearly introduces and 'presides' over the sketches: Verma has explained that this figure represented the prime minister Margaret Thatcher. The script on file has scenes of the police deceiving children, a party in which a young man is embarrassed by his name and denies his Asian identity, prejudice and insensitivity in schools, and a black ghost finally accepted by white ghosts but told that he is working for them in spooking people. This script was written by Balbeer Bahi, Helen Awan and Verma, and the cast on the flier included Rekha and Arti Prashar. Verma recalls that its major subject was the police and the use of 'sus' legislation, allowing the police to stop and search on suspicion, powers based on the Vagrancy Act of 1824, and that the scenes had a narrative thread of a disunited group of young people brought into unity by oppression.

Street credibility: *Chilli in Yor Eyes*

The professional company turned to a residency in Newham in April 1984 for research that led to *Chilli in Yor Eyes*, which is probably the culmination of Tara's original emphasis on the experience of young Asians in the UK. The research lasted three weeks, and involved the whole company of five actors, the director Yogesh Bhatt, the designer Arti Prashar and Verma as the writer. As the programme (DVD 94–99) reveals, the decision to focus on 'the lives of Asian youths in the borough' was taken after the first week:

> The following two weeks were then spent by the company in assembling more detailed information and impressions on the focus established; as well as agreeing on basic characters and story-line. (DVD 95.2)

The programme also provides a detailed account of the situation in Newham, with close attention on several pages to the issues of social deprivation, unemployment and racism, including racist attacks and violence. The immediate context for the research could be seen to be the campaign of

28 VHSTARA 0009.

1982–83 around the Newham Eight, Asian youths who 'in defending Asian school-children in Little Ilford School from racist attacks, were charged with affray' (DVD 98.1). The lack of local support facilities for battered wives or runaway women was highlighted, with the nearest provision being in Brent or Greenwich: 'the one attempt to provide facilities for Asian men and women to meet was thwarted by traditionalist community leaders' (DVD 98.2). Racist violence and the response to it was a continuing problem, and the play took its title from one incident:

> One of the youths had related the story to Company members of how, once when set upon by some racist youths, he had thrown chilli in their eyes.
>
> Unfortunately, he went on, he had not taken due regard of the wind, for it blew the chilli powder back into his face!
>
> (DVD 98.2)

The company took note of the popularity of Bhangra, and songs and a Bhangra dance were incorporated into what was otherwise street realism (DVD 100). The script has ease and fluency, and the cast settled well into the portrayal of characters who were now just slightly removed from them in age, revealing a confidence in performance that brought the script across to the audience. Those qualities are apparent in the video recording,[29] which shows an open playing space with a booth to the audience's right, used as a telephone box, another booth back centre, used for costume changes, and a scaffolding construction to the audience's left that functioned as a part of the youth club. The performance starts with the self-introduction of the characters, who step into a Bhangra dance, and the aspirations of the characters and their direct experience motivate the action. The play was performed at a variety of venues, from Cranford Community Centre in London to the Triangle in Birmingham, and was reviewed in the *Morning Star*, the *New Statesman* and the *Birmingham Post* as well as in the local south-west London papers. Critically, the most interesting review was by Sandra Williams in the *Middlesex Chronicle* (28 June 1984), who expressed a series of reservations, ranging from 'the stereotypical images ... like the heavy-handed father and the mean shopkeeper', to her concern that 'many women in the audience were angry that the sexism in the play was shown but somehow accepted', and that some young male members of the audience cheered the female rape but were revolted by the male rape, and to her general sense that the play lacked 'political punch'. She was also doubtful about 'how much can be achieved in a three-week visit to an area'.

Yet the play's vitality and conviction arise from the voices of the characters, as individuals and as a group, and their experience of survival

[29] Not catalogued: recorded 7 July 1984.

and frustrated hopes, and in that respect the issues are encountered and endured, rather than framed for presentation in themselves. Taking those dramaturgical decisions was a risk in what was a highly charged political location for the research, but the decisions were consistent with Tara's choice of direction for a British Asian theatre. Handwritten notes (undated) from Verma during the preparation period spell out those decisions consciously and unequivocally:

> The play is about five friends.
> We don't want to question in the play the variety of issues.
> The club is the structural focus: i.e. that structure is the focus of the five individuals.
> The main issues of the play are the issues which concern the five individual characters.

The rape scene has Rit on a bench on her own in Little Ilford Park at night, musing on the galvanising effect that the Newham Eight action had on a depressing life. The performance of this monologue by Naushaba Shaheen Khan in the video recording is clearly audible, compelling and sharply directed across the resources of the set. She is then abruptly and sexually confronted by two young men, who choose to interpret her presence there in accordance with her own summary of standard prejudice in her earlier monologue—'Allright for Sonny to sleep on this park bench, but Rit's a loose woman if she's out alone this time of night'. They close in on her and assault her together. The script includes a handwritten translation of the Punjabi lines.

FIRST LAD: Takko yaaro! Keylda phul ughda-ey es baagh-ich! [TRANS. Well, well, well … What have we here!]
SECOND LAD: (obviously) Phul nai, kuldi-a! [TRANS. A girl—!]
FIRST LAD: Kuldi nai—RunDhi-a! [TRANS. No … a whore!]
RIT: (To LADS) RunDhi teyri maa! (And gets up to leave) [TRANS. Call your mother a whore!]
FIRST LAD: (getting hold of her) Kaha chulli meyrey dhil ki savaari …! [TRANS. Where are you off to, my love!]
RIT: Let go of me!
SECOND LAD: Can't do that lass—not when you were waiting. Us lads have come to keep you company!—Cold this evening down here.
FIRST LAD: (to RIT) Bet you're warm though, init? Warmer'n the tarts we'd get up in Bradford!
SECOND LAD: Ever been to Bradford?
RIT: Me parents live across the park!
FIRST LAD: (to Audience) She thinks we're daft as well as

dangerous! (To RIT) On a works holiday off the mill, see. Only we didn't fancy the coach up to Scarborough.

SECOND LAD: Heard a lot about you girls in East Ham.

FIRST LAD: (violently pulling RIT to the ground) Maa-yev-i-ey, maa nuu RunDhi kayndhi-ey?! [TRANS. My mother's a whore, is she?]

SECOND LAD: Tha Tha, yaar!

(They proceed to rape RIT)

RIT: (crying out) Tan-zi-la ...!

(Enter SONNY)

SONNY: (hearing RIT's cry) Rit! (Checks lads, who check him) Bastards! (And charges into the LADS)

(Fight. SONNY faced with uphill task. Commotion builds up—NEIGHBOURS, etc.)

FIRST LAD: (on top of SONNY, pinning him down) Teach you what Bradford puddin's made of ...!

(Sonny dodges blow, but before can retaliate, other LAD's on to him.)

SECOND LAD: (to FIRST) Fuck 'im, Anwar!

RIT: Leave him be!

FIRST LAD: Oh-ho—like that is it? (To SONNY) Right, saaley-a—we'll sheep you! (To other LAD) Get 'em off!

(Both LADS pull off SONNY's trousers and roll him on to his stomach. SONNY struggles, only to get beaten further.)

FIRST LAD: (to SECOND) You first Gurmeet?

SECOND LAD: (struggling with SONNY) Holding 'im down—get on ...!

FIRST LAD: (distracted by movement off) Copper!

(Both LADS scarper)

SECOND LAD: (to SONNY) We ain't forgettin', git!

FIRST LAD: Next holiday!

(LADS exit. SONNY struggles on his trousers. RIT, concerned, helps him. Enter POLICEMAN)

Chilli in Yor Eyes, pp. 34–36

In the recording of the performance, which is dated just a week after the review in the *Middlesex Chronicle*, Rit is assaulted on the bench where she has been sitting, which is made of three plastic chairs placed together. The rape is interrupted by Sonny as she is struggling against the Lads, and the intended rape of Sonny is interrupted by loud music, with the script much abbreviated, leading to a blackout before the Policeman appears. It remains a powerful and disturbing scene, hectic and unpredictable in its outcomes, with attention firmly on the trauma of the victims, leaving an aftermath of false accusation in the place of any comfort (**DVD 101**).

A changing professional aesthetic: the influence of Shobana Jeyasingh and Anuradha Kapur

Two subsequent productions by Tara's professional company during the period of the Centre's refurbishment in 1984–85 registered a qualitative change in the mode of presentation and performance, and consequently in conceptions of what a British Asian theatre might be. Tara's first professional actors had been drawn from those in the group who were keen to make that commitment. Rita Wolf in *Lion's Raj* had not acted for Tara before, although she had experience with the Royal Court Young People's Theatre. Both Paul Bhattacharjee and Yogesh Bhatt had gained some directing experience by 1983, while Verma had gained confidence in directing the shows that had taken their dramaturgy from history. Support from David Sulkin and Anthony Clark had been instrumental in demonstrating the basic skills of direction and acting, but none of the performers who had emerged over the early years of the group was trained. The addition of Harmage Kalirai, who had trained with Jacques Lecoq in Paris, to the cast of *Chilli* brought a visible increase in physical confidence and an ability to engage an audience, which undoubtedly contributed to Bhatt's developing sense of direction. But with *Miti Ki Gadi* (*The Little Clay Cart*) and *This Story's Not for Telling* the company was re-directed by the expertise of two incoming practitioners, Shobana Jeyasingh and Anuradha Kapur, the one drawing on traditional South Indian dance (Bharatanatyam) and the other on Indian folk theatre techniques. Jeyasingh was based in Britain, and was becoming an established performer of the Southern Indian dance form Bharatanatyam, while Kapur had studied in Britain but was based at the National School of Drama in Delhi, and was a member of Theatre Union, a street theatre group in Delhi.

The emergent Tara Arts Centre had much to do with this sharp development. Workshops were held in movement, voice and classical Indian vocal music between July and November 1982, as previously noted, with a second series in the first part of 1983 which had included Indian classical dance. But the impetus to bring traditional forms into collision with Tara's predominantly naturalist style came from Jeyasingh, who had first met Verma at the Riverside Studios, where they had argued about 'the relationship between message and technique'. Jeyasingh at that point was a 'very committed and rather purist classical dancer'. Her argument was that 'the technique had to be part of the message', and that technique was not going to get in the way of the message, but 'it could enhance it, and it could be the message itself'.[30] Her view of Tara's work was that

> coming from a classical dance point of view I just found that production—I can't remember which it was—politically very engaging, but I just felt that to me as a dancer it looked rough. I mean the movements looked rough, and I could see how attention to physical crafting could make it really slick.
>
> [Jeyasingh 2008]

So Jeyasingh was surprised when Verma later asked her to give a workshop. His particular interest was in the storytelling aspect of Bharatanatyam and Jeyasingh recalls that, when she agreed to do some stories about Krishna, Verma said 'Why does he have to be called Krishna? Can't you just call him Harry?'; she remained convinced that he was 'resistant to anything heritage, culturally specific, classical' [Jeyasingh 2008].

Yet the idea of an Asian arts centre was bound to enhance this aspect of the Group's development, since a connection with Indian performing arts, in the traditions variously revived and shaped since independence, was almost inevitably going to become part of that centre's broad programme. That all three components—drama group, engagement with the traditional arts and a centre—were already anticipated in Verma's scheme for an Asian Drama Group (dating from 1979) should not be ignored. Circumstances had made this possible, but the remarkable possibilities that came with GLC policy and funding had coincided with a specific vision.

The choice of *Miti Ki Gadi* at this stage of Tara's theatrical development calls for explanation. Dramaturgically, the group had toyed with the Sanskrit epics as sources of fundamental myths, from *Diwali* (autumn 1981) through *Shikari the Bowman* (autumn 1983) to the joint exploration with Theatr Taliesin (autumn 1984), but the decision to produce a Sanskrit play cannot be seen as part of this continuum. Sudraka's play had none of the mythic qualities of the epics, and had appealed to modern audiences in India and elsewhere as an urbane comedy, pitting the ethical stature of an impoverished Brahmin against courtly power and featuring a courtesan who is both active in her own interests and also violently abused. In explanation, Verma recalls that in the middle of the tour of *Chilli*, as a dramaturg and script-maker wondering about form, it came home to him that he should look at the 'masters' of the craft, namely the classic Sanskrit playwrights including Sudraka.

But he also places the seed of this initiative much earlier, in the workshops given in 1981 at the Millan Centre to Tara members by Kirti

---

[30] Shobana Jeyasingh interviewed by Graham Ley, London, 15 May 2008.

Jain, visiting from the National School of Drama in Delhi, on movement patterns in Indian folk theatres.[31] He remembers, too, a discussion amongst Tara members at the Millan Centre in the same year about the style of Bollywood, which fixed on how the narrative was pushed along by song and dance. Those stimuli were followed by a Tara group visit to Jabbar Patel's production of Vijay Tendulkar's play *Ghashiram Kotwal* at the Riverside Studios in the Festival of India in 1981. The play was performed in Marathi and it changed Verma's mind completely 'about the possibilities of theatre, another way of doing theatre', with its incorporation of narrative, song and dance into a political drama.[32] But there can be little doubt that the impulse during the tour of *Chilli* to turn to the classic playwrights was the immediate catalyst that brought these underlying influences into effect. The choice of play was the choice of a translation, by the Sanskrit scholar and poet P. Lal,[33] which Verma adapted largely by cutting rather than rewriting. The political and satirical qualities of *Miti* not only recalled *Ghashiram Kotwal*, but connected for Verma with the social tensions of the current miners' strike in Britain.

Initially, his view of the prospective production in typed notes from 12 October 1984, and just before the auditions on 16 October, was unremarkable:

> A fable of a disintegrating society—symptomised by its material poverty and its moral depravity—ushering up its (inevitable?) forces of change; which are ultimately triumphant.

The 'forces of change' refers to the background power struggle in the play, in which the regime is replaced with a new, more popular ruler. The subsequent questions are of greater interest:

> —What is the relationship between this 'story' and us today?
> —Why is the story being presented?
> —Who are the 'presenters' of this story?

They are questions that arose with this choice of material, and to some extent they have haunted Tara's work from that point forward (**DVD 103–105**). What was envisaged for the production itself seems, even at this

---

31 Kirti Jain was later to become Director of the National School, from 1988 to 1995.

32 Jatinder Verma interviewed by Graham Ley, Earlsfield, London, 17 December 2008. On the influence of this production on Verma and Tara, see Ley 'Theatre of Migration', p. 352.

33 *The Toy Cart* is published in *Great Sanskrit Plays in Modern Translation*, trans. by P. Lal (New York: New Directions Publishing Corporation, 1957), pp. 75–188.

point of planning, not particularly distinct from the 'structural terms' of operation that Tara had consistently employed in performance:

> MITI as I see it in structural terms
> * Open stage. No sets. Minimum props. Costumes. Live music.
> * All performers on stage all the time.
> * No break from scene to scene or Act to Act (except interval).
> * An 'invocation' which leads into the story itself.

In fact, touring for many years with minimal resources had provided a basis onto which other performance skills and modes of presentation could readily be grafted. Handwritten notes by Verma for a 'Designers meeting' on 24 October show him calculating the input carefully for each component (DVD 106). So the musician may be an 'ironic commentator' or act as a 'vehicle' to support the characters, functions which were both realised by Baluji Srivastav; the non-acting performers will sit 'in a semi-circular fashion around each situation', and the 'containers [that] performers bring their initial costume change in can also feature in the play'. Most significantly, he has a brief for Jeyasingh, whom he had co-opted for the production:

> Where emotions come from/arise: that may be key to problem of inability to 'go for' simple representation of emotions. Shobana Jeyasingh to be clued into this need and should do work to realise this possibility.

The notes also refer to 'a flagpole in middle of acting area' and the need for performers to think about colours, with a reference to the colour codes attached to the *rasas* of Sanskrit performance theory, which were set out in the Sanskrit treatise on theatrical performance, the *Natyasastra*. Sudha Bhuchar and Shaheen Khan, two of the performers, recall that Verma gave them typed comments on the *Natyasastra*, which aims through the theory of *rasas* and associated *bhavas* to enable a performance to establish dominant emotions through the 'units of action' as Verma calls them in these notes, and in the play as a whole. The treatise also provides instructions for laying out and dedicating the acting area (hence the *jarjara*, or 'flagpole'), and devotes detailed attention to *abhinaya*, acting with the whole body and through properties.[34] The *Natyasastra* also prompted the choice of

---

34 For a clear summary account of the theory of *rasas* and *bhavas* in the *Natyasastra*, with other aspects of the treatise, see Farley Richmond, 'Characteristics of Sanskrit Theatre and Drama', in *Indian Theatre: Traditions of Performance*, ed. Farley P. Richmond, Darius L. Swann and Phillip B. Zarrilli (Honolulu: University of Hawaii Press, 1990), pp. 33–85, pp. 80–82 on aesthetics.

Shobana Jeyasingh as a choreographer, since the treatise also underpinned Bharatanatyam, her classical discipline of dance. Verma recalls that in their discussions they took as their starting-point that the Tara actors were 'never going to be dancers, we're not turning them into dancers but into expressive actors' [Verma 2008]. A workshop with Jeyasingh was scheduled for 29 October, and so she took the cast into the rhythms required for stylised walks, which brought them into and around the acting area, into each situation and change of character.

> It's a simple thing of looking at gait. Each character had a particular gait. The minute you get someone to do a walk in rhythm then you immediately stylise them. That was the big difference for me from the Tara I had known before, because Tara before was very much about the everyday person.
>
> [Jeyasingh 2008]

The basis for this practice was drawn from Bharatanatyam, in the Tamil term *araimandi*: '*arai* which means "half", and then *mandi*, which means "bent"—and actually in ballet you have the same thing, *demi-plie*, half bent'. The position relies on the turnout of the lower body, which the performers Sudha Bhuchar and Shaheen Khan remember as initially being extremely painful for them, but the effect even in the untrained is striking:

> You're lowering your body down the central axis. So immediately you're making of the body something completely non-pedestrian, because it's slightly alienating—it's not going to help you catch a bus, it's just a very stylised, quite an extreme way for the body to present itself. So the minute you get anyone doing that, you just take them from the twentieth century in London and buses and you put them somewhere special, quite rarefied ...
>
> Turnout is very, very difficult. But even just trying to do it, immediately the body looks incredibly hyper-energised and hyper-real.
>
> [Jeyasingh 2008]

The stylisation came relatively easily because 'the characters were immensely translatable into Indian classical dance—the courtesan, the prince, the clown, the warrior', fundamentally archetypes, and she and Verma 'used to have long conversations about archetypes as opposed to characters'. But with the process of stylisation came a far more important theatrical principle of performance, which she articulated to Verma at that time:

> I remember talking to Jatinder about inside out and outside in, because I think that's what classical dance, or any classical theatre gives you. When you create through movement, and you create archetypes, you

> do the opposite to psychologically-led theatre-making ... you have a belief that by getting the outside right, the inside looks after itself.
>
> [Jeyasingh 2008]

Jeyasingh also established a style of movement for the upper body, distinctly visible when the body is still, gradually incorporating a vocabulary of gestures of the head, hands, forearm, upper arms and torso during the course of the rehearsals.

> In Indian dance, especially the theatrical part, one develops characters by very small arrangements of the head, of distance between the gesture and the head. Very small, slight shifts, so it's almost like adjusting the picture that somebody's making. So one could only talk about the external, 'You can just tilt your head a little bit this way and put your hand like that', rather than 'You know you're in love, how would you be acting?'
>
> [Jeyasingh 2008]

The production rehearsed throughout November 1984 and opened at the Bharatiya Vidya Bhavan, a choice of venue that underlines the challenge that Verma was now posing to the Tara group and to notions of what Asian theatre in Britain could be. That challenge was to revisit traditional Sanskrit drama in what Verma hoped would be an act of skilled reclamation by Asian practitioners in Britain (**DVD 107–12**). The production also toured (December 1984–February 1985) to community centres, schools and community colleges, and arts centres in London, Northampton, Nottingham, Leicester, Huddersfield, Sheffield, York, Coventry and Birmingham, playing at the Oval House and Watermans in London and at the Midland Arts Centre in Birmingham (**DVD 109**). It was reviewed with enthusiasm by a range of national and regional newspapers, with both *The Guardian* and *The Morning Star* noting how far Tara had moved from its expected concern with the contemporary. The production was recorded on 24 February 1985[35] and, despite its relatively poor quality, the recording shows the extraordinary transformation of the mode of presentation and performance (**DVD 113–16**). It can be viewed alongside the recording of a subsequent workshop given by Jeyasingh on 3 December 1985[36] in preparation for a second production of *Miti* as *The Little Clay Cart*, which formed part of a Black Theatre Forum season in London early in 1986 (**DVD 117–19**).[37] In this workshop, as Bhuchar

---

35 VHSTARA 0120.

36 VHSTARA 0013.

37 See Alda Terracciano's account of the Black Theatre Forum, 'Mainstreaming African, Asian, and Caribbean Theatre: The Experiments of the Black Theatre

recalls, Jeyasingh took members of the former cast of *Miti* and new cast members through the movements and rhythms she had established for the first production, which was designed by Ann Hubbard, with costumes by Magdalen Rubalcava.

In July 1985 Tara invited Dr Anuradha Kapur to provide skills workshops, and she offered an open series during 22–26 July on 'Styles of Indian Theatre', for which the flier exists (**DVD 120**). The link between Kapur and Tara Arts was provided by Parminder Vir. Vir had recently met Kapur in India, but first got to know her just as Kapur was finishing her PhD at Leeds in 1980, with Martin Banham as supervisor. Vir was 'already interested in finding an interface with what was happening in India, because we were all doing a lot of political work and she was interested in the political moment', and so Vir facilitated the placement with Tara, which lasted about ten weeks.[38] In this period she also gave a lecture on the Raam-Lila of Benares at the Tara Centre, which was recorded but which does not now play back. The intention was that she would go on to work with the professional company on a project on communalism, or the definition and separation of communities by religious affiliation or traditions, which would be devised (**DVD 121**). The programme for the resultant *This Story's Not for Telling* set out the process (**DVD 123–26**). The devising was to rest on a distinctive mode of presentation derived from 'Indian Folk Theatre styles' and comprising 'minimal sets and props', 'a curtain, a chorus, a Sutradhar (story-teller) and masks'. An account of the process was then given:

> The Company set about the play by first exploring the tensions within itself: between being committed to an <u>idea</u> of being 'Asian/Black' and choosing or having choices thrust upon it, of being seen as separate identities: Hindus, Muslims, Sikhs, Indian, Pakistani, Bangladeshi, West Indian, Black, etc. The Company then began to improvise stories and fables that alluded to the points they wished to emphasise: of Greed, of Choice, of Refusal. In the final weeks, the task was to link these stories to the tensions between the idea and the reality of being Asians today, in Britain.
>
> As a Theatre Company dislocated from its historical traditions and alienated from significant realms of contemporary British life—and especially theatre—TARA ARTS has to adopt a position of extreme eclecticism: choosing from a whole range of traditions and practices in order to <u>achieve a way of seeing</u> its reality, in such a way that it makes sense to itself. Thus traditional stories were improvised

Forum', in *Alternatives Within the Mainstream: British Black and Asian Theatres*, ed. Dimple Godiwala (Newcastle: Cambridge Scholars Press, 2004), pp. 22–60.

[38] Anuradha Kapur interviewed by Graham Ley, Exeter, 13 April 2008.

> upon and traditional elements were used to present these stories, because these offered the best means for the Company to come to terms with a subject that was also itself.
>
> (DVD 124)

Kapur had been appointed to a post at the National School of Drama in Delhi in late 1981. During her BA she had set up a theatre group that worked in Hindi, which had produced a Hindi version of Brecht's *The Mother*, but was active at the time in the flourishing street theatre movement in Delhi and north India with her own company Theatre Union. With the riots that followed Indira Gandhi's assassination in 1984, 'communalism, the kind of past we were beginning to reconstruct, and our relationship to violence and how it was becoming routinised' seemed to her and Verma the most telling choice for the workshops and the development process (DVD 127). For the workshops and the process she came wanting to 'use as many aspects of street performance as possible', and she identifies three in particular:

> The primary one was music, and the way that it intervened, obstructed, sometimes stopped the performance, then actually sped it on ... Then we looked at the use of props, and I think the most mobile and interesting prop in traditional theatres—not classical, but traditional street theatres—is the curtain ... And the third part was the construction of the chorus in narrative forms of folk theatre, which is constantly a questioning voice, and that keeps the story going. Those were the three elements that we workshopped a great deal.
>
> [Kapur 2008]

The mask-work was not introduced by Kapur, but came from Verma, and the material was largely found by the performers, notably the folk tales, with the shadow of partition and colonial atrocity coming from Tara's work on General Dyer and the Manto story, *Dead Meat* (*Thanda Gosht*). Bhuchar led the narration on another story by Manto, *Open It* (*Khol Do*), while Nizwar Karanj introduced a fable about the Parsee immigration to India, in which the king is shown how sugar will mix in with milk and be invisible. Sudha Bhuchar and Naushaba Shaheen Khan were both in the cast for this production, and have recollections of the process.

> KHAN: A performing troupe comes to a place, and Ayub Khan Din was the leader. We're all behind the curtain and he comes out and says 'We're all going to do this show', bangs his stick, supposedly breaking his toe in the process. Then one story would turn into another.

BHUCHAR: Exactly, it was eight or nine stories. The whole idea was that you don't hide that you're performers, you're open, you're street performers but you're giving a message. So you never hide that you're performing. We did that exercise—'I lift up my hand'—in which you're voicing your own externalisation.

[Bhuchar and Khan 2007]

These accounts and recollections can be placed alongside a good series of photographs from the dress rehearsal in October 1985 (**DVD 128–36**) and an uncatalogued recording from 27–29 August 1985 of a stage in the process of development.[39] In the recording, for which the acoustics are not always good, a sequence of stories is run through by the cast, with the use of hand-held curtain, percussion, drapes as occasional costume, properties and masks in a controlled performance area immediately in front of a square, white screen. The narrative form is strongly marked and the scenes are fluently performed, with the cast in rehearsal clothes initially; there is a break after approximately one hour of the recording, and masks and a greater variety of props are introduced; in a third phase of the recording (after about 1 hour 20 minutes) there is an enhanced use of indicative costume and properties (**DVD 137–38**). The resultant production was reviewed, in national and local papers, with enthusiasm, with Kenneth Rea in *The Guardian* (5 October 1985) leading with a firm statement: 'it is clear that the Indian director Anuradha Kapur has given Tara Arts Group a tremendous boost of energy and discipline'. The selected scenes included the historically founded, with General Dyer and the Amritsar massacre and a version of Munoo's stark vision of partition underpinning 'updated folktales' (Tom Vaughan, *Morning Star*, 10 October 1985) of mindless violence and personal tragedy, and allusions to the Handsworth riots in Birmingham. Yet, despite the trenchant subject, direct connection with the contemporary in any location was slight. As Rukhsana Ahmad commented in *Spare Rib*, the performance operated on a principle of 'highlighting different aspects of the sensitive theme without making a definitive statement' (*Spare Rib* November 1985), while Rea was more bluntly critical:

> My one regret is that the manner of telling the story sometimes obscures the content. Ms Kapur's intention has been to avoid a 'cause and effect' analysis but by just presenting stories as illustrations of the problem of communalism.
>
> But without the point of each story being underlined, the audience

[39] The recording has the title: 'THIS STORY'S ... Devising 27–29 August'.

> is left to make what connections it can. I can't say I learnt very much about communalism, but I did enjoy some lively theatre.[40]

Rae may have been picking up not so much on language from the programme, which emphasised the alternatives being offered by the style of the production to the '"Cause and Effect" approach that dictates so much of our ways of seeing reality' (DVD 126), as on the summer Press Release, which had led with the contemporary:

> Events over the past two years in Britain and India have surfaced the issue of communalism amongst Asians in its most brutal form. In Britain, we have also seen communalism entrenched in the fabric of Northern Ireland society.
>
> (DVD 121)

The references here are likely to be particularly to the earlier disturbances in Handsworth on 10 July, which were followed by the greater violence and destruction of 9–11 September during the later stages of production development, and to the violence that followed the assassination of Indira Gandhi on 31 October 1984. What Rea observes is a possible disjunction between the vitality of the style of theatre and the engagement with the explicit subject, acknowledged as a disturbingly contemporary phenomenon, and Laurie Lee in *Time Out* expressed this same sense:

> The stories are as edifying as 'Aesop's Tales' seem to us now but though the content is simplistic and naive and the lofty themes not always apparent—the actual execution could not be bettered.[41]

Ideology of the new aesthetic: thesis and antithesis

There can be no doubt that Verma found inspiration from the process led by Kapur. In a short essay for the fourth issue of the *Asian Theatre Newsletter*, which had been introduced as part of the new Centre's activities, he summarised the key features and skills of this kind of theatre, and argued for a revision of Asian theatre in Britain in its light. The four features were the chorus, the story-teller/narrator (*Sutradhar*), the curtain (*Yavanika*) and masks, and the accompanying skills were those of singing, dancing and mime as well as acting.[42] His account preferred Indian Folk Theatre to naturalism as a means 'for the presentation of our themes': naturalism

---

[40] Kenneth Rea, *The Guardian*, 5 October 1985.

[41] Laurie Lee, *Time Out*, 10–16 October 1985.

[42] Jatinder Verma, 'Indian Folk Theatre in Britain', *Asian Theatre Newsletter*, 4 (September 1985), p. 1.

favoured the drama of 'particularities' and individuals, whereas 'Asian theatre is, for both practitioners and consumers alike, a theatre of issues.' With a sideways glance at the increasing number of '"Asian programmes" on TV', he argued that the urgent challenge was one of 'finding appropriate **forms** for our theatre', while not denying the importance of issues: 'if we do not perfect the **means** of our expression we will, inevitably, find it impossible to express'.

The third professional production of 1985 is inadequately documented, certainly by comparison, and as a consequence now relatively obscure. *Anklets of Fire* was scripted by Verma from a play by Kalaingnar Karunanithi, written in 1968, dramatising the classic Tamil epic *Cilappathikaram* of the first century CE (**DVD 139–42**). Verma's version of the epic story of the revenge of Kannagi for the murder of her husband Kovalan develops the role of a Greek trader into the Roman Marcus, who comes to symbolise imperialist oppression of the sub-continent. For Verma, in a note (dated 12 April 1985) introducing his script to the cast, Marcus 'becomes a synonym for early British imperialist intervention in India', which he justifies with the 'fact that as far back as the 1st century A.D., South India had active trading relations with the Roman Empire'. It is a relatively forced adjustment, even more so in the light of his accompanying observations that in South India '"Shakti" (Power)—which in Northern Indian tradition is normally associated with the male gods (Shiva, etc.)—is in South India strongly vested in Parvati (Shiva's consort), or Kali.' This might more readily account for the dynamic of Kannagi's revenge in the original epic, Karunanithi's play, and his own version, which encompasses the 'destruction of the whole city of Mathurai'. In a critical review for *Artrage*, Sabes Sugunasabesan emphasised the importance of this predominant quality of the original: 'the consistent nature of black women's struggles … and their anger over injustice is the message of Kannaki today', which had been obscured by 'the introduction of other elements into the play', including 'the inappropriate use of Tamil and other cinema songs'.[43]

There are thematically close connections with *Miti Ki Gadi*, in the central plot of a wife left for a dancer, but the mode of production was eclectic by contrast: Sugunasabesan wrote of 'a jocular style which showed a shallow understanding of the work' (**DVD 143–45**). The play had opened in May 1985 at the Tara Arts Centre, and was also reviewed in *The Scotsman* by Howard Purdie (*The Scotsman* 7 July 1985), who commented on 'the blend of Eastern and Western theatrical techniques', incorporating 'spoonfuls of sugary songs from Indian films', an element which Sudha Bhuchar from the cast recalls she felt to be discordant with the cultural setting.

---

[43] *Artrage*, nos 9–10 (Summer 1985), p. 53: MAAS/4/2, Warwick.

> I thought it had no integrity, because we used these songs from a language we didn't understand ... And you think what relevance is that music, because you don't know what it is saying.
>
> [Bhuchar 2007]

Specifically, Bhuchar remembers that Yogesh Bhatt

> went and got this record with songs in the Tamil language, which we didn't understand, and so you didn't know what they were saying and whether they were appropriate or not to underscore whatever we chose to do. Then we put on these English lyrics that went with the rhyme of the songs, and the whole thing was a complete mish-mash.
>
> [Bhuchar and Khan 2007]

Apart from criticism of the pace of the script and the accompanying direction by Bhatt, Purdoe for *The Scotsman* was full of praise, seeing 'Tara at its best: probing, exploring, experimenting; pioneering on the frontier of a future East–West theatre.' The date of Purdoe's review—7 July 1985—was, by coincidence, the date of the opening of Peter Brook's *Mahabharata* at the Avignon festival, and the review carries the enthusiasm for interculturalism that was becoming a vogue. In the same, fourth, edition of the *Asian Theatre Newsletter* (September 1985) in which Verma published his essay on 'Indian Folk Theatre in Britain', Hardial Rai expressed at length very different views from Purdoe in a review of *Anklets of Fire* with the subtitle 'Arrival of elitist Asian theatre?' (DVD 146–47). Rai, who had been instrumental in the formation and development of the Hounslow Arts Cooperative in the early 1980s, observed that the demise of the GLC would bring about a change in the emphasis of support for Black and Asian companies, since they saw 'Asian/Black arts through an historical development'.[44] Rai envisaged that the new criteria would stem from the ACGB, 'whose only base to give support is on the merit of "professional and artistic" credibility'. His argument developed that potential conflict in expectations:

> Asian theatre activists in this country can be said to therefore have been born and evolved out of a political ideology. It could be expected therefore that the work of such companies would remain faithful to their founding aims. Of course, this does not mean that overtly political plays be churned out, as the perspective could be present even in a classic or period piece.
>
> 'Anklets of Fire' raises the debate because it impresses me with contradicting some fundamental ideals. It is guilty of complacency in

---

44 Hardial Rai, 'Arrival of Elitist Asian Theatre?' (review of *Anklets of Fire*), *Asian Theatre Newsletter*, 4 (September 1985), p. 4.

> that any work produced by such companies would necessarily have an **Asian perspective from Britain.**

His first major criticism was of the design by Magdalene Rubalcava, which he felt brought the play close to the stereotype of costume drama.

> The second point of this production is of style. Any style must make a statement. 'Anklets of Fire' was produced in the wake of 'Miti Ki Gadi', a play which by its sheer audacity and clear purpose was a landmark in British theatre. It was an innovative work using a non-naturalistic stylised performance which extracted a statement from two very different concepts on theatre—Western and Asian. The Sanskritic movements and rasas (moods) brought a delight to a very wide section of the theatregoers. Any progression of this theatre was looked forward to. 'Anklets' surprisingly stumbles to find identity and fails because it lacks a purpose. Its use of movement and interplay of speech was unthoughtful and did not seem to address the audience the company has so far been used to—a wide section of the Asian community ...
>
> And this I feel is the basis of the argument. Should the move into a mainstream circuit (out of a struggle obviously) and a meeting of new criteria ask us to also indulge in the theatre practice of this country i.e. elitist and patronised only by a particular class?

On 6 September 1985 the Tara Arts Centre was formally opened. A year later, an application was made by Tara to the ACGB for revenue funding, which was successful.
[GL]

3

Hounslow Arts Cooperative

According to Poulomi Desai and Hardial Rai, the idea of founding a group came from a chance meeting at the Commonwealth Institute, where Desai was performing her poetry and Rai was recording on camera, as Desai recalls:

> That was 1980, it was definitely during 1980, and he was older, he must have been eighteen or nineteen at the time, and sort of came up to me and said 'Do you fancy starting up an arts group?', and I said 'What sort of arts group?', and he said 'Well, I don't know, you know it could be poetry and all this', so I said 'All right, then'. So we set up an arts group in Hounslow.[45]

Desai was fifteen at the time, a young punk poet who had been drawn into recitals by her mother, composing work mostly for Gujurati audiences but in English rather than Gujurati. As Hardial Rai recalls the meeting, he was reacting to being in the Commonwealth Institute, and Desai is clear about their sense of cultural politics at that time. They wanted to be a collective, from a 'throw back to the sixties' but also

> because of the influence of punk we wanted it to be ... much more open in the sense of being a challenge, but also a challenge to the authority within our own communities.
>
> [Desai 2006]

They also rejected the terms in which the British Asian experience was so often cast:

> It was a time of—whether from Local Education Authorities to god knows which city council—talking about [being] torn between two

---

[45] Poulomi Desai interviewed by Graham Ley and Sarah Dadswell, Exeter, 5 January 2006.

> cultures, and identity crises, and this had seemed to be going on for at least twenty years if not longer, and in our own mind-sets we thought this is our inheritance. And that was about it, and we had to do something about it.
>
> [Desai 2006]

Hounslow Arts Cooperative (HAC) had a range of activities from the outset, with a band, a magazine and a visual arts collective, and its involvement was part of a political scene in Southall in which the National Association of Asian Youth rubbed up against the Southall Youth Movement and the Southall Black Sisters, both relatively recently founded. The playwright Harwant Bains reviewed this broad context in an essay published in 1988, in which he reveals the disillusion typical of those who were part of the Southall Youth Movement with what he calls 'the professionalisation of ethnicity'.

> It is no exaggeration to say that nowadays there are two communities in Southall; the first, more visible one, is created and funded by various state agencies and run by 'career militants'; the second, more hidden one, is populated by the ordinary people who live and work in the area. The first community imagines it stands in a symbiotic relationship to the second—it is serving 'the people'; in fact, the relationship is largely parasitic.[46]

The immediate context was one of self-defence against racist violence. As Bains notes, the Southall Youth Movement was formed, 'essentially out of a coalition of local street gangs', after the murder of Gurdeep Singh Chaggar in 1976, and street action in Southall against racism and the intrusion of the National Front became intense in both 1979 and 1981.[47] In this context, the initiative taken by Desai and Rai is remarkably similar to that taken by the founders of Tara Arts some years before, except that it occurs in what was, by that time, a far more activist part of London's suburbs.

There are very few firm details about the first years of HAC as a theatre-making group, although the list of events is confirmed and many posters and even programmes have been preserved. An early (undated) statement of aims and objectives embraces 'activities in all artforms', and poetry, bands and the visual arts all flourished alongside theatre-making (**DVD 1–3**). Memories of the first performance, which was a presentation of Tagore's prose and poems, are very weak, but Rai is firm about inspiration

---

46 H. Bains, 'Southall Youth: An Old-Fashioned Story', in *Multi-Racist Britain*, ed. P. Cohen and H. Bains (Basingstoke: Macmillan, 1988), pp. 226–43, p. 240.

47 See Bains, 'Southall Youth', p. 237 on the formation of the SYM, and pp. 235–36 on the causes and community dynamics of the riots of 1979 and 1981.

coming from the enthusiasm of Desai's mother for Tagore's work.[48] Even Desai herself recalls very little, although it could reasonably be assumed that her performance skills and background in recitals may have been a basis for the event, which occurred in 1981 (**DVD 4–6**). By the following year it is clear that the group had expanded and that theatre-making had taken root, and both Rai and Desai remember a number of significant aspects that brought the production of *The Ramayana* into being in 1982. In the first instance there was the problem of rehearsal space, and both pay tribute to Dave Purvis, a teacher at Cranford Community School who offered and secured facilities for them in the school hall, where the show was eventually performed.

> He was a Geordie, I think, he went up to Newcastle afterwards. He was superb, not just in terms of supporting HAC, but loads of Asian arts organisations around then. The guy was gold, you know. He was brilliant, it was all extra-curricular and he ensured that people had a base there in Cranford.[49]

As a collective, the group had also grown:

> But by that time we had about forty people in the group, a multi-racial group, mainly teenagers and twenty-year-olds ... so it's a lot of college students and school students really who would come in, and whoever would come to the meetings would make a final decision: a collective, I suppose. So the way we went about it was discussing what we were going to do and what would appeal to people, but [also] what are the twists that we wanted to do with that, and the reasons why we were picking some of the epics, or something that was considered so precious in some people's minds.
>
> [Desai 2006]

The group had gradually expanded by means of invitations in leaflets and the encouragement of friends. Specifically, in relation to *The Ramayana*, the epic to which Desai refers above, they had subversive strategies, which picked out a north–south conflict and melded it with a white–black conflict. The group wished to turn these themes on their heads, and so the monkey king Hanuman was played by a white man, 'twisting a bit of the racial stereotypes'. In gender terms, Sita's traditionally passive profile in response to harsh treatment at the hands of her jealous husband Rama was challenged,

---

[48] This and subsequent quotations or citations of Rai come from Graham Ley's notes of an unrecorded conversation with Hardial Rai in the Lyric Theatre, Hammersmith, 14 November 2006.

[49] Ravinder Gill interviewed by Graham Ley, Hounslow, 13 November 2006.

in HAC's performance, by her reaction to being questioned by Rama about her virginity and by her own act of revenge on Rama.

The performance was devised with the influence of comic strips, among other things, and both Desai and Rai stress the importance of the skills of Harmage Singh Kalirai, who had recently returned from training with Le Coq in Paris, and whom Rai had met at the Institute of Contemporary Arts (ICA) in London in early 1982. Rai recalls that Kalirai came in alongside him in leading the workshops that took place on Tuesday evenings, while the rehearsals as the show developed took place at the weekends (**DVD 7**). There was a clear sense in *The Ramayana* process of a desire to build theatre skills, and the production itself featured painted flats, costumes and props. The programme exists, providing production credits, with Desai listed as the narrator and some doubling among what is predominantly an Asian cast of twelve actors. There was a tabla player, and two dancers are also listed, and the sole sponsor was featured on the back: 'Fulham Cellars, Wholesale and Retail Wines and Spirits, Cheapest Prices in London'. The figurative line drawings on the front and on the flier/poster are very fine, and the programme attributes the art and publicity to Manoj Anbaana (**DVD 8–10**). For this production the wider grouping of Hounslow Youth Arts Group was credited and reference was explicitly made to the full range of activities, including—alongside drama and poetry—a magazine, photography and visual arts. The production certainly played at the Cranford Community School in November 1982, but must have been performed before that date, since it is listed in later HAC documents as coming before *The Post Office* of August 1982.

For their third production HAC returned to Tagore, choosing to adapt a well-known play that existed in an English-language translation, *The Post Office*. Once again, memories of this piece are extremely vague, and there is hardly any further documentation. There were about three performances in Cranford in August 1982, and the adaptation was in what Rai calls 'contemporary language', with contemporary clothing. Desai notes that, like *The Ramayana*, '*The Post Office* had Caribbean members in it', and that for the early productions at the school in Cranford 'we did have mixed audiences'. She continues:

> But we were still ... it was still this sense of Asian-ness, starting from some point which would be understood by mainly Asian communities, because that's what our prime aim was, I think. ... They were not the only people who came, but they were primarily the people who came initially.
>
> [Desai 2006]

Tagore's *The Post Office* (*Dak Ghar*) was first performed in Britain in 1913, a year after it was written and one year before the translation was published. It is a symbolist drama of a young boy, Amal, who has been ill and sits at his window talking to those who pass by. He comes to invest a great deal of hope in the idea of a letter from the king that may arrive for him at the post office opposite, but his life is extinguished like the oil-lamp in his room. In common with *Sacrifice*, which was chosen by the Tara Arts group for their first production, *The Post Office* was not only a much-performed Tagore classic but was also subject to allegorical interpretations, with Amal readily seen as a life waiting for meaning to be granted, as much as for death. Such an aura could plainly lend itself to the kind of twist or challenge that HAC had brought to *The Ramayana*, and the contemporary could abrasively intrude upon or jar with the evocative timelessness that had come to be associated with the play as an icon of Tagorean spirituality. On the reverse of a flier, for a performance at the Meadowbank Community Centre dated 19 August 1982, the emphasis is placed on

> a young person growing in a world dominated by restrictions imposed by adults. Some of these restrictions are based on unfounded beliefs and rigid traditions but are carried on nonetheless because of the authoritarian relationships that adults have with children …
>
> Hounslow Arts Cooperative's adaptation of the *The Post Office* bites the universal elements of restriction and hope felt by young people all over. It further makes a point by changing the main role of a boy to a girl.
>
> (DVD 11–12)

At about this time, Ravinder Gill became involved with the group, after meeting Poulomi Desai in a band, and subsequently Hardial Rai. The involvement became a step into the unknown.

> Hardial said 'Do you want to be in a play?', literally. I had no interest in theatre, I thought 'Alright', I just shrugged, my life wasn't going anywhere. And I was in *The Sequel*, by Balbeer Bahi, which I threw myself into as the lead actor. I was unemployed at the time, so I would spend a lot of time just thinking about the play. With hindsight, what I was doing was a kind of method approach to it. I was really getting into the emotional and psychological state of the character.
>
> [Gill 2006]

Rai had met Bahi at Tara.[50] As the lead actor, Gill's memories give an insight into the production, which took place in 1983:

---

50 Bahi later co-wrote *A Cabaret for All Seasons* (1984) for Tara with Helen Awan and Verma, and co-scripted *Exile in the Forest* (1987) with Sankara Pillai and

> [Bahi's] play was based on a book called *The Sikh*—no, it was called *The Lost Soul* or something. It was a horrible book; it's terribly written. But it was a book, and I have to admire that. It was a novel ...
>
> So the play is about an Asian science-fiction writer who is rebelling at the idea of having to write stuff that is only to do with Asians. He wanted to write contemporary fiction, not historical, sari-costume drama. It's about his coming-of-age, and making decisions.
>
> And the play, in style ... there was an interesting, non-naturalistic aspect to it, where he [the lead character] would constantly talk to a shadowy figure, played by a woman, Shehnaz Khan, who later went on to work with Tara Arts for many, many years. She played my conscience.[51] So there was this angst between him and his conscience, and his problems with dealing with his girlfriend and his family who don't understand what he's about.
>
> [Gill 2006]

There was a limited range of other characters in the play, representing close relationships with family and friends, but also other shadowy figures resembling the role played by Shehnaz Khan:

> a bunch of other shroud characters. So it had this non-naturalistic aspect to it, which wasn't a dream sequence, it was literally his inner dialogue.

Gill recalls that the play ended in some kind of breakdown for the leading character, since he remembers 'doing an emoting scene, which I thought was really good'.

The production, which was directed by Rai, played at Cranford Community School and also toured to other community centres in London. The programme carries a Forward by Jatinder Verma which sketches a history of 'Asian Theatre', tracing its roots back to the eighteenth and nineteenth centuries, and emphasising that since 1976 'the Asian theatre movement in English' had drawn 'for its characters and situations on events and experiences of Asians in *this* country'. Inside the programme, a profile of HAC notes that *The Sequel* 'is HAC's first original play', describing the

---

Verma; his play *Vengeance* (1988) was also staged by Tara; he performed for Tara in *Tejo Vanio* and *The Broken Thigh* (both 1986).

51 Shehnaz Khan first performed for Tara in *A Cabaret for All Seasons* (1984); was a member of the Tara TIE (theatre in education) company in 1985, acting in all three productions; and performed in a series of productions for Tara between 1986 (with Bahi) and 1993. Gill acted for Tara in *Bhavni Bhavai* (1988, with Shehnaz Khan), *The Government Inspector* (1989), *Heer Ranjha* (1992) and *Troilus and Cressida* (1993).

Cooperative as a 'collective structured self-help group', and refers to a path from the earlier productions towards 'future work showing more and more evidence of a synthesis of old and new styles' (**DVD 13–14**).

Of *Heer Ranjha*, a previous production in 1983, very little information or documentation is available. Rai notes that it was a modernised version of the traditional Punjabi love story that had been shaped into a tragic, poetic form by Waris Shah in the eighteenth century. He gave it a Southall setting and worked through improvisation and music. Ironically, Gill was to perform in Tara's version in 1992.

In the early 1980s Rai went to the Edinburgh Festival and was struck by the cabaret style that he found there, and in 1984 Bahi co-scripted with Helen Awan and Verma *A Cabaret for All Seasons*, performed by Tara Arts, in which Shehnaz Khan was a performer. Gill recalls a performance of *Cabaret* at Cranford, by which he was impressed, and comments that HAC's subsequent *One Nation Under a Groove*

> was directed by Hardial from workshops that we created ... I believe he was influenced by techniques after attending directors' workshops at Tara. And they were good techniques, and threw up some interesting sketches. It was primarily written by Khalid Khan and Robin Mangtani, who were my friends from school, and myself. [Gill 2006]

Gill sees *Cabaret* and *One Nation* as 'the historical beginning of Asian comedy, which we carried on doing right up to 1996–97', and he is referring particularly here to the period when Hardial Rai was the Cultural Development Officer at the Watermans Arts Centre in Brentford in the 1990s, in which figures such as Sanjeev Bhaskar and Meera Syal emerged. He identifies multiculturalism as Tara's target in *Cabaret*, and sees *One Nation* as exploring the same territory.

> The theme was a satire on multiculturalism. It was about the double standards of places like the GLC [Greater London Council]. We were all very anti-racist. Hounslow and Southall had suffered racist violence, and we fought back ... We had the skinheads; we had the Hanborough tavern being burnt down in Southall. A lot of Hounslow people were there, a lot of my friends were there, fighting back against the skinheads. It created profound change in their self-image, which was very, very important. No longer were we victims, we were able to stand up and defend ourselves. We weren't cowering. And that came through in our comedy.
>
> It was also the post-punk spirit as well. I mean, a lot of people have criticised HAC for being too punky. But it was the zeitgeist in a way. It was about five years, no, eight years after punk, so it's a

> bit wild, really. But certainly the spirit was there, it came through in the anti-racism.
>
> And the themes ... the first half was a lot of sketches, primarily satirising multiculturalism and bureaucracy in the GLC. And the second half was a series of sketches again, but put together by a biography of a DJ. Because hip-hop was really taking off, it had come into this country.
>
> [Gill 2006]

Gill recalls that there were 'thirty different DJ sound-systems doing parties in and around Hounslow' at the time, 'all of them done by Asians', and one of those DJs was Parv Bancil, who became stage manager for this production. Mangtani played the DJ, and that part of the show 'tells his life story, but again it's more satirical sketches about racism, and anti-racism as well, the shortcomings of anti-racism, or the hypocrisy of it. The liberal guilt side of it.'

Of the other sketches, Gill describes one about two pregnant women, 'ostensibly an Asian woman and a white woman, both played by Asian women', with the white character doing all the talking, while the Asian character is shy and silent.

> And it's just natter, mindless natter—''Ere, aren't you a bit uncomfortable in what yer wearing? Well, I suppose it's yer culture'—and all that kind of stuff. It was a brilliant monologue ...
>
> And it's a fairly naive punch-line at the end: 'Anyway, I'd betta go luv, I'll see ya later. Good luck!' She goes off, and the silent Asian woman who has been sat there all this time finally speaks up to the audience: 'Thank god she's gone! Every bloody week's the same thing. One of these days I'm going to have to say something.' There were little twists like that.
>
> [Gill 2006]

The development process was very long, lasting eleven months according to Gill, with Rai promising performances and the show being refined all the time; performers included Gill and Mangtani, with Parminder Handa, Harmander Kundi, Satjit Heer and Khalid Khan, and it was directed by Shakiel Khan. Like Tara's *Cabaret*, *One Nation* was embraced in the GLC's anti-racism year, although performances continued into 1985, starting in February 1985 at the Cranford Community School, with a subsequent tour schedule from March into April largely at venues within London, including slots at the Tara Arts Centre and Watermans and ending in Nottingham (**DVD 15–18**).

From *The Post Office* forwards, the theatre group had minimal financial assistance from the Hounslow Arts and Recreation Committee, but Rai secured GLC funding for the production that followed *One Nation*. By this time, the theatre group had become more distinctly Asian, and debates began to occur about commitment, which turned towards the possibility of HAC becoming professional.[52] Gill recalls that Mangtani, Khalid Khan and he himself 'wanted to be involved in the management of HAC', and there were concerns that becoming professional would rob the group of its authenticity. In the event, Independent Theatre Council contracts were issued to the cast for *Pukh*, and the production was scheduled to open at the Cranford Community School on 19 October 1985, and take in the Oval House, Theatro Technis, Watermans, the Clockhouse in Woolwich, the Tara Arts Centre in London and venues in York, Leicester, Nottingham and Luton through to December (**DVD 19–22**). This was ultimately a devised script, and it was directed by Harmage Singh Kalirai. Desai believes that the idea for *Pukh* sprang from Gill's fascination with science-fiction, while Gill reports that Rai wanted the script to be 'based somehow on Knut Hamsun's *Hunger*', but that scripting proved to be a problem. He found the rehearsals very difficult, with Kalirai insisting on a physical training which Gill bluntly summarises as 'animal impressions which were horrible'.

Hamsun's proto-existentialist account of subjectivity and depression was supposed to feed into this process, but progress was frustrated by the absence of a script, and a substantial part of the tour that had been booked had to be cancelled. At that point, Kalirai sent the cast to see *Blade Runner*, and the film provided the needed catalyst.

> What we came up with was loosely based on the themes in *Blade Runner*. It was a science-fiction play set in a futuristic, fictitious, notional society, a three-tiered society of the underdogs, the privileged pure breeds, and then the hybrids, who are the mixed race ones. It was all a bit of a pantomime. I don't know if anybody made any sense of it ...

The programme for *Pukh* gives a further impression in a list of fifteen scenes, for which the settings included the sewer, the bar in the freezone, interrogation area, the freezone market and the subway. The scenario is also explained:

> The Daheru Race have decimated their own economy. Its sole purpose is to produce space craft and military hardware, which has caused unemployment amongst the settlers. The Daheruans are planning to leave the planet.
>
> [*Pukh* programme: **DVD 22**]

---

52 This was the period just after Tara Arts had become a professional theatre company with *Lion's Raj* in 1982.

The characters of the play are divided between the Daheruan security police and members of the Resistance that has materialised among the settlers. There was a cast of four, doubling nine characters: Preet Bancil, Gill, Satjit Heer and Naim Khan.[53] For the first time a HAC production was given a relatively elaborate design, by Chila Burman and Allan D'Souza, two members of the Hounslow Asian Visual Artists Collective (HAVAC), a part of the wider HAC. Desai recalls green and orange drapes, boxes in green and silver and futuristic costumes, while Gill adds detail about the set:

> There was a set of scaffolding, in an arc. And there was something draped down the back of that. The scaffolding was visible, so it looked very shiny and angular. And various blocks—coloured blocks—were used to stand on and create height. And various costumes were worn, very interesting costumes ... a lot of cloth, and netting would go over the head to create different characters ... You could reverse it, or one part of it you would lift up like a skirt and tie it round your waist, and it would become a different character.
>
> [Gill 2006]

Gill states firmly that the themes were 'race, racial purity, racial mixing and multiculturalism', and describes the play as a 'political thriller'.

The Naked Helmet, and the Problems of Coping With a Dominant Social Paradigm Under a Civic Culture 'was originally booked as a fascinating idea about an Asian policeman having to deal with the police force' [Gill 2006], and was to be written by Mangtani, since it was his idea. But Mangtani was expecting help from the group, while the group was expecting a script from Mangtani. 'So it was a misunderstanding; we booked a play, very silly, but we had to come up with something', and Gill suggested an inspiration in the comic *Viz*. The result was a collection of sketches, 'utterly pointless sketches' as Gill describes them, ranging from 'Sid the Sexist' to 'Tales of the Unexpected':

> I'd walk on stage, and I'd go 'Bugger me, a crisp packet on stage, that was unexpected! Bugger me, lights up in the lighting rig, that's unexpected! Bugger me, audience, what an unexpected day I've had!' And then Shakiel Khan would come up behind me with a big knife and stab me in the back and say 'I bet you didn't expect that, did you, you bastard!'

Gill denies that there was the same anti-racist satire in *The Naked Helmet* that there was in *One Nation*, with pointed exposure of the stereotypical

---

[53] Naim Khan was one of Tara's first professional actors, in *Lion's Raj* and subsequent productions.

representation of British Asians. He recalls one sketch in which he played 'a white director directing a scene about a typical Asian family'. He would ask for members of the audience to come out, and direct them:

> I'd say 'OK, you come home' to the husband, and say 'Ask for your dinner'. And the guy would say 'Hello honey, I'm home, I'd like my dinner'. And then the wife would say 'Hello darling, your dinner will be ready in ten minutes'. And I'd say 'Stop, stop, stop! That's not very typical. Come on, you're a macho Asian man. You demand to have your dinner served, so I want you to be a lot more aggressive.'
>
> So I would contrive this utterly absurd, stereotypical idea of a wife-beating Asian man, because that we know is very 'realistic' or 'typical'.
>
> [Gill 2006]

Both Gill and Desai recall a performance of *The Naked Helmet* at Southampton in June 1986 in front of a large Asian audience, containing a parody of the Cadbury's Milk Tray television advertisement of the time, in which a male cat-burglar delivered a package of chocolates to a woman, with the closing voice-over of 'And all because the lady loves Milk Tray'. HAC's parody concluded with the woman turning to the man who delivered the chocolates and saying 'I suppose you want to fuck me now?', at which 'the knackered stuntman looks at the audience and faints' [Gill 2006] This prompted the organiser to protest and try to stop the show, but when Rai, who was directing, invited the audience to leave no one did, and they were encouraged by applause to continue (**DVD 23**).

The Naked Helmet opened in late 1985 and toured in what was called the 'Road to Nowhere Tour' during 1986, listed on a publicity leaflet as taking in cities and towns across Britain, and 'Paris, Rome, Amsterdam, New York …'. The professional acting company was Gill, Preet Bancil, Shakiel Khan and Heer (**DVD 24–26**). In the summer of 1986 HAC also gave a small number of performances of their reworking of *Aliens*, a play by Karim Alrawi, directed by Rai and with the same cast members excepting Heer.[54] The theme of HAC's reworking was 'the British immigration acts discriminating against black people, particularly in the cases of re-uniting families from the Asian sub-continent' (**DVD 27**). The production was intended to work as part of a theatre in education (TIE) initiative, but the company was restricted to

[54] Alrawi was already an established playwright, and *Aliens* had been first produced at Soho Poly in 1981, directed by Madhav Sharma; Sharma mounted a second production for touring by Actors Unlimited in 1983: for Actors Unlimited, see the subsequent section of this book. Alrawi was working at the time at the Royal Court, where *A Colder Climate* was produced in 1986, with Janet Steel performing in it, who was later to become the artistic director of Kali.

operating in Hounslow by the terms of the support from Hounslow Council, and the initiative did not flourish. In leaflets advertising the TIE possibilities, the motives for reworking Alrawi's play five years after its first production were stated:

> Government policies on Immigration have not altered. Asian/black British citizens continue to undergo insensitive and hostile treatment and in many cases are being denied universal human rights ...

The short, hour-long reworking was set in a detention centre near a major British airport, with discrimination the primary issue. On the same plane are Ahmed, a British citizen with his pregnant wife, who is refused entry, and an Australian couple, with the husband living in Britain and the wife without an entry certificate, who have no problem at all, as Ahmed at one point protests [Desai 2006]. But the play itself consists of three characters: Ahmed, a security guard, and a woman detention officer called Higgs, played by Preet Bancil. Of the production itself there are limited memories, although Gill recalls feeling that it was a good play and that Shakiel Khan was impressive in it as the lead character, Ahmed.

After *Aliens* both Desai and Rai left the company, and the four actors spent a difficult six months trying to sort out a professional future. Preet Bancil agreed to 'get some sense out of the paperwork, and figure out if we have a company, and what to do with this company', as Gill describes it. The base of operations was the Bancil household and, significantly, Gill started 'hanging around' with Preet's younger brother, Parv, who was a DJ in the hip-hop scene. Parv Bancil had already been brought into HAC to work as a stage manager by Rai, but Gill was struck by Bancil's scripting ability. The genesis lay in 'drinking and hanging out with Parv's mates', notably on the roof of a shelter in the park that backed on to the Bancil house. As Gill explains, the funding that existed

> constrained us to write a play about Hounslow. And I thought 'There is nothing to write about this place. It's nowhere ...'. Up to now we were doing science fiction plays, or absurd comedy plays, pointless plays, maybe the odd sort of satire on racism. But here we were having to write something about Hounslow, like a school-teacher saying 'Do your essay'.
>
> [Gill 2006]

Gill describes what happened.

> One night I was just messing about on the typewriter, and I started writing what had just gone on on the roof with these mates ... And Parv saw this and he went 'Hold on, no, no, I don't think he'd say it

> like that.' And we were just drinking, we were pretty drunk. And we typed up one page, with Parv saying 'No, no, he would say' ... And he wrote that one page, and I thought 'This is really interesting, yes, it'll really work.' This one page had recognisable characterisation, lovely rhythms in the dialogue, and it was funny. So I said 'Parv, do you want to write a play with me?' And he went 'I don't know anything about writing plays.' And I said 'Don't worry, I'll type it and structure it, and we'll just work on it together', and he went 'Alright, then'.
>
> And we did, we wrote the first scene, which was brilliant. It was a classic first scene, it just flowed, it was superb. We came up with a story where his world and my world came together, and my world was represented by the female graduate who comes back to Hounslow and sees these odd characters.
>
> So this was *Curse of the Dead Dog*. I came up with the title because I found out that Hounslow was called 'Hound Slough', old-English 'Dog's Grave', and my own fatalistic attitude—maybe it's an Asian thing, I don't know—no matter what you're doing, no matter how hard you try, it never ceases to go wrong, the curse of the dead dog, the curse of suburbia, the curse of Hounslow ...
>
> Parv wrote [the dialogue] for the guys, I wrote for the women, and my part was really stodgy, I felt, and derivative, and his was just really flowing. And I had to take a back seat.
>
> [Gill 2006]

Gill's enthusiasm reveals the relief in finding a solution to the dilemma of the group of actors desperate to find a way forwards, and its sincerity contains sound judgment, although he is unnecessarily disparaging about his own part in the script-making. What Parv Bancil brought to HAC was a distinctive idiom that was rooted in Southall and Hounslow, and an ability to dramatise tensions and futilities that gave HAC a profile through dramaturgy. Bancil wrote good, terse dialogue that was actable, and provided the company reliably with a sequence of plays that carried them through to 1991, when HAC folded. With the core of a production now available in a script, the company auditioned for actors and a director, whom they found in Richard Hanson, director at the Old Red Lion in Islington. Of those performers who auditioned, Gill remembers that Neran Persaud was outstanding, since he was able to play any of the three male characters easily; Persaud had previously worked for Tricycle Youth Theatre and Red Ladder. They applied for sponsorship to Courage Breweries, 'who didn't feel that we were probably putting drinking in a favourable light, but offered to give us some crates of beer, which we would open up live on stage'. The set by John Williams had a podium about four feet high representing the roof of the shelter in the park, with a skylight set on it, and the rest was a bare naturalism.

Bancil's scripts from this period are unpublished, but he retains personal copies that are more or less complete. The programme for *The Curse of the Dead Dog* lists sixteen scenes, in two parts, with a running time of ninety minutes (**DVD 28–35**). There are three male roles, Charlie (Gill), Tez (Parv Bancil) and Spunky (Persaud), characterised by Gill respectively as 'a weedy wimp, a troublesome hard-nut, and a dreamer'. They are drinkers, particularly Tez, and their refuge is the roof of the shelter in the park. There are two female roles, flat-sharers Bal (Mary Charles) and Ammy (Preet Bancil); Ammy has just returned from university life in Southampton, but resists Bal's offer to join her at work, which would seem to be in social services or community relations, because she has an ambition to be a journalist. The two worlds literally collide when Tez drunkenly accosts Ammy in the park and she knees him in the groin. The script gradually brings Ammy into dialogue with the three youths in encounters in the pub, on a bus and in a cafe, and eventually on to their territory on the shelter roof in the park. She sees in them material for a feature, and the plot becomes active once she matches their experience in the faded hip-hop scene with the opportunity to run a fund-raising gig for the women's refuge with which Bal is closely involved. In the event, the revivalist gig is crushed by a gang run by the husband of the woman whom Bal has been sheltering in the girls' flat.

The scenic construction of the play not only highlights the separate dialogue worlds of the male and female characters, and brings them together, but differentiates between the characters in each, gradually exposing their weaknesses. In the final scene a bin-bag carried by Bal represents the destruction caused by the violence in the venue, as the constructive energy is crushed and the motivation dissipates once again (**DVD 36–38**). *The Curse of the Dead Dog* opened in October 1986 at the Cranford Community School and toured largely within London in October, November and December, but was still playing in March 1987, and in May 1987, when it was performed at the Oak Tree Centre in Acton, London, as fliers confirm (**DVD 39–41**).

The survival of the company until 1991 was largely due to the unremitting commitment of Preet Bancil to the administration, as Gill testifies, and the ability of her brother to produce scripts. Despite clutching success from the jaws of failure with *The Curse of the Dead Dog*, the company remained unconvinced, and felt it should look for a 'real writer' while coming up with some chosen themes. They approached Rukhsana Ahmad, who had started writing for Tara Arts some years before, with the theme of 'sexual identity, the confusion of sexual identity' [Gill 2006]. She declined, and suggested Kantha Talukdar, who accepted the commission and wrote a script. But the company decided that it was not what they were looking for, and they turned again to Parv Bancil, who wrote a script on the conflict between the desire for a career in the theatre and an unwillingness to compromise, which had a strong accent on sex and gender. The programme contains a Notice that the play, *How's Your Skull ... Does It Fit?*

> is not written by Kantha Talukdar, as previously stated. As the play now stands it has been totally structured and written by Parv Bancil from an idea initiated by the company. We apologise for any confusion!

The production was directed by Preet Bancil and designed by Charlotte Humpston, and it played for two weeks in March 1988 at Watermans after an intense meeting with the director of Watermans, Mary Allen, as Gill recalls. Inside the programme (**DVD 42–45**), there is a short characterisation of the work of HAC Theatre:

> HAC explores the present situation of social tensions, throwing perspectives on the future as opposed to grasping at the past. The plays originate from The Company's own direct experience as young Asians living in Britain and show the direction of the new generation's creativity.

How's Your Skull … Does It Fit? opens with a young Asian actress, Simi, performing an audition piece, which the director Wayne Kerr, who is placed in the auditorium, wants her to repeat by taking off her sweatshirt, pulling her tee-shirt off her shoulder, and being 'more feminine', putting 'more sex into it'.[55] The central relationship is between Simi and her friend Gurv, who refuses to compromise as an actor—'I won't sell my arse to anyone', and the cynicism about the way theatre operates and the pressures to take anything at all introduces caricatures of a seedy agent, Mr Chopra, a foolish young white actress, Jenny, and the conformist would-be actor, Aziz. Simi is offered a break working with Wayne Kerr, but only because he wants to do a realistic rape scene involving a young Asian actress, and in its conclusion the play unites the young Asian actors in their refusal to compromise.

Because of the run at Watermans in March 1988 the production was reviewed by both *Time Out* and *City Limits*, but without enthusiasm, and it is true that the theme is more substantial than the plot or the interaction in the dialogue. The script retained by Bancil is the stage manager's (Jill Biffin) copy, which has wardrobe lists, props lists and settings sheets attached to it, with a small preset diagram, all of which reveal a spare but relatively meticulous attention to a realist setting. The cast for this production was Stephanie Gabriella as Simi, Carolyn Christie as Jenny, Royce Ullah as Chopra and Wayne, Parv Bancil as Gurv and Persaud as Aziz.

With his subsequent *Bad Company*, Bancil returned to a reliance on dialogue, compressed to intensity by confinement, here in a police cell in what may be a police state in contemporary Tory Britain. The cast was Parv Bancil, Gill and Persaud, and the production was directed by Euton Daley of

---

55 From the script of *How's Your Skull* scene 1.1.2, in the possession of Parv Bancil.

the Pegasus Theatre, Oxford. Bill and Ash are members of the same gang, the Eliminators, who feel certain they have been grassed, but soon a third man, Jasbir, is thrown into the cell. In the background lie the activities of the People's Peace Not Politics Party, led by Mickey J. But in those sections of the script that exist (the first three scenes), the real tensions come from fury and frustration and the incompatibility of Bill and Ash with the more pampered attitudes of Jasbir. It is fiery work, and the consistent strain in all three scripts is that of being blocked, whatever the initiative and on whatever scale it is being pursued. The production rehearsed in December 1989 and played in London from January 1990 at venues that included the Tara Arts Centre between 23 January and 3 February.

The final script Bancil wrote for HAC was *Kings*, which played 6–11 November 1990 at Watermans and became part of a Hounslow Council for the Arts Drama Competition, bizarrely conjoined with amateur productions of Shakespeare and Gilbert and Sullivan (**DVD 46**). In some respects, *Kings* is a revisiting of the same milieu as *Curse of the Dead Dog*, starting on the roof of a park shelter but adding the threat that came with *Bad Company* in the presence of knives and the talk of guns. This hardening of the scene almost seems to find a reflection in the thoughts of one of the characters:

> JESS: (Jess sits down) I was thinking about things before you came up ...
>
> MICK: What things?
>
> JESS: Just about this place and the things that used to go on here and how much it's changed over the years ... It's not the same anymore ... I was thinking about the things we used to do as kids, me, you, Jag and Rat ...[56]

There were fights then, but Jess measures a qualitative change.

> JESS: Every night we used to have sessions. Where did we used to get the money from then?
>
> MICK: (shrugs his shoulders) Don't ask me. I can't remember ... Doesn't come that easy anymore.
>
> JESS: (after a short pause) I used to feel really safe here ... Get drunk, crash out anywhere and know that I'd be alright when I woke up ... If I did that now I'd never wake up again, they'd find me dead with a knife in my back.
>
> MICK: Or a bullet.
>
> JESS: Thanks for reminding me.

[56] From the script of *Kings*, scene 1/1/2, in the possession of Parv Bancil.

MICK: I didn't mean it like that ... I was just thinking out loud ... You're right, it's not the same. This used to be a sanctuary for us ... a trouble-free zone.

JESS: I've forgotten what it's like to walk down to the shops and have a look around without having to watch my back every five seconds ...[57]

Another two males, Roach and Rat, find a house in which to squat, with a chair in it that becomes the throne, and the final character, Jag, is introduced asleep in a graveyard. They are all in their early twenties, and Rat and Roach want to dethrone Jess. The plot hinges on the historic change identified through the nostalgia expressed in the opening scene (quoted above): in defending their notional territory, the gang comes to accept that it now needs a gun to counter the threats coming at it. Yet the leader, Jess, is reluctant to take this step, and fearful of its consequences. The pretender to the throne, Rat, supposedly sets up a meeting in the graveyard to receive a gun, but Jess contemplates death and leaves. The inner tensions of the group are once again the substance of the dialogue and the plot, but behind them the historical shift in the sub-culture of the gangs provides a ratchet to those tensions and the plot. *Kings* is an ominous play, whose expressionist and noir style contains a message about a deterioration that frightens those who are caught in it.

The programme for *Kings* provides short professional CVs for the cast and for the director, John Keefe, and states on the back page that HAC Theatre 'aims to produce and promote original work based on the second and third generation Asian/Black experience'. In a short profile of the play Jess is identified as 'the King', 'looking out in despair at the ruin and decay of the surrounding town', with *Kings* described as 'a dark new play about loyalty, friendship, power and the quality of existence' (**DVD 47–49**).

The final HAC production was a restaging of *Bad Company* that played in April 1991 at the Tara Arts Centre, in early May at Centrespace in Hounslow and then in late May at the Pegasus Theatre in Oxford, but funding for the company was not renewed.[58] Project funding for productions since *Curse of the Dead Dog* had come from the Greater London Arts Association (GLAA) and, to a lesser extent, the London Borough Grants Scheme. For *Bad Company* in 1989, the Arts Council of Great Britain had awarded £12,000.

A number of HAC practitioners became part of the initiatives led by Hardial Rai at the Watermans Arts Centre in Brentford during the 1990s. [GL]

---

57 *Kings*, scene 1/1/3.

58 *Bad Company* was restaged again, with a revised script, in June 1996 at Watermans, as part of the Asian Drama Festival organised by Hardial Rai.

4

Actors Unlimited

Actors Unlimited was officially launched by its founding actor-director Madhav Sharma in 1981, under the auspices of the National Association for Asian Youth (NAAY), with a production of *Our Own People* by David Edgar. The company represented both Sharma's long-standing battle against what he understood to be 'unfair discrimination in the British theatre' and his aspiration to create a multi-racial company in which 'actors would have more control over their talents' and casting would 'be done irrespective of race, colour, creed, political or sexual persuasion'.[1]

Sharma, originally from South India, had arrived in the UK in 1962 with a scholarship to train at RADA (the Royal Academy of Dramatic Art). In the 1970s he began to lobby for the rights of minority groups (gay, women, Afro-Asian) in British theatre, and became a member of the Executive Committee of Actors Equity Council.[2] In 1973 he joined forces with Margaret Morris, a producer in Drama for Granada TV, to mount a season of plays at The Howff, Primrose Hill, London, calling his company MS Productions in order to acknowledge Morris. The following year MS Productions mounted a second season of new plays, this time at the Terrace Theatre of the Institute of Contemporary Arts (ICA), The Mall, London. In line with his principles of equality and professionalism, Sharma states that only 'members of Equity were employed on no less than the Union's minimum terms and conditions ... Everyone was paid the same. We received no public funding, and the entire season paid for itself from takings' [Sharma 2009].[3] In the latter half of the 1970s Sharma continued

---

1 Email correspondence with Madhav Sharma, 9 May 2009.

2 Interview with Ravi Jain and Madhav Sharma by Sarah Dadswell, 12 March 2009.

3 The productions comprising the 1973 season were as follows: *Wait Till the Sun Shines Nellie*, by Lynda Marchal (now La Plante); *Kingdom Cottage*, by Bill Lyons; *Punch & Judy Stories*, by David Fitzsimmons; *The Love of Lady Margaret*, by Bill Morrison; *Hamlet*, by William Shakespeare; and a double-bill of *Home Life*, by Georges Courteline, and *Respectable Women*, by Georges Feydeau, translated and adapted by David Cohen. For the 1974 season, the productions were: *The*

to work as an actor and director, notably with Wakefield Tricycle Theatre Company and the Upstream Theatre Club, London. In 1979 and 1980 Sharma directed *The Promise*, by Alexei Arbuzov, and *Schubert*, by Ronald Duncan, respectively. These were co-productions between Actors Unlimited and the Upstream Theatre.

During this period Sharma continued to lobby for rights of minority groups within the theatre industry. But throughout this time it is fair to say that Sharma's direct work with Asian theatre practitioners was peripheral to his theatre activities. In the autumn of 1980 that changed when the actor Tariq Yunis introduced him to Ravi Jain, founder and General Secretary of the NAAY. For the past four years Jain had helped organise an annual Asian Youth Festival at prestigious London venues which attracted groups of Asian performers from across the country. The outcome of Jain and Sharma's meeting was that Sharma agreed to act as Artistic Director for the 1981 Festival, but under different conditions from previous directors. Sharma was to be the artistic director of an Asian Festival, but not a specifically youth festival, rather a more high-profile event showcasing British Asian professionals in which he would involve some Asian youth, especially for education, training and development. In return Sharma would receive a small salary and be given access to a room in the NAAY's Southall offices, a telephone and an assistant of his choosing. Once this policy was approved by the NAAY, Sharma would have 'total artistic control'.

So Actors Unlimited became a project of the NAAY; the NAAY had charitable status and this would afford Actors Unlimited more opportunities for fundraising for all performance events included in the Asian Festival. Sharma began work for the NAAY in December 1980, appointing Trisha Stovold as Festival Administrator and Christopher Bush Bailey as Production Manager, and creating a supervisory Festival Committee. Sharma immediately secured the Commonwealth Institute for the week of 5 October 1981. The Asian Festival included nine different theatre productions in addition to a book fair, various performances of South Asian music and classical dance, *Mehndi* (skin painting with henna), storytelling, art and photographic exhibitions, lectures and performances by community youth groups, including S. Singh Kohli's group from Glasgow, Seva Dhaaliwal's group from the Midlands, Rajinder Singh Suthar, Sanat Sinah, Pandit Das Mishra, eleven-year-old Sanjay Sharma, Sheila Chandra and Indipop with Monsoon, Asian Artists Association, Jazira, Jai Jalaram Arts Group, the L.I.F.E. Foundation and United Artists Association. Sharma also presented Zohra Segal with a lifetime achievement award [Sharma 2009].

Sharma finally consolidated Actors Unlimited with the production of

---

Importance of Being Neutral, by Royce Ryton; *Sam Slade is Missing*, by Bill Morrison; *The Iron Harp*, by Joseph O'Conor; and *Away From It All*, by Peter King [Sharma 2009].

David Edgar's *Our Own People*, a play which focused on the dispute at Darley Park Mills Ltd, Beckley, in the summer of 1975. It enjoyed a run at the Upstream Theatre Club, St Andrews, London, from 28 September to 17 October, but delivered one performance as part of the Asian Festival at the Commonwealth Institute Arts Centre on 8 October 1981.[4] It was directed by Sharma and designed by David Roger, with lighting by Graham Cull, and the predominantly South Asian cast was as follows: Tim Brierly (Clifford Kitchen), Deirdre Costell (Dawson), Shelagh Fraser (Cockburn/Visitor), Janet Key (Watts/Mrs Harper), Art Malik (Lateef/Sandhu), Zohra Segal (Bhandari), Geronimo Sehmi (Bartender/kadir), Dino Shafeek (Hussein/Faruqui), Terence Soall (Jowett/Harper) and David Yip (Ridley/Official). The production was subsidised by a British Equity grant. The biographical details in the programme (**DVD 1**) give Art Malik's training at the Guildhall School of Music and Drama (and various acting credits) and Dino Shafeek's time at the Guildhall and RADA (the Royal Academy of Dramatic Art). The intention of the company was communicated in this published statement:

> With the opening of 'Our Own People', a professional theatre company will have been formed which is dedicated to multi-racial and multi-cultural theatre. After the Asian Festival the Company will be submitting proposals for the renewed use of the Old Vic Theatre. This initiative by a Community Organisation and a Trade Union has important, positive, long-term implications for the future of all performers, particularly those who are not 'white'. (**DVD 1**)

Sharma recalls that the play received mixed reviews and that the Arts Council of Great Britain (ACGB) advisers disliked it [Sharma 2009]. The other theatre performances in the Asian Festival included *Borderline*, by Hanif Kureishi;[5] *East–West 3*, an Ensemble Dream Tiger production;[6] *Blind Edge*, devised for the Festival in collaboration with Karim Alrawi;[7] *Mowgli*, adapted from Rudyard Kipling, with music specially composed

---

4 Published in David Edgar, *Plays: Three* (London: Methuen, 1991).

5 Joint Stock Theatre Group and The Royal Court Theatre, directed by Max Stafford Clark, designed by Peter Hartwell, and cast including David Beames, Vincent Ebrahim, Deborah Findlay, Nizwar Karanj, Lesley Manville and Rita Wolf.

6 Directed by Paul Kriwaczek (producer of the BBC television Asian magazine programme *Parosi*) and narrated by Zohra Segal, with singers and musicians including Margaret Field, Kathryn Lukas, Rohan de Sa Ram, John Mayer and Douglas Young.

7 The Old Vic Youth Theatre, directed by Lucy Parker, lighting by Graham Cull and cast including Ashraf Mahmud Neswar, Riffat Bahar, Richard Bench, Howard Brown, Shreela Ghosh, Giselle Glasman, Kola Ilori, Edward John, Cathy Kilcoyne, Alphonse Mendy, Eddie Ofusu-Osei, Michael Quain, Mick Roch, Latifat Saka, Raymond Stevenson and Paul Tierney.

by John Mayer (a Christian Indian);[8] *The Ramayana*;[9] a production by Graeae Theatre Company with actor Nabil Shaban; a performance by the Tai-Shen Chinese Play Association of Liverpool of Folk Dance and Mime ballet; a multi-media dance performance by Flora and Ashvin Gatha; and a mime performance by Wayne Pritchett.

One element of the 1981 Asian Festival had been a playwriting competition 'for plays in English by or about Asians in Britain', with a closing date of July 1982 [Sharma 2009]. The competition had been initiated by Actors Unlimited, and was sponsored by Anthony Cornish, Drama Supervisor at Capital Radio, and the NAAY. The winner for the 18 years+ category was Karim Alrawi [Sharma 2009]. As a consequence of his success, in 1983 Actors Unlimited revived Alrawi's play *Aliens*. Sharma had met Alrawi through BBC Radio, and in 1981 he had directed a version of *Aliens* at The Soho Poly with a cast that included Art Malik.[10] The 1983 production was delivered as a double-bill together with Dilip Hiro's *Apply, Apply, No Reply*, directed by Tony Wredden (DVD 2). *Apply, Apply, No Reply* is a tale about a young graduate in Calcutta who is desperate to find a job. The play was originally written for television in 1976 but had also received a staged reading at the Maximus Club, London, with Sharma in the role of Anil Roy.[11] The cast of *Aliens* included Kevork Malikyan (Ahmed), George Irving (Miller) and Shelagh Fraser (Higgs); design was by Peter Ling. The cast of *Apply, Apply* was Derek Chabrol (Gour), Raad Rawi (Subodh), Lyndham Gregory (Tarun) and Dev Sagoo (Anil); it was designed by Suresh Vedak. Bosco O'Toole was the lighting designer for both, and the stage management team included Derek Chabrol, Raj Patel (of British Asian Theatre Company) and Colin Small. The double-bill was scheduled alongside a third play, *Hedda in India*, which was adapted from Ibsen's classic and directed by Sharma. The three plays toured across a number of London venues, including the Upstream Theatre, Jacksons Lane Community Centre, The Factory and what appears from a notated programme to be Walthamstow Youth Centre, from March to May of 1983. A note on the programme states that *Hedda* was 'Actors Unlimited's contribution to the Multi-Cultural Festival '83. Organised by the NAAY at the Commonwealth

---

8 Directed by Sharad Keskar, and performed by seventy-five children of all races from a London school.

9 Produced by Shilpi Gosthi, with a cast of forty-two, mainly Bengali singers and dancers (including the writer Tanika Gupta), accompanied by seven musicians.

10 Sharma dates the Soho Poly production to early 1981. It was produced in partnership with Verity Bargate (Artistic Director) and Bill Ash (Literary Manager), and designed by Dee Greenwood, with lighting by Graham Cull. The cast included Carol Gillies, Geoffrey Larder and Art Malik [Sharma 2009].

11 The play was published separately in India, and then as part of a collection, *Three Plays: To Anchor a Cloud; Apply, Apply, No Reply; A Clean Break* (London: Madison Books, 1985).

Institute' (DVD 3). The cast comprised Donald Gee, Jamila Massey, Raad Rawi, Jenny Seagrove (whom Sharma later married), Zohra Segal, Josephine Welcome and Tariq Yunis; stage management was provided by Chabrol, Patel and Small; lighting was by Christopher Bush-Bailey with Navin Thapar; the musical adviser was Anup Kumar Biswas; and design was by Peter Ling. This programme also contains photos of all the contributors, rather than biographies. Both programmes for 1983 include reference to the company's patrons: 'Lord Chitnis, Mr Maneck Dalal, Sir Alec Guiness, Sir Peter Hall, High Commissioner for India, Lord Jenkins, Ms Miriam Karlin, OBE, Mr Swarj Paul, and Dame Flora Robson'. The *Hedda* programme also lists all actors who have participated in Actors Unlimited, both in its present formation and as MS Productions in the early 1970s. Sharma notes the positive reviews that all three plays received [Sharma 2009], while Jamila Massey recalls good reviews but also the wonderful time she had working with Segal, an old friend and colleague (DVD 4).[12]

Until 1983 Actors Unlimited had not received any financial support from arts organisations except the Equity subsidy for *Our Own People*.[13] For these three productions in 1983 the company received funding (as guarantee against loss) from the ACGB, the Greater London Council (GLC) and the Greater London Arts Association (GLAA). Actors Unlimited described its identity and raison d'être on both 1983 programmes as follows:

> Actors Unlimited is a fully professional (using members of British Equity on no less than the appropriate minimum terms and conditions laid down by that Trade Union) Multi-Racial and Multi-Cultural Theatre Company.
>
> The current emphasis in our activities, which was inaugurated at the Asian Festival 1981 organised by the National Association for Asian Youth, means that in the immediate future affirmative action will be taken to ensure opportunities for artists of Asian origins.
>
> Ultimately, we aim to provide employment irrespective of race, colour, sex, class, political or sexual persuasion, or creed in a dramatic ensemble for professionals in the British theatre.
>
> (DVD 3)

In both programmes Actors Unlimited emphasises its financial vulnerability and requests direct financial aid from any prospective patrons, with letters

---

12 Interview with Jamila Massey, by Sarah Dadswell, 26 November 2007.

13 Sharma considers his quest for a multi-cultural, rather than strictly Asian, theatre company to have been a constant obstacle in his bid to secure funding for Actors Unlimited. For him, funders were seeking more 'specialist' theatre companies: [Sharma 2009], [Jain/Sharma 2009], telephone correspondence between Sharma and Sarah Dadswell, 14 May 2009.

of support to be sent to the various funding bodies (including the ACGB, GLAA and GLC). The short constitution printed in the *Hedda* programme includes this statement:

> It is intended that Actors Unlimited will become (by the summer of 1983) formally constituted as a democratic, non-profit distributing Company limited by guarantee, possibly applying for registration as a Charity. (DVD 3)

A later paragraph sub-titled 'Plans for Later this Year' set out the company's ambitious plans, which included commissioning plays about 'people of Asian origins' in the UK, in addition to productions of the classics with eminent actors and directors, work in Hindustani (Hindi-Urdu), and initiating exchange programmes with 'countries from where many new Britons originally came to this country'.

None of these plans came to fruition. Actors Unlimited was Sharma's company, his dream of belonging to a professional theatre company that embraced difference and rejected cultural and racial discrimination. In 1983, having fought for this dream for more than a decade, Sharma resigned from Actors Equity, and personal turmoil resulted in the end of Actors Unlimited. The company had offered a model for multi-cultural theatre and contributed much to the promotion of Asian arts and theatre in the UK. The productions and Asian festivals of the early 1980s undoubtedly signalled the depth of talent and political momentum that existed within the British Asian performance community as it entered a new era of professionalism and expansion.

[SJD]

5

British Asian Theatre Company

The short-lived British Asian Theatre Company (BATC) is associated with its founder and director Raj Patel. Patel trained at Mountview Academy of Theatre Arts, and in 1980 set up Star Studios in Hackney, London, with a view to making films about the British Asian experience. According to Dhirendra, who was later to join him and help set up the British Asian Theatre Company in 1982, Patel had been running theatre training sessions with young Asian runaway youths, who were mainly from the Midlands and Lancashire.[1] Patel had previously been involved with early UK-based Asian theatre practitioners Harbhajan Virdi (Artistic Director of the Asian Youth Festival for three years in the late 1970s) and Gurdial Sira. Sira ran paid Sunday actor training courses, held over thirteen weeks, for which he would issue a diploma. The classes consisted of breathing exercises and other activities based on scenes from Bollywood films. Patel used this model to help train the young runaways. These were youths, both male and female, from Indian, Pakistani and Mauritian backgrounds who had fled their homes, in conflict with their parents, and who used these sessions as a means of expression. Patel also wished to produce an autobiographical film *Caught in a Tangled Web*, which would tell his story of an educated actor forced to marry his older cousin in order to clear family debts. The young people he was training might later be recruited to act in the film.

Another key founding member of the BATC was Dhirendra. He had come to England from Tanzania in 1976 and settled in Birmingham. A huge fan of action films, he had responded to a newspaper advert to participate in a film workshop. This eventually led him to London, where he later met Patel. Dhirendra's theatre training included six to eight months with Theatre in Exile (based in Earls Court, London), an aspiring multi-racial company, including various people who had worked with Peter Brook.

---

1 Dhirendra Miyanger, more commonly known simply as Dhirendra. Raj Patel has passed away and the majority of the information presented in this section is taken from an interview with Dhirendra and Harmage Singh Kalirai by Sarah Dadswell with Susan Croft, 29 April 2007.

Here Dhirendra learned mainly physical theatre skills. In addition, he took a short course on sound and film editing at Beaconsfield Film School. In 1981 Dhirendra was filming an episode of a television series called *Mitch* for London Weekend Television in Keighley, Yorkshire, home to a predominantly Muslim Asian community. In one scene Dhirendra held hands with an Asian girl and walked down the street. The elders of the community considered this offensive and according to Dhirendra tried to stop the filming.

It was this incident that motivated the creation of the British Asian Theatre Company. For Dhirendra, there was no theatre company that portrayed the British Asian experience and the problems caused by intergenerational conflict of a relatively new migrant community. Although Tara would soon produce contemporary plays like *Chilli in Yor Eyes* (1984), Dhirendra and Patel felt distanced from Tara's historical plays and what they later perceived as Tara's more stylised form over content. They felt equally distanced from well-known Asian actors (including Saeed Jaffrey, Zia Mohyeddin, Roshan Seth and Renu Setna), whom they felt were only interested in a white mainstream theatre [Kalirai and Dhirendra 2007]. Although Patel had received formal actor training at Mountview, he was convinced that an inherent racism in mainstream theatre prevented many trained Asian actors from developing their careers to the full. The BATC's objectives, therefore, were twofold: firstly to offer a range of theatre training skills to Asian youths to equip them to gain access to the mainstream; and, secondly, as stated in the programme of their first major production,

> to produce plays about social issues facing Asians in Britain, since not enough were depicted in the past, in terms of true factual experience. It is committed to the development of a new blend of culture existing in Britain today and thus aims towards bridging the gap between East and West. (**DVD 1**)

The newly founded company was self-funded. There was no money to commission scripts and Dhirendra recalls how the Asian-led scripts that did exist focused on the Indian experience, which was alien to the many who had grown up outside India (e.g. in East Africa). So the BATC mostly employed improvisation and out of this process came the self-scripted first play *Ahmed the Wonderful Oriental Gentleman* [Kalirai and Dhirendra 2007]. The improvised sessions took place in Hackney at Chats Palace and the Hackney Community Asian Centre. Racism was rife in the UK and particularly in East London at this time. The play had originally been titled *Mohammed the Wog*, reflecting popular racist chants at the time. However, not only did this title offend funding bodies, but the BATC also received threats from Muslims and Bengalis in the Asian community centres, so the original title was amended.

Dhirendra considers *Ahmed the Wonderful Oriental Gentleman* to be a semi-professional play. The programme credits him and Patel as writers and Patel as the director. Dhirendra was both stage manager and administrator [Kalirai and Dhirendra 2007]. The actors wore their own clothes and the set consisted of a sole sofa. The play incorporated what would become defining features of BAT productions. Firstly, it was semi-bilingual, the predominantly English script punctuated with words from various South Asian languages, which were left unexplained. This aesthetic reflected real-life experiences and was also part of the devising process. Secondly, as later stated in a presentation in 1986, the BATC

> incorporates the conventions and styles normally associated with the hugely popular Indian film industry in an attempt to make their work more accessible to their audiences. They do not believe that theatre should be the medium of the elite only, and see themselves as reaching out to working class people as well.[2]

The company's work was multi-media and contained dance and music elements. *Ahmed* was a one-and-a-half-hour comedy that followed the migrant experiences of 'Uncle' Ahmed in England, which are contrasted with the loving memories he cherishes of India. Dhirendra explained the two formats of the play. 'The first piece was like a flashback Bollywood-style film, starts in the living room, the kid wants to be Amitabh Bachan and the father sits him down and teaches him a lesson. And then it flashes back to how the father came to England in the first place.' The second piece was in the style of a television sitcom charting the father's arrival and his meeting with an old friend Jake Ishan, now renamed Jackson because he could not get a job, and Dougal Singh, now renamed MacDougal.

The programme (**DVD 1**) states that the production premiered at the Hackney Arts Showcase on 22 October 1982 at Chats Palace. This London tour included the Tom Allen Centre (8–11 December 1983), North Westminster School (13 December) and Oval House Theatre (25–29 January 1984). At this stage the BATC was based at 61 Thistlewaite Road, London, Patel's home and also the base for Star Production's studio. The programme notes an earlier play, *An Experience*, but Dhirendra recalls *Ahmed* as the BATC's first full production [Kalirai and Dhirendra 2007]. The members of the group are given in the programme as follows: R[aj] Patel, J[ulie] Nanhoo, A[tia] Shah, D[hirendra] Miyanger, M[alkit] Bharj, H Mann, D Bhagri, R[ashid] Karapiet, H Mann [sic], M Digpal, T Gosh, J Ark, S Rai, H[emant] Kumar, M Miyanger, H Patel, Z[enab] Hussain, F[lip]

---

2 *A Meeting of Mother Tongues: Bilingualism, Theatre and School*, Conference report organised by the Royal Court Young People's Theatre held in November 1986, published by the Inner London Education Association (ILEA), p. 6.

Webster, R Asif, S Shah, Z Bibi, R[osie] Hussain and S[ultan] Farooqui. Funding is credited to the London Borough of Hackney and Greater London Council (GLC).[3] Rakesh Bhanot's review for *Artrage* also mentions the use of 'back projection of a very literal slide show', which points to the BATC's attempt to produce multi-media productions from the outset.[4] '[A]lthough the performance lacked polish and technique', Bhanot wrote, 'the audience responded with enthusiasm', particularly to Dhirendra's role. Bhanot, however, was critical of the clichéd characterisation and generally negative, stereotypical portrayal of Asians, especially the main character, played by Patel, who 'comes across as a fumbling idiot'. Bhanot worried that such portrayals, particularly by Asians, would reinforce British prejudices and preconceptions of Asians. (DVD 2–3)

At this time both Star Productions and the BATC were unable to finance full-time jobs, so most of the company had second jobs. Patel was stage manager of Madhav Sharma's Actors Unlimited (see Actors Unlimited section in this book) and a jobbing actor, like many. Star Productions also made wedding videos to finance the other activities [Kalirai and Dhirendra 2007]. Following *Ahmed*, Star Productions became a limited company and was contracted by the Economic Development Unit, Hackney, to produce videos of arts and entertainment events in the borough.

The BATC's second production was *A Man I Never Knew*. Patel had been the only Asian in the original version, which was devised and scripted by Belgrade TIE (theatre in education), Coventry, in c.1976 [Kalirai and Dhirendra 2007]. Patel credited a certain 'Ajnabi' in the BATC's programme as the writer.[5] (DVD 4) According to Dhirendra, this was a name conjured up by Patel to suggest an unknown author. The catalyst of the play is a racist attack on the house of Mohammed Sidat, who reports the incident to the police. The story follows the fate of Mohammed and his son as they strive to cope with the abundant racism and consequences of the attack and their actions at work, school and home. The 'in your face' political theme and aesthetic was typical of the BATC's aims to tackle pressing issues of the modern British Asian experience head on. The show was extremely popular and toured extensively in venues (theatres, community centres and schools) in the Greater London area in the autumn of 1984[6] and then nationally.

---

3 Funding may have been given through Star Productions rather than directly to the BATC.

4 Rakesh Bhanot, 'Still Struggling: Asian Theatre in Britain', *Artrage*, no. 6 (Spring 1984), pp. 4–5.

5 A copy of the programme is housed in the London Metropolitan Archives ref: GLC/DG/PRB/27/A5/098. At the time of writing it is available as a download on the online archival website http://www.movinghere.org.uk/deliveryfiles/LMA/GLC_RA_GR_02_050/0/1.pdf and 050/0/2.pdf.

6 The year of performance is that suggested by Dhirendra, since the archived documentation omits any reference to date.

A Man I Never Knew was produced with a higher degree of professionalism than *Ahmed*. Mark Salkild's design consisted of a chequered red and grey cardboard floor, a blackboard and two flats, behind which the cast changed. He, and by this time Dhirendra too, was employed by the Half Moon Young People's Theatre (YPT), East London; Atia Shah was employed by Watford TIE. The play was directed by Patel and the multi-racial cast (British, Asian, Turkish) with doubled roles included Misli Alan, Dhirendra, Patel and Shah. In a bid to engage a specifically Asian audience it was also bilingual, an element reflected in the poster and programme, designed by Sultan Farooqui. Dhirendra designed the costumes, Hemant Kumar was lighting and sound manager, Malkit Bharj stage manager, and administration was by Atia Shah and Carol Been. After the play the company held a type of after-show talk in which they used 'hot seating' to allow the actors to remain in character and talk directly to the audience.[7] This worked as an ice-breaker and encouraged the audience to talk about the subject of racism. The production was initially mounted without any direct funding. However, the BATC garnered support from their many host venues, who, at the company's request (as printed in the programme) contacted the potential funding bodies. The BATC finally received retrospective funding of about £14,000 from Hackney, the GLC and the Greater London Arts Association (GLAA) [Kalirai and Dhirendra 2007].

By this time the BATC was already a member of the Black Theatre Forum and Asian Theatre Activists, and played a role in the collective lobbying for Black and Asian theatre.[8] However, as many of the original company members now had other professional jobs outside the BATC, an ideological split began to emerge within the company. Some, especially Patel, wished to maintain the strong Indian idiom. They believed that this made the productions significantly more accessible to sections of the Asian audience than to the wider mainstream theatre audience, who did not necessarily understand the Bollywood idiom and considered the productions to be clichéd and amateurish. Others, however, wished to work within the mainstream and change the perceived racist system from within, and thereby increase access to it for Asians. This separatist versus mainstream argument

---

7 The above-mentioned ILEA report of 1986 states the BATC's 'policy of holding discussions after every performance, so that audiences can take up issues like the use of Asian languages, the teaching of languages in schools, etc.', p. 6.

8 See the section on the Asian Theatre Cooperative for more information on the Black Theatre Forum and Asian Theatre Activists. Raj Patel contributed to a conference 'Asian Theatre—Challenges and Concerns', under the auspices of the South Asian Arts Forum and Black Theatre Forum. Details of his presentation are recorded in 'A Summary of Presentations and Discussions Emerging from the Conference at The Drill Hall Arts Centre, [London] on Saturday 22 March 1986', a copy of which is archived in the Asian Theatre Cooperative archive currently held by Harmage Singh Kalirai.

was prevalent at the time and frequently discussed in the Afro-Asian Actors sub-committee of Equity Council, of which Dhirendra was then a member [Kalirai and Dhirendra 2007].

By the time the BATC produced its third show, *Anarkali*, the company had secured capital funding through the Hackney Inner City Partnership Programme, which enabled Patel to create his studio proper for Star Productions (also his home) and afforded rehearsal space for the BATC. *Anarkali* was the first BATC production that had funding up-front (Hackney, GLAA and possibly GLC).[9] It was also aimed at adult audiences, not the previously targeted youth audiences [Kalirai and Dhirendra 2007]. Although the original purpose of *Anarkali*, to represent the feminist voice of Asian women, was politically astute the production was generally unfocused. This was the consequence of ill-defined roles in the company and a clash of ideology between Patel, whose concept of the Asian woman was aligned with that of 'Mother India' (chaste, silently suffering, dutiful), and the female members of the company, who had much more progressive, western definitions of the modern British Asian woman. One advert read: 'The work deals with famous women in Asian history and their influence on Asian society. The play will seek to portray the role of these women in their societies contrasting their life-styles with Western European feminism.'[10] The story followed a young girl forced into marriage. She is a classical dancer and a flashback scene aligns her fate to that of the Indian legendary figure of Anarkali.[11] It is through the scenes played out as Anarkali that she finds her own expression. It also, quite daringly for the time, included references to lesbianism. Under the title 'Daughters of Asia strive to storm the political bastions', the programme (**DVD 5**) included a brief survey of Indian women who had, historically, been key to India's political development. The cast (which again doubled) included Venu Dhupa, Dhirendra, Charubala Chokshi and Misli Alan (who also helped devise the play), among others. The trademark multi-media production included dance and music elements. The company wished to raise the level of professionalism and hired the choreographer Nahid Siddiqui and the designer Suresh Vedak, who designed a rather ethnocentric set in the style of the Taj Mahal. The show toured to various London venues from September 1986, and outside London to Bolton, Manchester and Derby.

---

9 The funding bodies are recalled by Dhirendra [Kalirai and Dhirendra 2007].

10 *Black Arts In London*, Issue 59 (15–29 July 1986), p. 11.

11 According to the popular legend, Nadira Begum was a courtesan in the harem of the Mughal Emperor Akbar the Great; he gave her the title of 'Anarkali' in recognition of her beauty. But Akbar's son, Prince Salim, (later Emperor Jehangir), fell in love with this dancing girl; when Akbar discovered the relationship, the lovers rebelled in the face of his disapproval. The Emperor, however, ended the relationship when he ordered Anarkali to be buried alive in a brick wall. Her tomb is situated in the Punjabi city of Lahore.

After the experience of *Anarkali* the ideological and personal differences between various company members became too much and the company began to disintegrate [Kalirai and Dhirendra 2007]. There was another tour of *A Man I Never Knew* and Patel finally produced his long-awaited film *Caught in a Tangled Web* (c.1987). The BATC's final production was a comedy double-bill, *Curried Chips*, which included *Siege Mentality* by Gurmeet Mattu (a Glasgow-based writer) and *Mirza Ghalib in London* by Shamsuddin Agha (a writer based in Tower Hamlets, London), originally produced at the Commonwealth Institute as part of the Indian Festival in 1982. *Curried Chips* featured a cast of Patel, Paul Anil, Gerald Flood, Atia Shah, Khursheed Ullahkhan and Brian Poyser and played at the Shaw Theatre, London, in April 1988. Manick Govinda, writing for *Bazaar*, described the plot of *Siege Mentality*, written in the 'British tradition of farce and sit-com comedy' as follows:

> Elvis Khomeini, leader of the Islamic Worker's Rock 'n' Roll Movement and his comrade, Leila, storm into the grant-giving Commission for Ethnic Harmony to hold its committee members hostage. The police and army are called in to deal with the problem and rat charmer and mutant rat become embroiled in the plot.[12] (DVD 6)

But, according to Govinda, although the 'quaint' humour caricatured the British stiff upper lip and perceived racism within the police and army, it did not pack a big enough anarchic punch to really be effective. *Mirza Ghalib in London* follows the exploits of the great, late Urdu poet as he descends from paradise to join his followers in 1988 London, who have been chanting Hindu mantras (which is at odds with the Islam of the poet) at a *mushaira* (poetry recital) in his honour. What ensues, according to Govinda, is a rather 'dull' crash course in the history of India, Pakistan and Bangladesh, culminating in an 'affectionately exaggerated' scene of the *mushaira*, dramatically delivered with the usual 'wah wah's. Details of cast and production are absent from the review. It would appear that, without the input of earlier company members, the BATC failed to build on its earlier success and creative process. Having moved away from its earlier modern-day realist topics and devising process it pursued a comic production of existing texts, after which the company ceased to exist.
[SJD]

---

12 Manick Govinda, 'Curried Chips by British Asian Theatre Company', *Bazaar*, no. 5 (1989), pp. 23–24.

6

Asian Cooperative Theatre

The Asian Cooperative Theatre (ACT) was founded in 1983. Over the course of its six years it produced six plays including four original dramas, two bilingual plays and one adaptation of a European classic. According to Farrukh Dhondy[1] the idea to form ACT came from H.O. Nazareth.[2] Dhondy, originally from Pune, India, had vaguely known Nazareth as a poet from his time in Bombay. Together they drew up ACT's first constitution and chose the name, which was agreed by the other founding members: Tariq Yunis (actor), Dilip Hiro (writer)[3], Dipak Basu (activist), Kalim Janjua (actor), Hanif Kureishi (writer) and Jobaidur Rehman (actor) (DVD 1–2).

From 1980 to 1982 Dhondy had been a key member of the Black Theatre Cooperative.[4] ACT was based on the same model. For Dhondy, the concept was to write new plays and make use of the Asian/British Asian talent available and to 'display a culture that wasn't at all being catered for by any other theatre group'.[5] Specifically, the intention was not to perform agitprop

---

1 Farrukh Dhondy was a playwright, scriptwriter for television and activist. He described himself as a 'writer', 'agitator' and 'provocateur' at this time in an interview by Sarah Dadswell, 27 February 2009.

2 Hubert Oscar Nazareth was known simply as H.O. Nazareth.

3 Hiro's play *To Anchor a Cloud* was directed in 1970 by Harbhajan Virdi, with a design by Suresh Vedak; Saeed Jaffrey took the leading role as Shah Jahan, Massey played Mumtaz Mahal and Pamela Salem played Nur Jahan. There were five performances in total at the Collegiate and King George's Theatres in September and October.

4 The Black Theatre Cooperative (now known as Nitro) was founded in 1979 by director Charlie Hanson and writer Mustapha Matura. Dhondy, who had been a member of the Black Panther movement in the 1970s, wrote four plays for the Black Theatre Cooperative, including *Mama Dragon*, a reggae musical, which transferred to London's West End (Arts Theatre) and enjoyed a national tour and a successful LP of the songs featured in the production, and *Shapesters*, which played at the Cottesloe, National Theatre. All four plays were directed by Charlie Hanson and included a predominantly Black cast.

5 Dhondy includes Tara Arts in his assessment [Dhondy 2009].

or Indian classics (such as *Sakuntala*) but contemporary plays that reflected the British Asian experience [Dhondy 2009]. The aims and objectives stated in ACT's constitution, which was officially adopted on 6 May 1984, when the company became a non-profit-making voluntary organisation, were as follows:

> 1. To produce plays dealing primarily with the life and history of Asians living in Britain;
> 2. To encourage young Asian talent to participate and acquire theatre skills; by way of writing, directing, performance and management;
> 3. To conduct other activities such as conferences, training attachment programs, play-readings and workshops, related to the theatre.[6] (DVD 3)

Membership was obtained through a process of nomination. Newly proposed members would be expected to have worked on at least one production. Finally, in a bid to develop their careers, the membership was to 'have first priority of selection for work appropriate to their skills in any project undertaken by ACT'.[7] Harmage Singh Kalirai (actor, director and temporary administrator for ACT) and Dhirendra (actor) explained in an interview that 'ACT was the gap between leaving drama school, or some kind of training, and then going into professional theatre'. It was understood to be the equivalent of doing 'rep seasons' as an early training ground, because 'the Asians weren't getting in on that'.[8]

The constitution also stated that a rolling artistic committee, consisting of three members, which would 'normally function for a period of one year or three productions, whichever is less', would 'make decisions on the plays to be produced, [and] appointment of director'. Furthermore, it would 'oversee the productions and the administration of the company' and be 'responsible for the appointment and supervision of administrator/s appointed by ACT'. So although the entire membership was required at all meetings, unless 'unavailable through professional engagement', and temporary posts of chairperson, treasurer and secretary were appointed, it was the Artistic Committee which had direct responsibility for the artistic

---

6 ACT minutes dated 5 November [1983] state that the original constitution 'lacked the emphasis on "democratic decision", and leaned towards status quo', so Basu and Nazareth volunteered to redraft it. A copy of *The Asian Co-operative Theatre Limited: Constitution*, adopted on 6 May 1984, is found in the ACT archive, currently with Harmage Singh Kalirai. Archival documents are filed but not catalogued [HSK/ACT archive].

7 ACT *Constitution*.

8 Interview with Harmage Singh Kalirai and Dhirendra by Sarah Dadswell and Susan Croft, 29 April 2007.

output for any given period. As this section will illustrate, the lack of continuity within the company's structure and clearly defined roles and responsibility, in particular a lack of an administrator, were issues that ultimately undermined ACT's progress and creative ambitions.

By the time the constitution was adopted at the meeting in May 1984 the company had attracted a second tier of membership. Those present at this meeting included Dhondy, Kureishi, Hiro, Basu, Feroza (later Meera) Syal (writer and actor), Indira Joshi (actor), Rita Wolf (actor), Andrew Johnson (actor); Rehman, Kalirai and Maya Rao (writer).[9]

ACT's inaugural production was *Vigilantes*, by Farrukh Dhondy. Although Dhondy had offered to write a new play for ACT in November 1983,[10] *Vigilantes* was not performed until February 1985. In the interim, ACT membership met to build the company's infrastructure; to develop plans for future productions and training; and to coordinate activities with other Black- and Asian-led theatre companies.[11]

An un-dated copy of the company minutes (but likely to be from February 1984) records the Greater London Council (GLC)'s agreement to commission a play from ACT to be performed at the Arts Theatre, Leicester Square, as part of the three plays in the Black Theatre Season programmed for September 1984.[12] Further documentation clarified the GLC funding package: the funds were an 'administrative grant and not a revenue grant', but other money had been allocated to train a director; the GLC would handle the publicity for this first production, but ACT would require its own administrator. In addition, the Riverside Studio had agreed to offer

---

9 All names recorded on the adopted constitution.

10 See ACT minutes 5 November 1983.

11 In addition to membership of the Black Theatre Forum, from 24 March 1984 ACT became a member of the newly formed 'Asian Theatre Activists', which had met at the Tara Arts Centre. The first meeting was attended by representatives from Azadi (Hounslow), ATC, Hounslow Arts Co-operative, Tagoreans, British Asian Theatre Company (BATC), Tara Arts Group, Slough Young People's Publishers, Lokamaya Publications, Newham Borough Council and the Greater London Council (GLC) Arts Department. Information supplied in letter from Jatinder Verma, to membership, 30 March 1984 [HSK/ACT archive]. The 'Asian Theatre Activists' later became the 'South Asian Theatre Forum'. It was closely associated with the *Asian Theatre Newsletter*, which ran to approximately four issues in 1984 and 1985.

12 This initiative to promote Black (Black and Asian) theatre as an independent development in Britain to 'celebrate Blackness and [...] show Black people as they really are' was initially floated by Parminder Vir, Ethnic Arts Adviser at the GLC and Anton Phillips, then Director of Carib Theatre Productions (and later co-founder and Director of Talawa Theatre Company) in 1983. Alda Terracciano, 'Mainstreaming African, Asian and Caribbean Theatre: The Experiments of the Black Theatre Forum', in *Alternatives Within the Mainstream: British Black and Asian Theatre*, ed. Dimple Godiwala (Cambridge: Cambridge Scholars Press, 2006), pp. 22–60.

its space for rehearsal. Indira Joshi, H.O. Nazareth and Dipak Basu were elected as chairperson, treasurer and secretary respectively for the duration of ACT's *Vigilantes* only.[13]

The minutes of 1 April 1984 confirm that ACT operated from Nazareth's home at Goldhurst Terrace, London, where monthly meetings were held. During this time ACT also attended meetings with a group of other Asian-led performance and art companies and associations to explore potential solidarity, promotion of their work and lobbying.[14]

ACT's early consolidation of perceived infrastructure and purpose was rewarded with a grant of £21,130 from the GLC's Ethnic Arts sub-committee.[15] The company decided to concentrate its efforts on receiving and reading new scripts for future productions, either from members—to which end Dhondy suggested the company commission three writers with a payment of £500—or from other British Asian writers. Dilip Hiro outlined his play based on Robert Clive and Feroza Syal proposed a play entitled 'One of Us'. At this time the Artistic Committee consisted of Indira Joshi, Tariq Yunis and Dhondy, although Dhondy had recently been appointed as Commissioning Editor for Multicultural Programming for Channel 4 television.[16] Suresh Vedak, a designer, was also active within ACT at this point, as was Shreela Ghosh, who was then working as an actor for BBC television's soap opera *Eastenders*.

The rest of 1984 was taken up with searching for a director for *Vigilantes* and unsuccessful bids to the Arts Council of Great Britain (ACGB) for an open series of seven theatre workshops, originally proposed by Rita Wolf and scheduled to take place in the autumn.[17] According to the minutes of 11 November 1984, the GLC did award ACT a small grant to cover some costs

---

13 All information noted in the minutes dated 1 April 1984. Nazareth had already prepared the budget for the GLC, including three weeks' rehearsal and three weeks' performance for nine actors.

14 The meetings were frequently held at the Tara Arts Centre. Whilst ACT agreed it was 'impossible to have an[sic] united Artistic policy due to the diversity of groups [...] [it] could make a point political stance with Tara Arts and others, and [...] would contribute to a monthly newsletter for the purpose of keeping tacks on whats [sic] going on vis a vis Asian Theatre.'ACT minutes dated 1 April 1984. See also footnote 11.

15 This sub-committee had been set up by the GLC as part of its Arts and Recreation Committee following an Ethnic Arts Conference held in May 1982 and proved a very valuable source of funding before the restructuring that saw the end of the GLC in 1986.

16 ACT minutes dated 3 June [1984].

17 The workshops were to be led by Dhondy and Vedak (adapting stories into scripts and design); Franco Rosso (acting on camera); Frances Shepherd (Indian music); Keith Waite (sound and rhythm); Keith Waite and Nazareth (poetry and rhythm); Maya Rao (movement); and Cicely Berry (voice and the actor). The list and dates of proposed workshops were set out in a letter to ACT members dated 2

so the final voice workshop with Cicely Berry was to go ahead as planned on 16 December at the Riverside Studios.[18] At this time, with the first production imminent, it also became clear that the company was in urgent need of an administrator; this stipulation was imposed by funders for all professional theatres.[19] Nazareth met with Norman Sutherland of the GLC, which granted the company £3,000 for a part-time administrator and £1,335 to cover running costs. Shirley Escott was appointed as administrator. However, ACT still faced the very real possibility of a deficit after *Vigilantes* owing to initial under-budgeting.[20]

Vigilantes took place at the Arts Theatre from 6 February to 2 March 1985 as part of the Black Theatre Season. It was directed by Penny Cherns (not an ACT member, but a theatre and television director), who had also suggested a number of rewrites in its final stages.[21] It was designed by Suresh Vedak (who also designed the overall poster for the Black Theatre Season, incorporating Hindi to attract South Asian audiences),[22] and lighting was provided by Paul Armstrong. The actors were predominantly cast from ACT membership and included Shelley King (as Gita), Badi Uzzaman (Haroun), Rita Wolf (Hasna), Harmage S. Kalirai (Kas), Ursula Jones (Getty), Aftab Sachak (Feroze), Bhasker (Farid) and Kishore D. Chauhan (Fazlu) (individual biographies are printed in the programme: DVD 4). In line with ACT's principles of access to training and continuity of skills among Asian theatre practitioners, Shreela Ghosh worked with Cherns as trainee director.

Vigilantes is set in London's East End in a predominantly Bangladeshi community.[23] Dhondy offers a critical take on the male-dominated Bangladeshi community, which, in a bid to present a positive image to the wider British society, refuses to acknowledge its own inherent problems. This ultimately inhibits the community's progression. The plot follows the fate of a young Bangladeshi journalist, Hasna, who returns to her East End community to help a British television documentary team gain access to

---

October 1984. The failed bid was reported in the ACT minutes dated 14 October 1984.

18 Precise information about the workshop is given in ACT minutes dated 2 December 1984.

19 The need for an administrator is reflected in the company minutes. In addition, a few ACT members had been straining under the pressure of running a theatre company without some income in return.

20 ACT minutes dated 11 November 1984 for all GLC funding-related information.

21 There had been much discussion about the choice of director for *Vigilantes* for a number of months before the final selection. Dhondy stated that ACT did not have any directors at that time and he knew Cherns' work [Dhondy 2009].

22 ACT minutes dated 2 December 1984.

23 The script *Vigilantes: a play by Farrukh Dhondy* is published by Hobo Press, London, 1988.

Bangladeshi life. She wishes to film a short piece with the youth community, here represented by three Bangladeshi men in their twenties, Feroze, Farid and Fazlu, and their mixed-race (Bangladeshi/English) friend Kasim 'Kas'. This interaction is facilitated by Gita, an Indian migrant lawyer working in race discrimination and community law. Hasna wants to encourage the four men to recreate their vigilante, anti-racist activity of the 1970s so she can capture it on camera. However, following an incident, Feroze attempts to rape Hasna at the youth centre with Farid and Fazlu present, before Kas arrives and stops the action. A secondary plot follows with the older generation. Kas's uncle has come to visit from Sylhet and in the long-term absence of his father, to Kas's shame, ends up sleeping with his English mother, Getty.

Vigilantes played to mixed (Asian/non-Asian) audiences and received mixed reviews, although it was well-attended. Some felt it was 'negative, racist and sexist'.[24] According to Dhondy and Dhirendra there were many protestors from the Bengali community, who objected to this negative portrayal of their community [Dhondy 2009] and [Kalirai and Dhirendra 2007]. However, Dhondy states that *Vigilantes* was intentionally negative. He had no wish to produce a typical anti-racist play but to challenge the concept of Black theatre being about complaint. 'I think that it is only by looking critically at ourselves that you can advance theatre,' states Dhondy. 'I don't think that the function of theatre, or television, or novel writing is advertisement' [Dhondy 2009]. A draft document in the ACT archive that states the company's dramatic policy echoes this political and ideological objective. It identifies a three-stage development of Asian engagement in theatre in Britain, starting with an assertion of the skills the diasporic community brought with them, progressing to 'looking forward in anger: drama designed to express simple protest [...] intended basically for ideological assimilation by already sympathetic white people', and culminating in the present and final stage whereby some trained themselves to act and write and then 'sold our skills' to work in the 'brutal marketplace of commercial TV and competitive world of fringe theatre'. ACT wants to emulate modern Indian theatre, which is 'full of "modern" plays that are not dedicated to being the public relations department of a community' (DVD 5).[25]

Although Vedak designed the *Vigilantes* set, there were many problems with the Arts Theatre as a venue. Apart from the lack of rehearsal space (ACT used The Drill Hall and Upstream Theatre Club) and 'get in' and 'get out' time, the cast also felt a degree of discrimination by the venue's crew.[26]

---

24 ACT minutes dated 10 March 1985.

25 Anon., 'A Brief Statement of the Dramatic Policy of the Asian Co-operative Theatre', draft document [HSK/ACT archive].

26 ACT minutes dated 10 March 1985.

The delay in securing a director and Dhondy's hugely delayed delivery of the final script (one week before the performance was scheduled) meant that both designer and actors were not as prepared as they might have been. In the meeting that followed this production the company hotly debated the issue of casting outside ACT for actors. They also discussed the limited nature of the company's membership—an issue which continued throughout the company's existence. The minutes of 17 February 1985 confirm that Newham Council awarded ACT £4,500 to tour *Vigilantes* in its borough in March. By this time ACT had acquired Independent Theatre Company (ITC) membership and also voted in a new artistic committee comprising Dhondy, Basu, Syal and Andrew Johnson.[27]

In the wake of its successful inaugural production ACT struggled to find its focus for further development and even a script for its next production. The company's cooperative structure, with rotation of administrative and artistic committee roles, may have added to the slow pace of progression. For example, regarding the selection of playscripts, all were supposed to be circulated to the Artistic Committee, then the membership, but this rarely happened. The report from the Artistic Committee meeting of 18 July 1985 agreed that without an artistic director steering the ship the artistic policy of the company was problematic. They concluded that, while the constitution covered most issues, 'the direction of the company heavily depends upon the funding that we are able to achieve'.[28] The company needed a proper space for meetings and play readings; what Suresh Vedak refers to as 'a home for the company' 'to stop the Coop disintegrating any further'. So, in light of the newly acquired ITC membership, the Artistic Committee laid out a few guidelines to tighten the company's aims and objectives: the company should function as a general training ground for Asians for entry into mainstream theatre and television; it should provide a forum for writers to develop their ideas (something currently absent from the mainstream), particularly for 'writers who want to represent the historical and contemporary theme on British/Asians'; regarding casting and employment '[t]he Coop employs the right person for the job, regardless of race, creed or colour'; finally a 'script, scenario or outline' required approval by the Artistic Committee before any investment in workshops or development can commence. The minutes from this era also show that Rita Wolf and Harmage Singh Kalirai are regularly attending meetings of the Black Forum Theatre on ACT's behalf.

ACT's second production was *Film, Film, Film*, again written by Farrukh Dhondy. It was an adaptation of *King Lear* set in the context of modern India and the Bollywood film industry. In November 1985 ACT received its GLC grant of £26,000 to be used for the company's next production by

---

27 ACT minutes dated 10 March 1985.

28 ACT minutes dated 28 July 1985.

April 1986.[29] Although some of the money was used to facilitate workshops directly related to *Film, Film, Film*, it was also used to fund a number of workshops similar to those planned for the previous autumn (but which had failed to go ahead owing to insufficient funds) and to employ a much-needed administrator. Workshops were therefore arranged to take place between 17 and 28 March 1986. The first two-day workshop was taken by Lawrence Boswell on the theme of improvisation based around a Shakespeare text. This was followed by two days with Andrew Dickson on song and singing practices, workshops on voice and dance and a possible workshop on masque and mime (no doubt to be taken by Kalirai, who had trained with Jacques Lecoq for two years in Paris in the late 1970s).[30]

Film, Film, Film was a joint production with the Shaw Theatre and took place in June 1986. ACT had been in negotiations with the Shaw Theatre since November 1985, when the theatre's director, Ian Bowater, had offered ACT rehearsal space, technicians, scenery and publicity (up to £5,000). The larger venue suited the epic themes of the proposed play and the planned multi-media production. The director, Laurens Postma (who had trained at RADA (the Royal Academy of Dramatic Art) and the London International Film School, had an established reputation in both film and theatre, and was then Associate Director at Bridge Lane Theatre, but also working on a drama for Channel 4), was already committed to the production, with workshops taking place at the National Theatre. These combined elements suggested that *Film, Film, Film* would be a larger-scale play than *Vigilantes* and would raise ACT's profile.[31] The play included elements of film (which provided the opening scene), contemporary Indian music (composed by Baluji Srivastav and orchestrated by Graham Pike), and song and dance (choreographed by Astad Deboo)—all elements which reflected the Bollywood aesthetic. Postma began workshopping the play in November 1985 and, according to Dhondy, it was his creative team that was responsible for the set design, which benefited from this relatively long developmental period [Dhondy 2009] (in stark contrast to the rushed schedule for *Vigilantes*' design). The cast included both ACT and non-ACT members but the 100% billing in the publicity went to Zia Mohyeddin (**DVD 6**). Mohyeddin was a celebrated actor from Pakistan who had trained at RADA. In the 1980s he was well-known for his theatre and television roles, and had just starred in two popular television series *Mountbatten—The Last Viceroy* and *King of the Ghetto* (Channel 4), written

[29] ACT minutes dated 10 November 1985.

[30] ACT minutes dated 12 January 1986.

[31] Postma was appointed by Dhondy as director because of his experience in mixed-media [Dhondy 2009], and no doubt a connection through Channel 4. However, as the ACT were not consulted about the appointment this seemingly undemocratic decision inevitably caused much consternation among the ACT membership, which is reflected in the minutes of this period.

by Dhondy.[32] Obviously the company perceived Mohyeddin as a big draw to attract wide audiences. Other actors included Nizwar Karanj, Ayub Din Khan, Sumar Khan, Bhaskar, Shelley King (also in *King of the Ghetto*), Aftab Sachak, Shireen Shah (whose role was initially given to Indira Joshi, who later resigned as the script was unavailable to read before agreeing to take on the role) and Meera Syal (who had now adopted her new name).

In *Film, Film, Film* Dhondy attempted to bring the worlds of Indian film-making, the reality of Indian life and the interests of the Indian diaspora together. The plot follows the fate of a Bollywood movie mogul (Mohyeddin) who wishes to retire and leave his considerable empire in the hands of his three daughters.[33] The elder two daughters agree to continue making films in their father's style; the third daughter, however, has been to film school in London and claims that her father has ruined the potential of the Indian people by feeding them this frivolous stuff. Having promised not to interfere with his elder daughters' film-making, the mogul and his fool set out into the storm; here a storm-version of India's street poverty. In his films the mogul has always depicted the poor as pure and the rich as vice-laden, but he soon comes to realise the poor too can be nasty and kill easily. He falls ill and is rescued by his third daughter and her husband, a film writer from London. The mogul helps them produce their film, which does better than that of his elder daughters. According to Dhondy, the audience clap and it is only then they realise the whole play they have been watching has been the film as written by the youngest daughter, produced by the elder daughters—hence a play, within a play, within a play or *Film, Film, Film*. The play's programme (DVD 7) states the multiple narratives as 'parody of the Indian film, the echo of the Shakespearean grand theme and the real voices of today's theatre'. A closer reading of *King Lear* with alternative endings is given in an earlier outline of the play (DVD 8). Anecdotal evidence suggests that the production received a mixed response.[34]

---

[32] *King of the Ghetto* depicted the Bengali Housing Action Group in which Dhondy and others encouraged more than 700 families in the Tower Hamlets area to squat in disused and rundown buildings. This eventually provoked the government into taking positive action and ultimately providing better accommodation for these families. As with *Vigilantes*, *King of the Ghetto* showed the Bengali community in a critical light and provoked more protest.

[33] The script is unpublished but an early outline of the plot is archived in the HSK/ACT archive. The synopsis given here is taken from information supplied by Farrukh Dhondy [Dhondy 2009].

[34] In addition to the anecdotal evidence, a review by Tim Robinson, 'Shakespeare Wallahs', with the caption for the photograph 'Lear's daughters curry favour' (DVD 9), stated that although the play is 'thought provoking: cinematic escapism is attacked, only to be accepted as a necessary release' and praised what he perceived to be the play's ironic humour, his 'overall impression is one of confusion' and he

Although the extant archival records do not present a definitive funding picture at this stage, a document prepared by Shirley Escott on 10 October 1986 states the following: the projected budget for *Film, Film, Film* was £44,637 and projected income was £47,000 (based on grants and box office). Actual budget was £51,413. It appears that actual total income was £46,876. The income was derived from grants of £38,158, box office takings of £1,723 and other portions of income, including the first instalment of a Greater London Arts Association (GLAA)[35] grant for the year 1986/87 of £6,995. Altogether this left a deficit of £4,537. However, Escott also notes that she had just signed for the second instalment of a GLAA grant (£5,067) and expects further grants from Camden [Borough Council] of £4,658 and Richmond [Borough Council] of £9,317, which would put the company in a current surplus of £14,506. (The minutes of 5 April 1987 state the production's budget overran by about £15,000.) Escott's documentation also records that *Vigilantes*' budget was 'close to £30,000'. She concludes that it is, therefore, impossible to 'mount a full production in the coming year—it is simply not viable'.[36]

But this is exactly what the company did. On 4 January 1987 ACT voted in a new play by H.O. Nazareth, *The Bhangra Dancer and Her Man with Cancer*, which was performed as *The Bhangra Dancer* at the Young Vic Studio on 17–28 February 1987. A three-hander with Harmage S. Kalirai, Shelley King and Janet Steel, it was directed by Sue Pomeroy and designed by Suresh Vedak.[37] The brief synopsis printed on the single page programme (**DVD 10**) is as follows:

> 'The Bhangra Dancer' charts the lives of Shiv, Tara and Maya, three young Asians living and working in present-day London and Bombay. With the aid of traditional masks and the music of hugely popular Bhangra funk pop groups ALAAP and HEERA [...], we see them attempting to come to terms with their two differing cultures, particularly in the tricky area of love and romance!

Anecdotal evidence suggests this was not a particularly engaging or successful play. Manick Govinda, writing for *Bazaar*, described the improbable plot as a *ménage à trois* with Shiv, 'a college student by day and telephonist at the exchange by night, with rather thin dreams of being a Bhangra

---

criticised the 'weak' dialogue and 'repetitive parody [which] verges on the puerile'. This may, of course, reflect Robinson's unfamiliarity with the Bollywood aesthetic.

35 Reference to this association is abbreviated to GLAA in the ACT minutes, and GLA in the letterhead of correspondence with 'Greater London Arts'.

36 Statement and letter from Shirley Escott, addressed 'To All Co-op Members', dated 10 October 1986 [HSK/ACT archive].

37 Janet Steel was later Artistic Director of Kali Theatre Company 2002 to present (2009).

popstar and pretensions towards creating Bhangra 'protest music', 'his pregnant girlfriend Tara who is a fashion student attempting to portray the independent British Asian woman', and 'Maya [...] a woman from Bombay with an unhappy arranged marriage who comes to England in search of knowledge and the selfish flirtatious Shiv' and what appears to be clunky pseudo-feminism.[38] The minutes from the meeting of 5 April 1987 show that the play's realisation was based on a point of confusion over funding. Evidently many understood that the requirement of the GLAA grant obliged ACT to mount a full production by the end of the financial year, when in fact the company could have used the GLAA funds to 'concentrate[] [its] efforts on locating [itself] in a proper office with a full-time administrator'. What ensued was a rushed process in which the play was written over a couple of days; a contract was quickly signed with the Young Vic, set designed, music selected, publicity printed and play rehearsed with a number of late changes to the script. The minutes state Nazareth's dissatisfaction with the alternative ending created by Pomeroy, problems over outstanding bills and a problematic relationship with the Young Vic. While the show could not truly be described as a development in ACT's aesthetic output or company profile, Escott and Kalirai state the 'considerable interest in the show as regards touring', and the box office returns which 'had not been at all bad considering the length of the run. Congratulations to the cast and production team.' The show did not tour.

The rather chaotic production of *The Bhangra Dancer* reflects the company's continued internal problematic infrastructure and financial instability. Dhondy had recently left the company, but before going reiterated his advice that ACT should seek an artistic director and administrator.[39] Tension existed between members who wished to take the company in a particular direction, taking on greater responsibility (including Wolf and Kalirai), and those who championed a perceived cooperative stance where decision-making was done by committee and broader membership. A compromise was reached in which Kalirai and Wolf (who led this discussion) and Vedak would take on the 'responsibility of running the company for the next six months'. ACT, however, was soon to be in great financial difficulty. The GLAA had refused ACT's request for £36,000 in the coming year's budget and put the company on a standstill. The company recognised the need to register as a charity and to seek private sponsorship to raise funds.[40]

But the financial crisis worsened. On 15 April 1987 Kalirai received a letter from Tim Brinkman, Assistant Arts Officer (Drama) for the GLAA,

---

38 Manick Govinda, 'South Asian Theatre', *Bazaar*, no. 2 (Summer 1987), p. 18.

39 ACT minutes dated 5 April 1987. Dhondy also felt that the company's next work should be a commission that would allow the actors to play characters other than Asians.

40 All information in ACT minutes dated 5 April 1987.

in which he stated that the GLAA would renew its annual support for ACT for the financial year 1987/88, but had decided to 'issue notice that no funds will be available to support the annual programme of work taking place in the financial year 1988/89'.[41] Three representatives from ACT were invited to a meeting with Brinkman, Anna Stapleton (Arts Development Officer, GLAA), Anton Phillips (former director of Black Theatre Forum), Dhirendra (former member of British Asian Theatre) and Carin Mistry (these final three were to observe and monitor ACT's work on behalf of the GLAA).[42] ACT were to undergo a six-month review process by the GLAA, the results of which would be considered by the Performing Arts Committee on 10 September.[43] During this review period the GLAA confirmed its grant to ACT for 1987/88 on a standstill level with the previous financial year of £9,320, but this was awarded on the following conditions: ACT should produce at least one full production in the next financial year which satisfied the aims of the cooperative; deliver workshops for Asian theatre practitioners; secure a permanent office base; contract permanent administrative staff; and significantly improve the quality of its artistic and administrative output.[44] Reported consultation between GLAA and ACT reveal GLAA's criticism of ACT's choice of productions to date and of an absence of Asian directors, a concern that major decisions are 'bulldozed through by one or two individuals within ACT', and a lack of continuity and company development over the course of the previous three productions.[45]

The second half of 1987 was taken up with the development of the company's artistic programme and infrastructure. On 7 June ACT produced a staged reading of Lorca's *Blood Wedding* at the Riverside Studios. This was a fundraising event attended by 160 people. According to an article by Rita Wolf, veteran actors Saeed Jaffrey and Zohra Segal and colleagues conceived the idea twenty years earlier in India.[46] Now, reunited for the television comedy series *Tandoori Nights* (Channel 4), many of this cast (of which roughly half were ACT members) decided to remount the staged reading with Jaffrey as director under the auspices of ACT. In an interview Jaffrey remarked 'I [...] felt it was a good chance for some of the fine

---

[41] Tim Brinkman (GLAA), letter to Harmage S. Kalirai, ACT, dated 15 April 1987 [HSK/ACT archive].

[42] ACT minutes dated 10 May 1987.

[43] The ACT minutes of 10 May 1987 state that, since the recent demise of the GLC, the GLAA had taken on many of its former clients, some 'very disorganised', and some who have since folded.

[44] Anon., letter on behalf of the GLAA, addressed to Harmage S. Kalirai, Administrator, ACT, dated 14 May 1987 [HSK/ACT archive].

[45] ACT minutes dated 10 May 1987.

[46] 'Doing the Write Thing', by Shaila Parthasarathi, including contribution by Rita Wolf, dated 21 August 1989, in *Bazaar*, no. 9 (1989), p. 4.

actors involved to exhibit their classical talents, dispelling the widely held notion that black actors and actresses can't do Shakespeare or Lorca'.[47] Certainly the cast list boasts some of the most well-known Asian actors of the time and is testament to ACT's aspiring professional standards and wish to be taken seriously by the mainstream. The cast included Tariq Alibai, Shireen Anwar, Bhasker, Tanveer Ghani, Kusum Haider, Andrew Johnson, Harmage S. Kalirai, Nizwar Karanj, Shaheen Khan, Shelley King, Art Malik, Cheryl Miller, Aftab Sachak, Zohra Segal, Roshan Seth, Meera Syal, Gordon Warnecke and Rita Wolf (**DVD 11**).[48] The programme (**DVD 12**) lists funding by Camden Borough Council, London Borough Grant Scheme and GLAA.

Other activity that year included filming a programme, *Asian Family*, for the Open University at Mulberry School and Montefiore Community and Centre, Tower Hamlets. An administrator, Manjit S. Rooprah, was finally in post. He and ACT's coordinators attended a range of training courses. In September the London Borough Grant Unit (LBGU) awarded ACT £9,783 for 1987/88 (conditional upon the GLAA review) and in December the company finally moved into new offices at 25/31 Tavistock Place, London.

The following year was taken up with a wide range of workshops and funding applications to develop *Blood Wedding* into a full production. The GLAA's Performing Arts Committee recommended the withdrawal of annual funds (which Kalirai attempted, unsuccessfully, to fight through an appeal process) and both Camden Borough Council and the LBGU also withdrew their funding. Documented income, however, includes £30,000 from the Arts Council and £3,000 from the Commission for Racial Equality (CRE) towards ACT's programme for 1988.[49]

Artistic output, however, included a staged reading of Dilip Hiro's *In Search of Lord Clive's Corpse* and a double-bill of bilingual work *Jawaani*. Hiro had been commissioned by ACT for this play in May 1986 with the aid of an Arts Council theatre writing scheme and the company had developed it in the intervening period through a series of workshops. It was advertised as a 'Contemporary Satire on Money and Military Power' and dealt with the mystery of Clive's death (**DVD 13**). According to Hiro, Clive's actual grave is unmarked. Understanding that Christians were denied a burial if they had committed suicide, Hiro's play follows three characters who wish to buy Clive's house in London, but to do so they have to solve the mystery of his death. As they pass from room to room of his house they experience

---

47 Neema Kambona, 'Centre Stage', *The Voice*, 23 June 1987.

48 The programme includes two slightly different cast lists with a note that 'several of the original cast have been changed'. I understand that the above list was the actual cast on the night (**DVD 12**).

49 Letter from Kalirai to Bramwell Osula, LBGU, dated 25 May 1988 [HSK/ACT archive].

scenes from Clive's life, and eventually one of them, a Lebanese woman working for a rich Sheikh, sees Clive cut his throat. The moral of the story is the permanence of money, regardless of who owns it.[50] This was the last play Hiro wrote.

Jawaani comprised two bilingual plays, *Heartgame* (English–Bengali), by Mary Cooper and the Harehills Bengali Women's Drama Group and directed by Hettie MacDonald, and *Prem* (English–Gujerati), by Jyoti Patel[51] and Jezz Simons and directed by James MacDonald. As Dhirendra notes, various Asian theatre companies were experimenting with bilingualism in the mid-1980s, including Tara Arts and BATC [Kalirai and Dhirendra 2007].[52] During this time Kalirai was drawing a salary as administrator for ACT and received a credit as producer (**DVD 14–15**). *Jawaani* enjoyed a four-week run (23 November–22 December 1988) at London's Soho Poly Theatre and later toured to Leicester's Phoenix Arts Theatre (29 and 30 December), Derby and a school in North London. The designer was Ellen Cairns. *Heartgame* is a simple tale about young love, arranged marriages and family duties set in Leeds and Sylhet. A young college student, Raju (played by Kulvinder Ghir), is secretly seeing his classmate Reeta (Sudha Bhuchar), but when Raju's parents (Gian Bhandari[53] and Dhirendra) get wind of this they promptly send Raju to Bangladesh to marry his cousin, Anju, a young peasant girl, and bring her back to Leeds. Reeta is ignorant of Raju's marriage and both girls are unaware of each other's existence until they happen to meet at a bus-stop and each realises the implications of the other's true identity.[54] Cooper's use of bilingualism was essential to the play's development, with women aged between fifteen and twenty, based in Leeds and attending an English class. The women had all come from villages in Bangladesh and had varying levels of written and spoken English and Bengali. The play reflects many elements of the biographical stories which they shared during the discussions. The different languages, like the parallel stories of Anju in Bangladesh and Reeta in Leeds, are beautifully interwoven in the play, even within a sentence, so that Bengali and English-speaking audiences can follow the action. The cast did particularly well under the

50 Information given by Dilip Hiro, in interview with Sarah Dadswell, 26 February 2009.

51 Jyoti Patel's first play, *Awaaj*, won an award in the Young Writers Festival, the Royal Court Theatre in 1986.

52 In November 1986 the Royal Court Young People's Theatre held a conference on the use of bilingualism, from which the report 'A Meeting of Mother Tongues: Bilingualism, Theatre and School' was published by the Inner London Education Association (ILEA).

53 More usually known as Kristine Landon-Smith, who later founded Tamasha Theatre Company with Sudha Bhuchar in 1991.

54 The script is published with an author's note in *Plays by Women: Eight*, selected and introduced by Mary Remnant (London: Methuen, 1990), pp. 31–105.

coaching of translator Mohammed Abdullah, with Wolf as the only Bengali speaker.[55] Wolf recalls that it was a very simple plot and 'you had also almost to be able to understand it without really following it verbally' for it to work well. She describes it as a comedy which received a warm reception from the young audience who came in school and college groups and for whom 'it's both embarrassing [...] and they can't believe that you're talking about this stuff', that is the reality of their modern lives (DVD 16–17).[56]

The second play, *Prem* ('love' in Sanskrit) was first staged at the Battersea Arts Centre as part of the British Petroleum (BP) Young Directors Festival. It follows the relationship of Prem, a young Hindu woman, and Rashid, her Muslim boyfriend. *Prem* is a *Romeo and Juliet* scenario in which the parents are unhappy with the match and do their best to separate the couple. Prem and Rashid steal a few moments together when they can, as on school trips, and share laughs. Against her parents' wishes and with Rashid's encouragement Prem leaves school and home and sets herself up in her own flat, waiting for Rashid to join her. But he cannot sever the ties with his bachelor life, does not commit fully and eventually abandons Prem altogether, leaving her heartbroken and cut off from her family and social group (DVD 18).[57] The young lovers were played by Sudhar Bhuchar and Dhirendra (DVD 19). *Jawaani* received almost unanimously positive reviews, both for acting and use of bilingualism. Interestingly, it was the *India Weekly* review by Sashi Deo that dismissed *Prem* as 'long-winded', noted the 'free love with minimum hindrances from their elders', the lack of 'roots in Gujarat culture' and 'bilingualism [that] has been used thinly without any confidence'. A contrasting view was shown by many British critics, whose reviews bordered on or were openly patronising. Robin Thornber, writing for *The Guardian*, was quite taken aback by his ability to understand the language from the 'ringing conviction and sprightly vitality' of the actors: 'Can intonation really be so similar in all three languages?' he asked. 'I guess, from the company's obvious commitment, that the players are close enough to the issues to recognise their urgency. [...] I just hope that the company can reach the Asian ghettoes as well as well-meaning white liberals. Take it to Blackburn.'[58] Many of the reviewers criticised the recent withdrawal of funding from ACT, particularly as the GLAA had recently advertised for theatre companies to apply for funds from a Black Development Fund in the publication *Black Arts in London* but had not approached an existing company like ACT to apply.[59]

---

55 See author's note in published script, p. 104.

56 Interview with Rita Wolf by Sarah Dadswell, 22 February 2008.

57 As far as I am aware the playscript is unpublished, but an outline of the plot is in HSK/ACT archives (DVD 17).

58 Robin Thornber, 'Derby: Asian Co-operative Theatre', *The Guardian*, 7 January 1989.

59 Harmage Singh Kalirai wrote an article in protest about the state of funding

Jawaani had been produced on a minimal budget and exhausted ACT's remaining funds. Just before the show opened Kalirai sent a letter dated 14 October to all ACT members in which he stated his deep concern for the very existence of the company and felt the only solution was to restructure it with a board of directors that would be active and willing to take artistic and administrative decisions [HSK/ACT archive]. Although this eventually provoked a change of personnel in artistic committee (Dilip Hiro and Jobaidur Rehman replaced Kalirai and Wolf), it did not solve the problem of infrastructure, administrative responsibility and the company's aesthetic and ideological development.

ACT's final play was a full production of Lorca's *Blood Wedding*, which had been in development since the staged reading in June 1987. In the interim the company had organised a number of related workshops exploring both Spanish classical texts, dance and movement with Shobana Jeyasingh (credited as choreographer) and the text itself. The director was Jonathan Martin, then a specialist in Spanish classical theatre, who, with Mary Ann Vargas, produced a new translation of Lorca's original script. Having stepped down as principal members of ACT's Artistic Committee, Kalirai and Wolf were now responsible for producing *Blood Wedding*. The play was initially planned as a co-production with Theatre Royal Stratford East in autumn 1988, but ended up as a co-production with the Half Moon Theatre in London's East End, where it played 3–28 October. It had already opened in Newcastle's Playhouse (25–30 September), and later toured to Sheffield's Crucible Studio (30 October–4 November) and Bradford's Alhambra Studio (6–11 November).[60] Ashley Martin Davies' design was rather spare, what Nicholas de Jongh for *The Guardian* described as 'a bald open space, with an occasional silvered tree brought on',[61] and featured five musicians playing live at the sides of the stage. ACT's version of the Spanish classic had been inspired by the direct historical link with Spain's gypsies, who are said to have originated in India, and the similarities between aspects of Rajasthani dance, music and itinerant culture and Spain's gypsy culture. The multi-racial cast included (in order of appearance) Mona Hammond (mother), Paul Bhattacharjee (bridegroom), Jacqui Chan (neighbour/beggarwoman), Peggy Phango (mother-in-law/servant), Meera Syal (wife of Leonardo), Okon Jones (Leonardo), Badi Uzzaman (father),

---

and this particular incident in 'One More Time, With Feeling: Asian Cooperative Theatre', *Artrage*, no. 22 (Winter 1988), p. 43. In it he states that ACT's annual budget from the GLAA of £28,000 was completely cut for the financial year 1988/89. He rails against the funders and the colour bar that exists and denies Asian theatre companies access to the mainstream.

60 Tour dates taken from 'ACT's Blood Wedding', *Artrage*, no. 24 (Summer 1989). There is some suggestion in other documentation that the play premiered at the Half Moon and the Newcastle dates actually ended the tour.

61 Nicholas de Jongh, 'Sex, lies and Lorca', *The Guardian*, 16 October 1989.

Janet Steel (bride), Sayan Akaddas, Tracy Harper, Yogesh Bhatt and David Mishra (young girls, youths, moon, woodcutter, guests and musicians). Baluji Shrivastav returned as sitar player. Rita Wolf was assistant director to Martin, the composer and music director was Akintayo Akinbode and John Turner was producer for the Half Moon with Kalirai. Akinbode's music incorporated flamenco, Indian, North and South African music and Peggy Pango also sang. The play received very mixed reviews in the national press and more favourable reviews in the regional press. Many remarked on the performance of Mona Hammond, which was interpreted as either passionate or melodramatic (**DVD 20–23**). Without a doubt the play, perhaps because it was a European classic, attracted attention across the mainstream press, so ACT ended on a crescendo.

Blood Wedding was a large undertaking, but it is now impossible to track the funding for this production. One projected budget suggests £110,000, but there are no final accounts and it is difficult to see how a company which had lost much of its funding and vacated its previous office space at Tavistock Place in March of that year could have obtained that level of funding. Earlier archival documents reference a £30,000 grant from the Arts Council for the production.[62] ACT had lasted six years, produced six plays, attracted the cream of Asian theatre talent, bridged the older and younger generations of actors, commissioned new plays, produced new writing, including the community-inspired *Heartgame*, successfully delivered bilingual plays to a mixed audience and, finally, produced a European classic. Some members wanted to take the company forward to build on the bilingual work, continue to develop new writing and explore the possibility of more cultural transposition of adaptations in the vein of the 'Rajasthani' *Blood Wedding*. Sadly, in the end, a member of factors contributed to ACt's demise: the desired democratic, cooperative model of decision-making, the pressures of jobbing actors with unstable paid work commitments, the general lack of experience of running a theatre company and a lack of overall commitment to the project from many, the absence of a permanent administrator and office space, and possibly an artistic director or board of directors. This combination of factors ultimately undermined the company's creative output and left its potential unfulfilled.
[SJD]

62 All documents referred to are in the HSK/ACT archive. See also footnote 42.

7

Tamasha

from 1989 to 1997

Tamasha is an enterprise artistically conceived and run by its joint artistic directors, Kristine Landon-Smith and Sudha Bhuchar. But, in addition to this core relationship, there is also the question of the division of artistic roles, and in this aspect they must be joined by a third figure, the designer Sue Mayes, who has remained as the designer for the company throughout. So in artistic implementation through the production process there is a firm triad: regularly Landon-Smith features as director and joint script-maker with Bhuchar, who also takes leading acting roles, and Mayes designs.

The account that follows leads through from the foundation of the company to the point at which it gained revenue funding from the Arts Council, discussing the evolution of the company from production to production. To an unusual extent, much detailed evidence for the formation of the company and its aims over this period is contained in the documentation available in Tamasha's ample archive (on which see footnote 4 below). So this remarkable evidence not only illuminates the conception and development of productions, but also how the profile of the company was shaped and presented through engagement with the leading funding bodies.

Untouchable, 1988 (Delhi) and 1989 (London)

Tamasha was founded to mount a theatrical production of an adaptation of Mulk Raj Anand's novel *Untouchable* in London. Anand's novel was published in English in 1935, and is evidently responding in some part to the agitation on the caste system that formed part of the platform of Mahatma Gandhi and the Indian National Congress party in India, since that is where it concludes.[1] The circumstances and context of this first production by Tamasha, which took place in 1989, are complex. They involve not just the foundation of the company and the background to this event in the professional lives and aspirations of the founding personnel, but also a

---

1 Mulk Raj Anand, *Untouchable* (Harmondsworth: Penguin Books, 1940).

previous production of *Untouchable* in India in the preceding year, which had been directed by Kristine Landon-Smith.

Landon-Smith's immediate family was in Australia, and she used to travel there via India, where she visited relations. One of her cousins suggested that she should write to the National School of Drama in Delhi, which she did, and on her way back to the UK she was interviewed by the director, Ratan Thiyam, who offered her a job. Some weeks later the director confirmed that the School had gained funding from the British Council to employ her for three months, directing second-year students towards a production of Chekhov. Once she had started, she believed that the students 'needed to really identify with the characters they were playing, to look at how to observe people', and she proposed that they work instead on Mulk Raj Anand's novel, *Untouchable*.[2] As she recalls, she had chanced upon the book, but 'as soon as I picked it up I could see my students in the novel, and that's what happened, and so I read on.' She spoke to Thiyam:

> I said 'Look, I don't think that Chekhov is a very useful exercise for these students. I would prefer to do an adaptation of the book. They can go out in the streets, they can observe, it's a great character study for them. More importantly, we will be devising that work, we will be adapting the book together in the rehearsal room.'
>
> [Landon-Smith 2007]

The process was that the students worked in Hindi, although Landon-Smith was not herself fluent in Hindi.

> I don't speak Hindi, although I'm half Indian, I have learnt it periodically. I could understand quite a bit, but I developed this kind of shorthand with my students and there was always somebody who could translate, so we'd do the improvisations, we'd write them down, they'd translate back for me and then we'd formulate a script. It was a very arduous task, but it was rewarding.
>
> [Landon-Smith 2007]

The result was a Hindi script in a production for which Anand gave his approval, and which he came to see. It was performed in the grounds of the Drama School (**DVD 1–9**).

> It was a promenade production, and it wasn't on the lawns, it was in the courtyard. The reason I chose that was because there was a disused building on one side which had these huge white steps, and I

---

2 Kristine Landon-Smith interviewed by Graham Ley, London, 30 October 2007.

> could see that we could use those steps for the temple. Over this side there were trees, and I could think I could put a well there, we could put a stage there, we could put the slum colony in the background.
> [Landon-Smith 2007]

The professional prelude to this crucial experience was that Landon-Smith had trained at the National Institute of Dramatic Art in Sydney and at the Royal Scottish Academy, and subsequently worked as an actor and gained some awareness of directing, although not much concrete experience. She had been at the Royal Court and with Hull Truck Theatre and Durham Theatre Company, and worked alongside Sudha Bhuchar for six months when she joined Tara Arts to act in *The Broken Thigh* in 1986, when they became good friends. On returning from India she showed Bhuchar a video of the *Untouchable* production in Hindi, which Bhuchar understood fully, and they both felt they there was nothing like it in the UK.

> And it was there that we said why don't we set up a company to do this here. Certainly at that point both of us recognised that there was nothing like that on the Asian theatre scene, or in terms of the British theatrical scene.
> [Landon-Smith 2007]

Bhuchar herself was by now an established professional actress who had worked extensively with Tara Arts and on television, and Jatinder Verma offered them an opportunity to do a reading at the Tara Centre in Earlsfield, and a small subsidy. They were determined to maintain the Hindi version but also to perform in English, although finding a sufficient number of bilingual actors would prove to be extremely difficult.[3] In addition to the support from Verma, Harmage Singh Kalirai advised Bhuchar and Landon-Smith to apply to the Arts Council for development funding.

The original application for Project Subsidy to the Arts Council of England (28 November 1988) was followed by a set of Amendments (12 January 1989) which were addressed to Tim Brinkman, to whom Landon-Smith and Bhuchar were later to express their gratitude for his continuing support for Tamasha (letter, 9 February 1990).[4] In the original

---

3 Sudha Bhuchar interviewed by Graham Ley, London, 31 October 2007.

4 In 2007 Tamasha's archive was organised in 'Areas' of the storage room. Area 1 was 'Finance, education, development, administration', and within it 'Box 1—Funding Bodies' contained further ring binders and box files, including two for applications to the Arts Council, supposedly dividing at 1997: the first was labelled '1993–1997', but it actually contained applications from 1988 to December 1995, while the second ran from February 1996 forward. This large 'Box 1' also contained ring binders for applications to the London Boroughs Grants Unit, the London Arts Board, and further files that came outside the period under consideration here. Some

application, the Aims and Objectives of the company were 'to deal with contemporary and relevant issues in a "theatrical form"', and to bring Anand himself 'to advise and help us in our research'. The intention was to perform in both Hindustani and English, and to that end there was to be a preparatory language week in Hindustani for actors. Tara Arts was to provide support: Jatinder Verma had 'given a subsidy of £1,800 for script development and initial setting up costs', and the idea was to make some use of the Tara Arts studio. There would also be an exhibition 'on the plight of the untouchables'.

The Amendments show some interesting developments. There was an insistence on 'a great need from within the Asian community and the theatre going audience at large for plays in Asian languages', and a shift in thinking about venues to prominent London-fringe possibilities—the Drill Hall, the Battersea Arts Centre, the Almeida, the Half Moon and the Young Vic Studio. Most significantly, there were some striking statements about the aesthetic and approach to be adopted by the company in the description of the intended production: 'The production will be done in a totally realistic style. The town ... will be recreated on stage. All the different locales will be shown.' This observation is followed by a handwritten insertion in the copy in the archives: 'The production needs to recreate the environment and atmosphere of life in a small Indian town—the social background of the characters is sketched in great detail and they are portrayed with humour and spirit.' The Aims and Objectives have also been expanded:

> We see *Untouchable* as launching our style of work both in terms of language and also as an example of plays being devised from literature. This format will be employed by subsequent Tamasha productions ... We also see the company covering contemporary issues both in Britain and the subcontinent ...

Seldom can a major funding body have received so accurate a projection of future work in a first project application. There are commitments here which suggest an awareness of the need to achieve a close definition of the 'product' from the outset, an objective sense of what will be delivered. The applications are also interesting in acknowledging debts—to Asian Cooperative Theatre (ACT) and to Tara Arts, in different ways—but firmly marking a departure in terms of career development. The Amendments express this plainly: 'We also aim to promote the Asian actor/producer. This would enable us to exercise our own artistic choice in what we perform and makes us more in control of our careers ....' A handwritten

---

other relevant documents are stored in the 'Show Boxes', by production, in 'Area 2', and specific reference will be given to those when cited or quoted.

note inserted in the original application under Aims and Objectives had expressed the same feelings more personally:

> To exercise an artistic choice in what we perform. As Asian performers our experience to date has been one of either being typecast or working within Asian companies where one is merely an actor. We feel that being actor/managers would enable us to have more control over one's careers.

That the applicants are women receives no mention in itself, but it may be seen as a strong and purposeful subtext.

The advice from Brinkman at the Arts Council in these early stages had pushed the original application into the amended version, which was seeking a modest development subsidy for a three-week workshop for ten actors, 'forming a pool from which subsequent productions will be cast'. The resultant 'moved' reading was to be in both Hindustani and English at the Tara Arts Centre (letter, 13 February 1989), and an Arts Council of Great Britain (ACGB) subsidy for £5,000 for this purpose was awarded (24 February 1989). In this period Tamasha applied for charitable status (letter, 27 February 1989), and the reading of *Untouchable* subsequently took place on Sunday 2 April 1989. The Report for ACGB (6 May 1989) states that the 'audience was there by invitation', numbering thirty-five for the Hindustani reading and fifty-five for the subsequent English reading, which retained many of the first audience: 'Many of the audience were directly involved in the theatre either as actors, designers, directors or administrators.' There had been a language week for the actors, led by Bhuchar, and the moved reading had material support in the space: 'There were crucial elements of design so that those present would get a very clear idea of what a full-scale production would look like.' In fact, these were properties found or bought by Landon-Smith, working from her own design concept for the production in Delhi [Landon-Smith 2007].

What stands out here is not only the meticulous character of the planning, and its care in gathering the necessary support, but also the role assigned to the script in the process. The adaptation of Anand's novel occupies a central place, but it is functional in the preparation of actors and the elaboration of a basic design concept for its realisation. The Report was soon followed by an application to ACGB for Project Subsidy and Small-scale Touring (14 July 1989), which promised a rewriting of the script. Sue Mayes now appeared as the designer. She and Landon-Smith had recently met again at Rose Bruford College in London, where Landon-Smith had been a visiting director and Mayes was 'tutor in properties and scenic techniques'. This application reveals that Mayes had already been awarded research grants for *Untouchable* from the British Council and ACGB, and would be in India from 3 to 16 August 1989. Mayes and Landon-Smith had first met in Jeff

Teare's production of *The Lost Ring* for the Theatre Royal, Stratford East, in which Landon-Smith had played the lead, Shakuntala, and which Mayes had designed.[5] Mayes had worked for the Theatre Royal before then, but *The Lost Ring* started her connection as a designer with India: 'It was the start of this love affair. I borrowed a book on the cave paintings at Ajanta, and I used those to inspire and inform the design' [Mayes 2007].

Mayes went to India, working from contacts given to her by Landon-Smith, including Anand's adopted son, and taking a new camera bought from the grant. She went round the old city in Delhi and then took the train to Amritsar, visiting the Dalit or 'untouchable' village, compiling a dossier of photographs of living conditions and material items, 'the string beds, the big earthenware water jugs, specific things I could get to know and identify in their natural setting and then recreate when I came back here' [Mayes 2007]. Jonathan Lamede had come to the reading at Tara and had invited them to perform at the Riverside Studios in London. Mayes and Landon-Smith knew that they would remove the seating at the Riverside and create an open performance environment. Both Dennis Charles, the production manager, and Richard Moffatt, the lighting designer, were professional contacts whom Mayes brought into the show. The named cast included Dhirendra as the sweeper Bakha, the leading figure of the novel's narrative, and Naushaba Shaheen Khan and Sudha Bhuchar, who had worked together for many years at Tara. Consolidation had proceeded at a pace. Tamasha was now a registered charity with an established management committee, and was to be a limited company and a member of the Independent Theatre Company (ITC). An instrumental figure in the relatively frustrating push for private sponsorship had been Stephen Hayklan of Wiggins plc, who is thanked in the programme of *Untouchable*, and became a member of the Tamasha board. Applications for funding had been made to private sponsors and foundations, as well as to London Borough Grants (for £10,000) and the Greater London Arts Association (GLAA) (for £8,000). Touring plans included Glasgow as part of the City of Culture festival in 1990, but the opening venue had been determined as the Riverside Studios in London, with dates of 4–30 December 1989.

There were some interesting developments of rationale in the Project Description of the application (14 July 1989). So the company aimed to be 'providing the Asian community with theatre in their mother tongue thereby reaching a wider Asian audience than ever before'. This strongly contrasts with the stance taken by Tara Arts in its foundation and development; this organisation had achieved ACGB revenue funding on a very different basis. A further statement records plans to produce 'both Indian classical and contemporary plays both in English and Hindustani and other classical languages'. The suggestion of a 'mother tongue' is odd in the light of the

---

5 Sue Mayes interviewed by Graham Ley, London, 1 November 2007.

diverse language communities of South Asians in the UK, and the associated and flourishing language-theatres. The Project Description promises a production that has

> a truly Indian subject matter and allows audiences to see Indian village life depicted in a totally naturalistic style. Up till now theatrical experiences such as this have been 'imported' from the Indian sub-continent.

A similar idea covers the opportunities the production would offer to professional Asian actors 'otherwise denied them in this country and too often given to actors "imported" from the subcontinent'. This seems to have been a relatively casual reference, and Landon-Smith confirms that she knew very little about the established South Asian language theatres operating in the UK. The production concept remains much the same, with the addition of a 'musician to punctuate the action. The period will be authentically recreated by the choice of music, costume and the use of language.'

The ACGB subsidy of £39,820 (20 September 1989) stipulated a minimum of seven weeks' touring (thirty-seven performances), with no fewer than fifteen performances outside Greater London, but this total was later reduced to two weeks (13 November 1989) and finally included Leicester, Manchester, Derby and Bolton. The production ran in Hindi and English versions at the Riverside Studios from 4 to 30 December 1989 and toured in January 1990. The Report and statement of income and expenditure submitted to ACGB in February 1990 contained an interesting further adjustment to the aims of the company, 'our objectives being to produce Indian cultural, Indian classical and contemporary and Indian influenced plays'. In relation to that stronger emphasis on the sub-continent, it is worth noting that Oxfam had awarded £3,000 towards the production. The Report of February 1990 firmly places an accent on the mise en scène, in relation to the notion of authenticity and the suitability of the design for touring.

> The original Indian production was done as an outdoor promenade by Kristine ... A vast space was used and the design was built around the existing environment. It was very important for us to maintain the size and 'promenade feel' for the London production, yet still have a show which would be easy to adapt on tour. This was achieved by Sue Mayes' environmental set and her very detailed and authentic props. Riverside Studios proved to be the ideal venue, as we were able to remove the existing seating and create an Indian village in the round and thus a 'seated promenade'.

Mayes' research trips gave her ideas, and her props 'were authentic re-creations of what she found in India'. The set itself was suitable only for the Riverside, so the props alone went on tour, 'but due to their authenticity they in fact conjured up the whole feel of the Indian village which we achieved at Riverside'. Although the audience was estimated to be 70% Asian, the English-language performances were more strongly attended, and the company's self-assessment in the Report concluded that Hindi was seen as potentially 'intellectual and therefore inaccessible'.

The available documentation on *Untouchable* includes a hard-backed notebook containing the Show Reports by the Stage Manager Varinder Dhaliwal, essentially notes on missed cues and various minor shortcomings, but also other information, such as running times.[6] On Tuesday 5 December the audience at Riverside numbered eighty-five for the Hindi version preview, 'Sudha had too much water in her bucket', and the 'singing was a bit off-key'. This aspect apparently did not improve—on 6 December 'wedding song off key', and again on 8 and 9 December ('I could be heard in the lighting box laughing')—and the hookah proved a trial: it was not lit on the first preview, 'still not lit' on the second, and remained noted as in that state on 6 and 7 December. There is also an exchange of letters between Landon-Smith and Jonathan Lamede, Director of the Riverside Studios (in the same box), with Landon-Smith thanking Lamede for 'taking the chance' in booking a company 'with no reputation behind us': 'had it not been for your belief in the project we could never have got started'. Landon-Smith also acknowledges Lamede's advice not to run so many Hindi performances, which had proved correct, 'but as you have experienced we are both very stubborn and therefore have to learn the hard way' (DVD 10–25).[7]

House of the Sun, 1991

Anand's *Untouchable* was a modern classic, and in the programme to the Delhi production Landon-Smith states that she 'found the novel perfect for adaptation with so many interesting characters to be portrayed on stage'. This same quality is even more pronounced in Tamasha's choice for a production scheduled for 1991, Meira Chand's novel *House of the Sun*, which, by contrast, had been published very recently, in 1989.[8] This was a co-production with the Theatre Royal, Stratford East, who

---

6 Archive: Show Boxes: 1—*Untouchable*.

7 The Tamasha website currently includes images of some production materials for all its productions (notably programme covers, and occasionally inside pages), and details of cast and production credits: www.tamasha.org.uk. Scripts of all the productions mentioned in this account were published by Nick Hern Books in an initiative in 1999, partly funded by 'Arts for Everyone' from the National Lottery through the Arts Council. The exception is *East Is East*, for which the publication details are given separately below.

8 Meira Chand, *House of the Sun* (London: Hutchinson, 1989).

part-commissioned the development period and also contributed £47,000 towards production costs. In March 1987 the director, Jeff Teare, had staged his own adaptation of Kalidasa's classic Sanskrit drama *Shakuntala* at the Theatre Royal with a cast that included only a small number of Asian actors. The music for this production was provided by Baluji Srivastav and the choreography was by Shobana Jeyansingh, but the production had been poorly received as evidence of a new interest at the Theatre Royal in reaching out to British Asian audiences. A co-production with Tamasha represented a different approach by involving a new, British Asian-led company which had the additional advantage of containing two practitioners, Landon-Smith and Mayes, who were known to the theatre from *The Lost Ring*. Tamasha's application to ACGB for a Project Subsidy (20 September 1990) noted that a three-week workshop with six actors had already been completed, which Landon-Smith recalls took place in the Theatre Royal's portacabin. It also stated that this would be 'a large-scale production to be performed in a main theatre', and that it would not be possible to tour, in contrast to *Untouchable*. This decision is bound up with the design and production concept: 'The design will incorporate a realistic representation of the block of flats, a working lift and many of the outside locations in the play'. Fourteen actors were to play thirty or more characters, 'and the piece will be performed in a realistic style'. A guarantee against loss of £28,330 was later confirmed by ACGB (31 January 1991), and the production, subtitled in the promotional material 'A Bombay Comedy', took place at Stratford East from 12 April to 11 May 1991. There was once again a grant from Oxfam of £3,000.

Chand's *House of the Sun* is set in a block of flats known as Sadhbela in Bombay, and the action takes place while, in astrological terms, Saturn has entered the house of the sun. The residents in Sadhbela are predominantly members of the refugee Sindhi community, displaced from Sind in the Indus valley at the time of Partition, who administer the block on a communal basis. In the application for Project Subsidy it was suggested that the Sindhi community in London was a target audience, and that the immigrant Sindhi community in a big city such as Bombay is 'not unlike the immigrant experience in this country', with additional mention of issues such as the generation gap and dowries. This dual focus on the collective 'immigrant experience' and a specific community represents a significant shift from *Untouchable*, and one of the stated aims in the application was 'to heighten the awareness that Asians are not a homogeneous group', noting 'the diversity that exists within the Asian community in terms of language and culture'. The production was to consider 'how language changes with the influence of migration', although Chand's novel, like Anand's, was written in English. Both Sindhi and Hindi were to be reflected in the script, as in the Sindhi experience in Bombay. So there is a clear attempt to mirror the British Asian experience in a novel set in India.

Mayes, Landon-Smith and Bhuchar all went to India in October for ten days as part of the research for the production, visiting downtown Bombay. Bhuchar had family connections with the Sindhi community in London, and to a degree research into the community combined with outreach promotion for the resultant production [Bhuchar 2007]. Landon-Smith had some cousins who happened to live in a block of flats with predominantly Sindhi residents in Bombay, and Mayes began to match the housing she saw in the city with the conditions in the proscenium space of the Theatre Royal, choosing eventually to slide the lower panels of the facade up in order to bring the interiors of different flats out on the revolve. She gained a sense of the vertical strata of the dwelling in Chand's novel, with the sweepers out on the street at the bottom of the lift, and the richest family at the top in the penthouse [Mayes 2007] (**DVD 26–36**).

The aesthetics of adaptation in *Untouchable* (London) and *House of the Sun*

Untouchable was performed in the round at Riverside Studios, with the extensive latrines set to one side and Bakha's family's cramped, bare room to the other, the musician on a raised platform set just in the audience, and a modular, stepped focal area to the rear of the space. The design created an environment with a central open space for the actors to be seen performing tasks of labour—of which the most emblematic was sweeping—collective actions, and dialogic or physical interaction. Suggestions of dwellings were conveyed in a facade behind the stepped area, and on a raised platform set in the audience to one side, but were rarely used. In *House of the Sun* the facade of the block of flats in three stories confronted the audience in proscenium, with the lift shaft centrally placed. The opening scenes were played in a room in part of the facade and immediately at the foot of the lift, but subsequent scenes were introduced on a large revolve, with components of setting defining them consistently as the flats of the families involved in the story. There were rare moments when the action played in the open, and the wider world was conveyed in only one or two moments by street sound effects. The music was used for continuity, with no musician visible.

In aesthetic terms, the kinds of 'realism' or 'naturalism' involved are clearly very different in the two first productions, and the relationships to the source novels are also interesting. Anand's novel is a third-person narrative of the experience and perceptions of the young sweeper Bakha during the course of a day, and its radicalism is not just in its politically and socially charged subject matter, but in the identity and status of the novel's subject, Bakha. The sights and sounds of the town and the surrounding countryside are described much as they appear to his senses, and in that respect the novel leans far more to expressionism (or even symbolism) than to realism, which is not surprising for its period. The dialogue is relatively sparse, and in the climax of the novel his hesitant and confused consciousness is assaulted by the persuasive rhetoric of others: a Christian missionary, Gandhi himself, and debating intellectuals. Much of the novel is internalised, and that imagined and vicarious 'reality' could not be represented in the selective material environment of Tamasha's production, which objectifies Bakha to our view alongside all its other characters.

Chand's novel is less ambitious in relation to any individual, and distributes its attention across couples and families and characters within them. The coherence is supplied by a multiplicity of narrative threads, although the superstitious mentality of Mrs Hathirami moves restlessly throughout the period of time which she alone sees as significant, with Saturn in 'the house of the sun'. Yet the physicality of the city, its sights and sounds and its material presence, punctuate the domestic settings that regularly provide the milieu for dialogue. The choice of a facade, which is turned inside out in the staging of interior scenes, inevitably stills this fluidity, and curiously removes just that sense of the street which was established for 'reality' in the production of *Untouchable*. The adaptation, despite its interest in generations, does not explore the experience of the young men (notably the despairing Sham) as much as does the novel, while a trio of idle girls on sofas gains a compensating prominence which has little or no significance. So both the mise en scène and the adaptation are a strange compromise between a monumental scenographic backdrop and barely indicated studio scenes, with the revolve substituting for the narrative flow and roving eye of the novel.

Both novels have at their core, alongside other more routine humiliations, the degradation of young women, which stretches to beating and murder in *House of the Sun*. Chand's easygoing style tears open at the moment of the pathological violence inflicted on a young bride, Lakshmi, by the mother-in-law, and Anand describes an incident involving Bakha's sister, Sohini, and a priest in the environs of a temple which Bakha is aware he may pollute. Sohini tells Bakha that the priest made suggestions to her while she was cleaning the latrine of his house, and when she screamed the priest came out shouting that he had been defiled.[9] In the production, the priest assaults Sohini in the central space, pushing her to the ground.[10] The production of *House of the Sun*, in some contrast, is rather sparing in its omission of the beating inflicted on Lakshmi by the mother-in-law, which leads inexorably to a horrific and contrived domestic burning.[11]

---

9 Anand, *Untouchable*, p. 62.

10 This is no more than a staged interpretation of what Sohini's modesty may have implied, but it is interesting in the light of later reactions to a similar theme with Gurpreet Kaur Bhatti's *Behzti*.

11 Chand, *House of the Sun*, pp. 127–28.

Women of the Dust, 1992

Oxfam provided support for both of Tamasha's productions, and indeed by early 1991 had already approached the company in connection with the charity's fiftieth anniversary in 1992; a basic agreement was reached in a meeting at Oxford. This connection suggested a departure from the company's practice to date, and an application was submitted to ACGB (12 February 1991) under the 'Working with a Writer' scheme. The development process of a three-week workshop with six actors was by now standard practice, but it was to be followed by a ten-week writing commission which broke new ground: 'We see this as a development as we would now be looking at very contemporary issues and writing a play from scratch with no novel as a starting point but rather a community as our starting point.' A supporting argument was that this 'process of work enables Asian actors to help contribute to new literature'.

It is not specified in the application itself who the writer was going to be, nor are themes or location identified, and ACGB declined funding in May (letter, 7 May 1991). At the end of the same month an application for a workshop under the Project Subsidy scheme was submitted, with an accent on subject matter: one week with actors to decide on the theme, and one to work further on it. The proposed themes were tentatively prostitution or widowhood, and this was approved by ACGB to the sum of £4,960 (letter, 31 July 1991). But both Landon-Smith and Bhuchar recall that Bhuchar had been shown photographs by Sunil Gupta of Rajasthani women working on construction sites, wearing their thick jewellery, and had talked to her about them, and that this theme appealed to Oxfam, since the charity provided some support for them. This resolution may have occurred in the summer, since by late August 1991 ideas had moved on, with the emphasis now falling on structure. In a further application to ACGB for Project Subsidy (20 August 1991) the project carried the provisional title of *Musafir* ('Traveller'), and the writer was identified as Ruth Carter, whose career had been established in writing for film and television. Landon-Smith recalls that Max Stafford-Clark, whom she knew from her time at the Royal Court, had come to *House of the Sun* and suggested that they should think of employing new writers. Carter came to their notice after they had contacted a few literary agents for scripts. An undated draft proposal for a video project documenting research in India explains the search process undertaken by Landon-Smith and Bhuchar.

> Tamasha chose Ruth Carter, who will be visiting India for the first time ever, after reading plays by dozens of contemporary writers, including several nominated by the Royal Court. Their attention was caught above all by one play—Ruth Carter's *A View of the Ngongs*—which impressed them enormously with its humour, its

> sharp observation and the fact that its African characters were convincingly written 'from the inside'.

A View of the Ngongs had not been performed, and the draft offers some interesting thoughts from Landon-Smith:

> 'We anticipate [a lot of flak—***crossed out; pencil substitution of***] some objection for not automatically choosing an Asian writer', comments Kristine Landon-Smith, 'but the most important point was to choose the writer who could respond in the most open and imaginative way to the brief; we don't intend to limit our scope by imposing dogmatic restraints on our choice of collaborators'.
>
> Although Tamasha's two previous and highly praised productions were in emphatically naturalistic mode, there is no house-style to be imposed, and Ruth Carter has already found herself musing on the fantastic possibilities of a grotesque and rather sinister puppet character, inspired by a development video she saw where puppets were being used in a health teaching scheme.

In the application for Project Subsidy (20 August 1991), the locale for research was identified closely, as the village of Tilonia in the district of the town Ajmer in the region of Rajasthan, some 200 miles south-west of Delhi. The Riverside Studio was named as the London venue, with a tour envisaged to Leicester Phoenix, Bolton Octagon, the mac (Midland Arts Centre, Birmingham), Manchester Green Room, Oxford Playhouse, Belgrade Coventry and the Courtyard of the West Yorkshire Playhouse in Leeds. Oxfam had already committed £14,000, and the GLAA £7,500, which embraced a research trip to India, part of the writer's commission and a small production contribution. The section on Aims in the application charts this profile for the company, which it states was formed

> to bring Indian contemporary drama to the British stage. Using literature as a basis and through research and development work with actors, Tamasha has developed a unique way of producing new writing. Tamasha aims to provide large scale plays depicting authentic Indian life previously unseen on the British stage. Tamasha's commitment to presenting innovative Indian work has attracted a new and large multicultural audience.

The Project Subsidy, for a guarantee against loss of £37,020, was only approved by ACGB six months later (letter, 11 February 1992), and stipulated an eight-week tour, with a minimum of three weeks outside London. A response to that condition from Bhuchar (12 March 1992) noted that Bristol Old Vic studio had now offered three weeks for the production, making an extended tour difficult. Landon-Smith had been working extensively with the Bristol Old Vic as an actor and director in the last two years, and some of the production staff for the eventual *Women of the Dust* were drawn from those contacts. In the letter to ACGB (12 March 1992), Bhuchar sketches a potential conflict between the investment in touring favoured by ACGB and Tamasha's own sense of its best future:

> Our future aspirations are: we would like to co-produce with regional theatres and also have a sizable London venue for each of our shows. This obviously has repercussions on how the Arts Council views Tamasha …

Small-scale touring was inconsistent, Bhuchar continued, with raising the profile of Asian theatre, something to which Tamasha was firmly committed. The eventual compromise, after meetings with Tim Brinkman and Ian Brown at ACGB, combined an opening three weeks in Bristol followed by three further weeks at the Riverside in London, with periods of a few days at Leicester Phoenix and the Arts Centre at the University of Warwick in Coventry. The production ran from 7 October to 12 December 1992 (**DVD 37–49**).

The planning for the research and development process proved to be extremely protracted, since the core components of the research by Landon-Smith, Bhuchar and Mayes as designer, and the subsequent script-development by a group of actors, were in this case complicated by the need to generate a theme with the writer, Ruth Carter. Workshop dates were arranged and changed, and the internal politics of collaboration surfaced in debates about who would hold copyright, which affected the ACGB writing commission for Carter (letter to ACGB, 1 October 1991, and letter from ACGB, 17 October 1991, respectively). The intention was that Landon-Smith and Bhuchar would accompany Carter on research in India, but then there might not then be sufficient funds for Mayes to go with them. That indeed proved to be the case, and it was Landon-Smith on this occasion who compiled the dossier of photographs from which Mayes was to work. The emergent idea was that in the workshop after the research trip they would 'flesh out characters and storylines', and that there would be 'a substantial input in terms of the Indian language which will also be a feature of the piece' (letter to ACGB, 1 October 1991). Further detail was set out in a subsequent letter to Brinkman (12 November 1991). On the return from India there would be a process of 'collation, translation and collaboration' with Carter before the workshop with actors, since Carter wanted to 'clearly sketch out characters that she knew she would be using and to ask the actors to improvise with all that solid material at their fingertips'. Bhuchar had primarily conducted the interviews in India, which had been taped but only vaguely explained to the others on site, so this process was essential. The undated report on the workshop confirms that once again Mayes 'participated by building various surroundings for the actors to work in'.

In the village of Tilonia, with its non-government organisation project, they had the strange experience of being kept away from the women who were weaving baskets there as an alternative to working on the construction sites in the city. Landon-Smith feels that this was 'a catalyst for the whole script, because then Ruth was able to contextualise it and in the script she was writing about the do-gooders and the people who want to do good, and the real people' [Landon-Smith 2007]. Bhuchar had been able to gain access to building sites as her uncle was a contractor and could provide them with the appropriate contacts, and Oxfam also operated a mobile creche for the women, which they were able to follow. In a short film held in the Tamasha audio-visual collection, produced and directed by Sara Jolly and called *Women of the Dust: A Play in the Making*, Carter states that the idea for the situation of the play came not in the village setting, but in the city:

> As soon as we hit the Delhi building site, and started talking to the women, I felt ... this is where it has to happen, this is the centre of the drama, that cement-mixer, and what happens around it.

She also states later in the film that she began the dialogue in Rajasthan, with scenes written around the pregnant girl, and then left the script. She completed it in a month in the UK. For her, the play tells 'a simple story ... about a peasant girl who wants to get home and have her baby ... and through that simple story we explore the women's lives'.

In the rehearsal process before the production in late 1992, a great deal of attention was given to vocal rhythms and projection. In Sara Jolly's film Carter comments on how the Rajasthani women do not speak in an 'intimate tone' but 'announce what they are doing', and, although she did not initially like the idea of actors 'shouting', she acknowledged that the women 'did have to shout above the noise of the machines'. In the same film, Landon-Smith talks of a division between urban and rural: 'We found that in fact it was very difficult for the actors to completely change their urban speech to real rural speech.' The accounts of voice are slightly different here, defined diversely as 'rural' or the product of an urban working environment, but in notes written by the voice coach, Jill McCullough, for actors in the rehearsal process (Archive: Show Boxes: 14—*Women of the Dust*: title, 'Rajasthan') the emphasis lies on vocal adaptations in the building site:

> The women are speaking in a relatively high pitch, and when they talk over one another, or interrupt, they will use a different pitch to do so. This is probably a technique learnt on the building site. So they would use a combination of volume increase, to make themselves

> heard over the noise of the mixers and also pitch changes, which are a way of signifying a change of direction in speech and speaker.

The notes provide comments about nasality, about the 'narrow pitch band', about carrying vocal strength through to the end of the speech line, and about tight and closed off vowels, with 'sliding on the vowels, which gives it a sing-song sense'. There are clear instructions on how to express various consonants, alongside the emphasis on stretching the vowels. The curious feature is that all these observations on speech had to be applied within a predominantly English-language script. John O'Hara, with whom Landon-Smith had worked at Bristol, composed the songs, working as Bhuchar recalls from a recording of one or two of the women's songs they had made, but composing his own and fitting Carter's lyrics to them. The movement was taught by Shobana Jeyasingh, and had been identified by Landon-Smith on the construction sites as a key element of any production:

> It was how you bend, how you would lift believably, how you would then walk with the bricks. We had bricks made up, which were not heavy, but [the challenge was] how to make them look as though they were heavy, how to help us with the patterns of movement, because that was a big thing for me.
>
> [Landon-Smith 2007]

A bid for three-year revenue funding

During the long preparation for *Women of the Dust* the idea of working with a writer had become entrenched, despite frustrations with funding the commission. Encouragement from ACGB to take this path still came, and early in 1992 Bhuchar submitted another application to the ACGB 'Working with a Writer' scheme (20 February 1992). The proposed format was the same, with a three- to four-week research trip to India in January 1993 and a workshop with actors on return followed by the commission for writing the script. The writer was Carter, who had an idea 'about the lives of domestic servants in the big cities of India', and the play was to be 'a combination of her imagination and "social realism"'.

> Previously one has seen servants depicted in plays mainly as secondary characters and more often than not from the eyes of the employer. We aim to get beyond this and see life from behind the doors of the servants' quarters.

The application was rejected (23 April 1992), but the role of the writer in the vision of future work remained. When Tim Brinkman left ACGB in January 1993, the letter from Tamasha (26 January 1993) thanking him for his support mentioned that the company 'probably will apply for revenue funding'. After looking at examples of revenue bids by Gay Sweatshop and Trestle, a bid was submitted (30 March 1993). The development plans were crucial to this, and included a transmutation of Carter's idea for a sequel to an adaptation of Lorca's *Yerma*, which was said to have themes relevant to India and Rajasthan. The commission would occur in 1993, and it would be produced in 1994/5. In thc same year, 1994/5, a second project would be started.

> Commission, research, develop second idea based on the Indian community in Britain.
>
> As a British Asian company we feel it is important to develop work based on Asians in this country and we feel we have the expertise and contacts to get inside a community and find the seed for a fictionalised drama based on documented research.
>
> Ruth Carter is a possible writer, but we may look at others for the commission.
>
> Possible themes:
>
> — joint family relationships
> — fostering and adoption of Asian children
> — depression and mental illness among Asian women
> — Asian community in the Hebrides (they began as door-to-door salesmen)
> — the journey of immigrants to this country (from India to east Africa to Britain)
> — how this passage has affected assimilation—how does it feel to look back.

This was to be produced in 1995/6. The third project would start in the same year, was placed in the Indian sub-continent, and would depend on 'discussions with Save the Children and Christian Aid', who had become involved with funding for *Women of the Dust*. The plan was that that would be produced at the Bristol Old Vic, presumably because of the success there with *Women of the Dust*.

The required three-year plan was qualified by a bid for continuing freelance status for Landon-Smith and Bhuchar, entailing one project a year. Landon-Smith was still with Rose Bruford and Mountview, and was also 'part of a new ensemble under Andy Hay at the Bristol Old Vic'; Bhuchar was involved with broadcasting. It was this aspect of the application that resulted in its rejection by ACGB (letter, 20 May 1993), which encouraged the continuation of Project Subsidy applications.

So the pattern was established, of writers' commissions followed by Project Subsidy, and in some respects the following years almost inevitably represent marking time. *Women of the Dust* continued to occupy some attention, with Bhuchar receiving a writer's commission award to translate the script into Hindi in preparation for a proposed tour to India, and Landon-Smith preparing to direct a version for BBC Radio 4 (to be broadcast on 14 April 1994). Funds were raised for the India tour during 1993 from trusts, companies and banks, with the four cities of Delhi, Bangalore, Bombay and Baroda the initial target. Four actors, including Bhuchar, came from the UK, and four from India, with the production team being largely drawn from India, including the design. It was eventually produced in the original English version in Delhi and Bombay, with a cancelled production in Baroda, in January–February 1994 (DVD 50–52).

A Shaft of Sunlight, 1994

Carter's adaptation of *Yerma* was pushed back to 1995, despite an early application to ACGB for a writer's commission (2 April 1993). In its place, Tamasha applied to ACGB for a Commission or Option award (24 June 1993) for a 'new stage piece' based on Abhijat Joshi's radio play, *A Shaft of Sunlight*. Joshi was a lecturer in English at Ahmedabad College in India, and an actor, director and playwright, and *A Shaft of Sunlight* had been produced by the BBC World Service, with Bhuchar playing the leading role. Tony Clark, whom Bhuchar had met during her work with Tara, and with whom she had recently worked, was now at the Birmingham Rep. When she showed the script to him he was keen to programme it, partly because the Rep wanted to reach its Asian communities. The core of the play was the tension caused by religious conflict in a marriage between a Muslim man and a Hindu woman. The play was set in Ahmedabad, but Tamasha made a strong case in the application to the ACGB for a Commission for its having a wide application.

> We feel that this play would have great relevance ... The Asian community in Britain is very affected by what takes place in the Subcontinent and Hindu and Muslim relations have been badly affected by events and the communities are now experiencing mutual distrust and lack of understanding of each other.
>
> The whole issue of religious bigotry needs to be aired and also the question of Hindu/Muslim marriages needs to be addressed as they are still largely not accepted in Britain today ...
>
> [***handwritten, pencil addition***] Although the piece is specifically set in INDIAN society—the issues it raises are very relevant to current political situations being addressed in the world (BOSNIA—Northern Ireland—RUSSIA to name a few). The resurgence of cultural and religious identity as important factors in territorial power and the feeling that one race or religion is superior over another (for example the practice of 'ethnic cleansing')—are issues

> that are in the forefront of world politics today. In *A Shaft of Sunlight* the writer manages to cover the broad subject by looking at one specific domestic situation.

Tamasha was convinced of the value of 'grass roots marketing', an emphasis that had formed part of its bid for Revenue Funding. This belief sprang from the success of outreach work to the Asian community in Bristol with *Women of the Dust*, and from the contrasting disappointments where it was not applied, as for the subsequent run at the Riverside in London. The Project Subsidy application for *A Shaft of Sunlight* (20 December 1993) included a reference to it, and the project was to be a co-production on this occasion with the Birmingham Rep. An award of a Guarantee against Loss of £34,000 was made (3 May 1994), and the tour included the Battersea Arts Centre and the Tom Allen Centre in London, Oldham Sixth Form College, Cellar Theatre in Huddersfield and Phoenix Arts in Leicester, with the opening in Birmingham on 13 October 1994 (**DVD 53**).

With *A Shaft of Sunlight*, Tamasha moved abruptly from the panoramic to the intimate, with the set representing a domestic interior and a small cast of five playing a family in three generations, a friend whose arrival shakes the household, and a cameo role for a sweeper. Yet, as in the previous productions, there is a core of personal distress or tragedy, with a consistent sense of disempowerment in the face of social pressures. This is unquestionably a different kind of 'realism' aesthetically and indeed dramaturgically, with the intensity of exchanges in closed rooms between the members of one family framed by the set, which compresses the energy from actors in a constant charge released to the audience. The set was a gauze box, with a central entrance and rooms suggested beyond, carefully designed for touring to small venues and representing the closed interior space (**DVD 54–56**). The language of the play has not been shaped to place the characters closely in a given milieu, as had been the case—in different ways—in the previous productions, and this curiously neutral impression is if anything enhanced by the colloquialisms of the sweeper. The evenness of diction is very rarely broken by Hindi words, and the referentiality is slight and relatively non-specific: we hear of Partition, of curfew and of armed Hindu and Muslim militants, but of little else.

A Yearning, 1995

Almost immediately after *A Shaft of Sunlight* opened, Tamasha prepared an application to the Arts Council of England (ACE) for a Project Subsidy for *Yerma* (01 November 1994). Tamasha had previously written to ACE before a September meeting setting out the *Yerma* project once more in a Rajasthan setting, and stating that 'we will be working in the same naturalistic and carefully researched way but are now applying this to a classic text' (undated letter), in which it seems that 'classic' must here signify a European text, granted the production of Anand's *Untouchable*. In the application for Project Subsidy the emphasis remained on Rajasthan, and on issues of fertility and parenthood in that context, and the award for £36,250 was made (13 January 1995). Two months later, in the application to ACE for the writer's commission, the context had shifted from Rajasthan to the UK, almost as if the experience of *Women of the Dust* had finally faded, although the writer remained Ruth Carter. The application states that

> there are startling parallels between the Punjabi community and the rural communities of Spain in the 1930s. Our play will be set in modern day Britain and the Punjabi community now settled in Britain which has its roots in rural Punjab seem to be caught in a time capsule where traditions and culture have become almost fossilised ...
>
> In the usual Tamasha style the play will be based on extensive research in Punjabi communities throughout Britain. The play will have a large cast and will be a spectacle to look at. Original music will be composed and played by Ansuman Biswas.

This would be the first production Tamasha had set in the UK and the first occasion on which the research process was conducted in UK communities; so, if the research process was 'usual', the British context for it was not. Nonetheless, the company had gained experience of the value of outreach work in the community from previous productions. With a second co-production with the Birmingham Rep the resolution of bringing the contexts of both play and audience together proved attractive, as Bhuchar recalls:

> I do remember why the Punjabi community was chosen, because they are a community with such rural links. The Punjabi community in Britain is so rural now, let alone when we did the production. So it seemed like a really good fit, and we had those connections with the Birmingham Rep, so setting it in Birmingham just seemed to make sense.
>
> [Bhuchar 2007]

Perhaps decisively, the London Arts Board (LAB), which had supported *Women of the Dust* and *A Shaft of Sunlight*, also supported this production with £8,000, a grant which was used to employ an Education officer to run workshops in Birmingham, Leicester, London and Sheffield, adding schools to the existing audience-building strategy with community groups.

In what was finally called *A Yearning*, the experience of India is largely compressed into the character of the young wife, Amar, and the setting is contemporary Birmingham. Yet, like *Women of the Dust*, the play contains songs from Amar, her cousin Arvind and a chorus of women, and musical composition is again prominent. Landon-Smith recalls that initially the design for *A Yearning* was what she calls 'heavy', but that she and Mayes

> basically stripped everything away, because there were so many domestic locations, and if you made it too domestic it didn't resonate to the rural force, since there was still a rural feel, a poetic feel, and an epic feel beneath it. The more domestic you made it, you lose that. But you needed the domestic settings, and you needed this epic quality and poetry to it as well. So Sue and I ended up stripping everything away ... and Sue came up with this fantastic disc that was painted to move between inside and outside. We lit the disc so there would be darkness around it—it was just this floating disc.
>
> [Landon-Smith 2007]

The production opened in Birmingham on 26 September 1995 and toured to the Lyric Theatre, Hammersmith; Theatre in the Mill, Bradford; High Wycombe Town Hall; The Nettlefold, Norwood, London; and The Crucible, Sheffield (**DVD 57–62**).

East Is East, 1996

The Birmingham period represents a remarkable change of emphasis and also status for Tamasha, since their profile up to and including *A Shaft of Sunlight* had gained them two-year fixed-term funding from the LAB in May 1995 (letter, 26 May 1995). This success came two years after the failure of the bid to gain revenue funding from ACE, and although the annual sums of £30,000 awarded by the LAB were no more than the average guarantee against loss for a production, they provided a bridge of security between specific project funding. Tamasha's application to the LAB (undated, but probably early 1995) set out aims and plans in section 16:

> Our initial aim to cultivate Asian audiences for not only Tamasha but also producing houses has been a success ...
>
> We are influenced by the best values of contemporary theatre and we are keen not to limit ourselves to the notion that Asian theatre in order to be relevant has to take a diametrically opposed stance to British realistic forms of presentation.

This must be a reference to Tara Arts, but it also may reflect sensitivity about Tamasha's relatively conventional aesthetics in the demanding context of London theatre. New writing featured prominently in these aims—'To nurture new writing from British Asian writers ...'—and the company was working with a group of young Asian writers in collaboration with the

Royal Court, following a discussion at a conference organised in October 1994 by Sampad, the South Asian arts agency based in Birmingham.[12] This was a significant departure for Tamasha, bringing together growing attention to the British Asian experience with the company's recent determination to work with outside writers. The short-list in the application was Ayub Khan Din, Joyoti Grech, Tanika Gupta, Neil Biswas and Parv Bancil, who were said to be working on ideas for a possible Tamasha/Royal Court co-production for 1996. There was to be a two-week workshop in January 1996:

> The two week workshop will consist of a skills week (tutors will include Cicely Berry, Hanif Kureishi and Stephen Jeffrey) followed by two days each per writer to work with actors, director and dramaturg on the rehearsal floor.

After this workshop, the Royal Court 'may choose to pick up one of these scripts and Tamasha is committed to producing one of these scripts'.

The workshop was held in January 1996 at the Royal Court, and by February Tamasha was applying (26 February 1996) to ACE for Project Funding for Ayub Khan Din's *East Is East*, which was awarded at £13,274 (28 May 1996), with a projected opening at Birmingham Rep followed by a tour at Crucible Sheffield, Ambassadors London (temporary home of the Royal Court) and Bristol Old Vic. Plans for 1996–97 were submitted to the LAB in March (4 March 1996), and the Aims section repeated the statement on theatrical aesthetics forcefully:

> To challenge the notion that all 'Asian' theatre in order to be relevant has to be ritualistic, and in some way to take a diametrically opposed stance to British 'realistic' forms of presentation.

Tamasha was to co-commission Ayub Khan Din's *East Is East* with the Royal Court, and co-produce with Birmingham Rep and the Court, and had been 'developing this play for some months now'. Ayub Khan Din had been teamed with David Lan, then writer-in-residence at the Court. Some of the other writers from the January workshop were also developing their ideas, but Harwant Bains was to write *Partition* for the 1997–98 production by Tamasha. Bains had been a workshop leader in January, and his play *Blood* had been produced in 1989 at the Court, where he had also been a writer-in-residence. In contrast, Khan Din's play had been written over a decade before and had received a reading at the Albany Empire in which

12 South Asian Theatre Conference, 'A Question of Identity?' 20–21 October 1994, held at the Birmingham Rep. On the second day there were focus groups on Theatre in Education, Youth Theatre, New Writing and Audience Development. On the evening of 20 October there had been a performance of *A Shaft of Sunlight*.

Bhuchar had participated. She was strongly committed to the play, despite Khan Din's reservations about it as an early script which had failed to gain interest at the time.

The two-year fixed funding from the LAB was awarded on 26 May 1996, the ACE Project Funding for *East Is East* two days later. In addition, Tamasha had applied (15 May 1996) to the LAB's Diverse Acts scheme, and was awarded £20,000 in September for *East Is East* (19 September 1996). This was the first award under the scheme, which was set up to respond to new work from communities or individuals originating from the Caribbean, India, China, Africa, Latin America and the Pacific rim. Commissions were sought from ACE for *East Is East* (2 April 1996) and Bains' *Partition* (26 June 1996), and were both awarded: £2,000 for Khan Din (11 June 1996) and £2,215 for Bains (21 August 1996).

East Is East is far more explicitly funny than any previous production by Tamasha, bordering at times on farce, and far more firmly placed in a 'British' convention of 'realistic' drama. Its subject was British Asian experience, and it was written by a British Asian about a family of seven children, with a father of Pakistani origin and an English mother, and set in Salford in 1970. It opened at the Birmingham Rep on 8 October 1996 and transferred to (the Royal Court Upstairs at) the Ambassadors London on 19 November 1996, where it sold out very quickly. It was a comprehensive critical success, and a second production was very soon organised for February and March 1997 at the Theatre Royal Stratford East in London and the Royal Court Downstairs (**DVD 63–67**). Later Tamasha statistics (3 July 1997) state that it was 'the most successful show in six years at the Royal Court', seen by 36,500, of whom half were Asian and half 'other'.[13] In the report to ACE (7 January 1997), Tamasha stated that '*East Is East* has shown the demand for a voice for the British Asian experience', and that the company would 'continue its commitment to developing new writing from British Asian writers with our project for 1997, *Partition* by Harwant Bains'. A Project Funding application for *Partition* had been submitted in October 1996 (30 October 1996), and £40,529 was awarded by ACE under the Cultural Diversity heading (4 February 1997). In January 1997 the LAB had confirmed its second instalment of £30,000 in the fixed funding for 1997–98 (24 January 1997), and in November 1996 Tamasha had sought (29 November 1996) letters of support for a renewed bid for franchise funding from ACE: letters were written by Felix Cross (Black Theatre Cooperative), Deborah Paige (Sheffield Theatres), John Stalker (Birmingham Rep) and Philip Hedley (Theatre Royal, Stratford East), and were received during December.

---

[13] The play was published by Nick Hern Books in association with the Royal Court in 1997, after appearing as an 'Instant Playscript' from the same publisher in 1996.

A new bid for franchise funding

In the event *East Is East* did not lead on to the development and production of more 'new writing from British Asian writers', since by July 1997 the commission for *Partition* had come to nothing, and work of that kind was not to follow in the next ten years. But its critical success did lead directly towards the goal of Franchise funding from ACE for Tamasha. In April a letter was sent from ACE inviting the company to make an application (1 April 1997), and a period of three months was spent compiling the application. The terms set out by ACE for 'Non-Building Based Companies' stated that 'a limited number of new companies that meet the initial criteria for eligibility ... are also invited to apply'—that is, alongside those seeking renewal of their three-year funding. Basic eligibility consisted of the receipt of funds from ACE or a Regional Board for a minimum of three years beforehand, with an accompanying track record, and current priorities at that time were Theatre for Children and Young People and Cultural Diversity, 'in particular investment in black and Asian companies, disabled artists and companies working with people with disabilities'.

The application is a curious mixture of ideas co-existing with one another, almost all of them expressed at various points in Tamasha's development. So, in the section on Artistic Policy, what is expressed is a history of activity rather than a policy:

> Tamasha Theatre Company aims to reflect through theatre the Asian experience—from British Asian life to authentic accounts of aspects of life in the Indian sub-continent, through a range of forms from adapting works of literature and classics to commissioning new work from contemporary writers.

This is followed, in the section on Artistic Achievements, by an interesting claim:

> Each production has spoken to a different section of the British Asian community: *Untouchable* through its Hindi language performances to an elderly section; *House of the Sun* to the Sindhi community; *A Yearning* to the Punjabi community, to take just three examples. The most common response to the productions from Asian audiences is 'You told my story'.

Part of the weight behind the application came from the evidence of solid support from other sources. So the LAB's fixed-term funding had 'enabled the company to stabilise its administrative structure' and had 'resulted in a core of people who now see Tamasha as an integral part of their working life'. This statement firmly countered the previous objection to the freelance status of Tamasha's key figures in the first bid of 1993. In addition, a three-year scheme with Marks and Spencer had allowed the consolidation of the approach to education and development, building on earlier minor support from trusts such as Esmée Fairbairn and Paul Hamlyn. These were signs of permanence, and they were accompanied by a promise to create a website and a confident vision of Audience Development and Marketing Strategy.

> Tamasha has successfully cornered the Asian niche market and over the years increased its market share in the mainstream. While Asian theatre is burgeoning, very little of the work filters into the mainstream stage, now attracting a 50:50 mix. Asian audiences therefore feel isolated. Adjusting to cultural conflicts with society the Asian community has little access to seeing their story portrayed on these mainstream stages. Tamasha gives this community a voice ... Each show has spoken to a different section of the British Asian community. What we have been successful at is in keeping that particular section of the audience throughout the body of work so that they return to see a Tamasha show, not just the actual production.

For all the confident tone, which is understandable, some of the claims made here might be questioned, and once again there is more of a sense of history than of policy for the future. With the section on type and style of work that follows, covering new, classical and devised, clear statements offer a sound, programmatic account:

> new work is developed through workshops and commissions and Tamasha's style of research-led projects where the research is the starting point for the text. These productions result in an authenticity which speaks very directly to our audience ... For classic adaptations to work the reason for transposing one world to another has to be clear in order for the final adaptation to illuminate the original.

In January 1998 fixed-term (Revenue) funding was awarded by ACE from April 1998 for three years, with £128,000 in the first year.

A Tainted Dawn, 1997

The projected script by Harwant Bains was eventually not taken up. With a commitment to the Edinburgh Festival creating a tight deadline, Landon-Smith and Bhuchar put together in the summer of 1997 the script for *A Tainted Dawn*, after improvisations by actors from nine short stories written about Partition. According to the report on *A Tainted Dawn* submitted to ACE (8 December 1997), 'due to the late delivery and content of the play by Harwant, the company decided not to produce this'. *A Tainted Dawn* already appears as the next intended production in July 1997 (ACE application, 3 July 1977), less than six months after the award by ACE of Cultural Diversity funding for the production of Bains' *Partition*. The theme remained constant because of the fiftieth anniversary of the event of Partition itself, which coincided with the fiftieth anniversary of the Edinburgh Festival, at which the play opened in a co-production again with Birmingham Rep. Landon-Smith was working as a producer for BBC Radio and for one project had provided a season based on short stories, and was confident that this could be the source for a production on the theme of Partition.

> So Sue, Sudha and I chose our stories, and took them to the rehearsal room, and in five weeks we improvised around the stories and rehearsed the work and put it together. Some of those stories were told just through the moving image; this was the first time we worked with Lawrence Evans, our movement director ... So some of those stories, which were lorries leaving and people dashing to get on the lorries and leave Pakistan and go to India were done just as a moving image and no real text.
>
> [Landon-Smith 2007]

The final script wove segments of the some of the stories in a sequence through to the end, with a central position held by a boy who is separated from and then re-united with his parents. The stories were by S.H. Ajneya, Lalithambika Antharjarnam, Jamila Hashmi, Leila Keys, Saadat Hasan Manto, Ali Imam Naqvi, Mohan Rakesh and Bhisham Sahni. *A Tainted Dawn* opened on 11 August 1997 for a week at the Gateway Theatre in the Edinburgh festival and toured to Tricycle London, Haymarket Studio Leicester, Birmingham Rep (7–25 October) and the West Yorkshire Playhouse Courtyard (**DVD 68–72**). In January 1998 confirmation was received from the Arts Council of the award of revenue funding for Tamasha from April 1998 for three years, with £128,000 awarded for the first year; and, in the same month, the LAB confirmed the award of £30,000 for 1998–99 and committed to three-year revenue funding for the period 1998–2001.

Tamasha was from the outset conceived as a professional company, drawing upon the professional experience of its principals. It was, at the same time, an initiative in women professionals exercising control over their theatre practice. After limited success with raising private sponsorship, Landon-Smith and Bhuchar pursued public arts funding for each specific project, adding to that an emphasis on funding for script development. The principals, including Sue Mayes, made constructive use of networks of professional contacts and placed an accent on high production values.

A standard process was adopted, with a research period (in India for the first productions) followed by a script development period with actors, and the close professional practice of the company has given rise to what is currently an impressive training programme for young professionals. But this accent on professionalism should not conceal that the fact that until the achievement of revenue funding both Bhuchar and Landon-Smith had to rely on other sources of income, and were adding this work to other major commitments. The emphasis in the choice of material during this early period shifted from a diasporic interest in India to a more direct connection with British Asian audiences, and this was partly because of a close link with an immediate community at the Birmingham Rep. In principle, Tamasha has either adapted or devised materials on a regular basis, but other writers have also brought the company considerable success.

[GL]

8

Kali Theatre Company

Song for a Sanctuary and the formation of Kali

Kali Theatre Company was founded in 1991 by actor/director Rita Wolf and writer Rukhsana Ahmad. The account given here follows the formative years of Kali, from its first production of *Song for a Sanctuary* with Wolf as Artistic Director to the transition to Ahmad as Artistic Director and the ensuing decade of the theatre's development, before Ahmad stepped down in 2002 and Janet Steel took up her post.

Song for a Sanctuary, which received its first full public performance on 8 May 1991 at the Worcester Arts Workshop, Worcester, hailed the directing debut of actor Rita Wolf. Wolf, originally from Calcutta, was one of only a handful of Asian actors at the time who had received formal training in the UK. Having begun her career in 1979 with the Royal Court Youth Theatre, she had acted with a number of companies, including Tara Arts, Asian Cooperative Theatre (ACT) (which she also helped to run for some time with Harmage Singh Kalirai) and Joint Stock (including the co-production with the Royal Court Theatre of Hanif Kureishi's *Borderline*). Her film and television credits included the celebrated British 1985 film *My Beautiful Laundrette*, Channel 4 comedy series *Tandoori Nights* (1987) and, most recently, a role in the major UK television soap *Coronation Street*: a significant achievement for an Asian actress in the 1980s. However, Wolf gave up this lucrative role to embark on her work with Kali, which she understood to be 'probably the most important work I would ever do' and 'something that had some lasting value'.[1]

Rukhsana Ahmad, who had moved to the UK from Pakistan in the early 1980s, had been educated in Karachi and the UK. Although *Song for a Sanctuary* represents her first three-act non-theatre-in-education play, to date she had received a number of theatre and radio commissions, including from the Theatre Centre, Black Forum Theatre, Monstrous Regiment,

1 This and all further direct references to Wolf are taken from an interview with Rita Wolf by Sarah Dadswell, 22 February 2008, unless otherwise stated.

Tara Arts (two theatre-in-education (TIE) productions) and BBC Radio 4. In addition, she had written short stories, newspaper articles and reports, and run a range of creative writing and adult learning classes in London and the regions. Perhaps Ahmad's most fertile training ground as a writer was the Asian Women's Writing Collective (AWWC), founded by Ravinder Randhawa in 1984. The AWWC's aim was 'to promote creative writing by Asian women through a supportive environment and make their writing more accessible to publishers',[2] a principle that underpinned the emphasis on writer development that Kali was to champion. Although London-based, the collective was attended by Asian women writers from all over the UK, including invited speakers. It provided a forum in which the work was immediately understood in all its cultural complexities and was rigorously critiqued by its members. Crucially, for Ahmad and the development of Kali, the AWWC provided a platform which was both multi-lingual and politicised, and also introduced her to the workshop principle as a means of supporting and developing the work of others. The success of the AWWC is evidenced in the large number of participants who have enjoyed successful writing and theatre careers, including Maya Chowdhry, Leena Dingra, Joyoti Grech, Rahila Gupta, Tanika Gupta, Shamshad Khan, Parminder Sekhon and Meera Syaal Meera Syal to name but a few, many of whom later worked with Kali.

The inaugural production of Kali Theatre Company began life as *Sanctuary* and had originally been commissioned by the feminist theatre company Monstrous Regiment in 1987. The initial stirrings of the play were formed when Ahmad heard accounts of a lockout in an Asian women's refuge, which circulated in the media. 'After a serious row some residents [had] banded together and locked out the workers for [a number of weeks]'. Ahmad was 'bewildered' by a 'division between women who should have been on the same side'. She 'researched the setting and the situation visiting at least two refuges and running writing workshops in a third for four weeks'. During the rewrites, however, Sue Parrish (then Artistic Director of the Sphinx) 'insisted that the lockout did not work and was redundant' and Ahmad was persuaded to remove it from the final draft.[3]

The narrative of *Song for a Sanctuary*, which shaped the final production, was inspired by the real-life murder of an Asian woman, Kulwant Baur, by her abusive husband as she sought safety in a women's refuge.[4] In the end the play did not reach production with Monstrous

---

2 Ravinder Randhawa, *Asian Women Writers Collective (1984–1997)*, http://www.salidaa.org.uk/salidaa/site/Collections?mode=catalog&adlib_id=900000001.

3 Information supplied by Rukhsana Ahmad in correspondence to Sarah Dadswell, 14 February 2009.

4 Ahmad knew very little about this event, except that Kaur had been murdered by her husband in a refuge. Correspondence with Ahmad, 14 February 2009.

Regiment. However, Wolf, who was horrified by the real-life story and the lack of media coverage the incident had received, came to know about the play and was 'thrilled that someone had engaged with the subject' and was disseminating the information at a very grassroots level. She contacted Ahmad with a view to exploring the possibilities of producing the play. In the first instance Ahmad re-wrote the play as *Song for a Sanctuary*. It was then given a rehearsed reading organised by the AWWC on 3 December 1989 at Common Stock Theatre, Hammersmith, London, with Wolf in the role of Kamla. The script underwent a number of drafts before its full premiere in 1991, but the essence of the plot remained the same: a first generation Sikh woman, Rajinder, seeks safety for herself and her children from her violent and abusive husband in a women's refuge. The refuge is run by the easy-going Eileen, of similar age to Rajinder and herself a victim of domestic violence, and Kamla, a young Asian woman whose reformist zeal to deal with domestic violence effectively and publicly is in conflict with the traditional values and privacy that Rajinder holds so dear. Jackie is another resident of the refuge who befriends Rajinder's daughter, Savita. On a brief return to the family house Rajinder discovers that her husband Pradeep has also been sexually abusing Savita. They return to the apparent safety of the refuge, only for Pradeep to break in one night and stab Rajinder to death in front of Savita.[5] In an interview in *SpareRib* Wolf stated her reasons for wanting to produce the play: 'Child abuse and violence towards women reveal very basic core emotions, but we don't always have the language to deal with them and that's why this play is important.'[6]

Wolf initially approached ACT to produce *Song for a Sanctuary*, but the play, which required five female actors and only one male, was not taken up by the then predominantly male-orientated company. She then tried many theatres that specialised in new writing, including Soho, the Bush and the Royal Court, but none was interested. Wolf observed the 'gap between a[n Asian] community and its way of seeing itself and its needs, and the established theatre', and decided to set up a theatre company with Ahmad and produce the play herself.

Ahmad and Wolf decided on the name Kali, which embodied many of their founding feminist principles. In Hinduism and earlier Vedic writings Kali is a goddess of great female power or *shakti*. In Bengali it means black ink, and in contemporary Hindi black woman. The goddess therefore

---

5 The script is published as Rukhsana Ahmad, *Song for a Sanctuary*, in *Six Plays by Black and Asian Women Writers*, ed. Kadija George (London: Aurora Metro, 2005), 2nd edn, pp. 204–41.

6 Kamila Zahno, 'Rita Wolf directs *Song for a Sanctuary*', *SpareRib*. The copy of the interview lodged in the Salidaa archive is undated, but it may be from February 1990, issue 54; it is pp. 6–8.

denoted the idea of 'female power, regeneration, fertility and strength'.[7] Wolf's experience of theatre management and production and her belief in the potential of a company like Kali gave the company momentum, a fact openly acknowledged by Ahmad.[8]

Following the first rehearsed readings, in 1990 Wolf successfully applied to the Arts Council of Great Britain (ACGB) under its Development Subsidy of £6,000 for a three-stage process of 'development work with director, designer and writer', followed by a 'workshop period using actors plus the above' and concluding with a staged reading.[9] Understanding the need to establish a durable company structure, the funds were also to cover the 'development of administration and infrastructure of the company'. Wolf stated the company's intention to apply for future funds to mount a national tour the following year. In the same application Wolf set out Kali's aims and objectives in a mission statement which has remained remarkably constant over the course of the company's development to date:

1. To create opportunities for Asian women in the field of theatre, and especially to give them a voice in the field of new writing.
2. To show a commitment to the work of new women writers in Britain as well to showcase work of existing South Asian writers who may not be known in this country.
3. To train Asian women as theatre practitioners as well as writers in Britain.

Wolf's justification for producing the play itself is based on raising awareness of the issues the play identifies and giving voice to Asian women who are a 'sadly neglected group lacking an identity in the artistic life' of the UK. She highlights the important potential of *Song for a Sanctuary* to draw in a new and diverse theatre audience. She also references the support of Jatinder Verma, Artistic Director of Tara Arts Group, and Julie Parker of the Drill Hall, London. In an additional single-page document Kali justifies its positive discrimination towards 'black and ethnic minority women ... for all employment opportunities' within the company, which seeks to redress the 'biases working against women on grounds of race, religion, disability and sexual preference'.[10]

---

7 Dimple Godiwala, '*Kali*: Providing a Forum for British-Asian Women Playwrights', *Studies in Theatre and Performance*, 26.1 (2006), pp. 69–83, p. 69.

8 Interview with Rukhsana Ahmad by Sarah Dadswell, 31 May 2006.

9 This and subsequent quotations taken from the following document: Application for Development Subsidy, to The Drama Director, Arts Council of Great Britain, by Rita Wolf, Director, Sanctuary Productions, for the project 'Sanctuary', dated 3 April 1990, 9 pp. [Kali Archive]. All documents in the Kali Archive were uncatalogued at the time of research.

10 Undated, but must date from around 1990 [Kali Archive].

From the outset, Kali sought to establish its identity as a company which was writer-led. Through its company profile, its writing development process and its choice of production subject matter it was specifically targeting women from the Asian community in the UK, supporting them professionally and raising the profile of issues that affect them.

Following a successful application to the Arts Council of Great Britain, *Sanctuary* received a rehearsed reading on 29 September 1990 at the Riverside Studios, London. Ahmad then continued to redraft the script and it finally received its first full performance with the more elegiac title *Song for a Sanctuary* on 8 May 1991 at the Worcester Arts Workshop before continuing on a national tour. The original cast was: Rajinder (played by Kusum Haider); Savita, her daughter (Sanny Bharti); Pradeep, her husband (Simon Nagra); Amrit, her older sister (Simon Nagra again); Sonia, another resident (Jackie Cowper); Kamla (Sayan Akkadas); and Eileen (Joanna Bacon) (**DVD 1**).

Song for a Sanctuary is shot through with the themes of alienation and vulnerability and its complement, fear. It is Ahmad's ability to create understated, complex characters and unresolved situations that brings depth and texture to the play which is set in the context of the stark and tragic reality of domestic violence. Rajinder's stoical composure in the face of her desperate circumstances conceals a married life of oppression and fear, which Ahmad reveals through subtle references and a series of brief flashbacks. Ahmad creates a world in which nothing is clear-cut and decision-making is a complicated process with no definitive positive outcome guaranteed. For example, Rajinder turns to her sister Amrit for help, but her sister is more concerned with the family's honour. In desperation, Rajinder asks Amrit if she would prefer her to set herself alight in her back garden. Amrit's response is: 'Honour is always preferable to disgrace, but the choice, of course, is yours.'[11] Ahmad uses the contrast between the determined Kamla and easy-going Eileen to explore the pros and cons of following strict protocol, which is there to help women in this crisis. Similarly, she contrasts the traditional, first-generation Rajinder and westernised, second-generation Kamla to explore the multi-layered issue of ethnic identity and the value systems that accompany women of different Asian backgrounds who have different experiences of migration and different levels of engagement in the British system, as illustrated in the following exchange, in which Rajinder refuses to publicly admit the child abuse her daughter has experienced:

RAJINDER: I'd like to avoid a scandal. She's got to marry one day. But then you don't know what it is to live within the community. I don't know where women like you come from. Call yourself an Asian, do you?

---

11 Ahmad, *Song for a Sanctuary*, p. 221.

KAMLA: I am one.

RAJINDER: I wouldn't go that far! Black you may be, Asian you certainly are not.

KAMLA: You can't deny me my identity. I won't let you. You people with your saris and your bloody lingo and all your certainties about the universe, you don't have a monopoly on being Asian. You can't box it and contain it and exclude others. I'll define myself as I bloody well want to.[12]

Although Rajinder lacks support networks within her Asian culture, she also fears engagement in the institutions of western culture, which prevents her from taking up Kamla's help to talk with the social services to procure accommodation for herself and her children. Her daughter Savita, also a progressive young second-generation Asian woman, can see the potential in an alternative life choice: 'If we had our own place it would have been different. We could've made it nice. Got little bits an' pieces, and made it our own.'[13] These analyses of social and ethnic relationships and group dynamics located in the microcosm of a refuge had formed the basis of Ahmad's original narrative of the lockout of the workers by the residents.

The play received broadly positive reviews in local and national press for the spring national tour that played in eleven venues from Glasgow to London.[14] Ahmad was also nominated for the Susan Blackburn Smith Award.[15] Antonia Denford of *City Limits* praised the subtlety of the play's focus and flagged up the set designed by Catherine Armstrong in which '[i]nsecure makeshift walls riddled with doors represent the battered women's refuge [...]' (DVD 2). Both Denford and Louise Kingsley for *The Independent* praised Wolf's directing and the 'committed performances' from the actors (DVD 3–5).[16]

Song for a Sanctuary enjoyed a second national tour in October and

---

12 Ahmad, *Song for a Sanctuary*, p. 236.

13 Ahmad, *Song for a Sanctuary*, p. 233.

14 A document in the Kali archive states the tour schedule as follows: 8 May, Worcester Arts Workshop; 10 and 11 May Cumbernauld Theatre; 13–15 May, Mayfest, Mitchell Theatre, Glasgow; 17 and 18 May, Old Bull Arts Centre, Barnet; 21–25 May, Derby Playhouse Studio; 28 May, Weymouth College; 29 May, Hazelwood House, Loddiswell, South Devon; 31 May and 1 June, Spilsby Theatre; 3–15 June, Tara Arts Centre, London; 19 June, Centre Stage, Stockport; and 20–22 June, West Yorkshire Playhouse, Leeds.

15 Ahmad also adapted *Song for a Sanctuary* for radio in 1993, for which she was awarded Runner-Up in the Council for Racial Equality's Race in the Media Award.

16 Louise Kingsley, 'Song for a Sanctuary', Tara Arts Centre, London SW18, *The Independent*, Friday 14 June 1991 [Kali Archive].

November 1991, playing at major British theatres including the Lyric Theatre Studio, Hammersmith, London (a two-week opening run); the Unity Theatre, Liverpool; Hoxton Hall, Hackney, London; Rotherham Arts Centre, South Yorkshire; Norwich Arts Centre; and the Birmingham Rep Studio (**DVD 6**). This tour was originally organised with the co-production of the Tara Arts Group. Although, owing to unforeseen financial difficulties in the summer of 1991, Tara was unable to keep its originally stated level of support, Jatinder Verma's aid was still considerable. He offered to underwrite Kali's two-week run at the Lyric, supply his stage manager Hitesh Chauhan for this period and the one-week rehearsal period, negotiate a straight two-way box office split between Kali and the Lyric (not usual practice) and provide transport for the cast, set and Kali members for specific dates of their tour. Until this point he had also offered administrative and publicity help to Kali to facilitate their first production's tour. In fact, Kali procured the Lyric's programming partly as the result of Tara Arts's need to withdraw its own production and hence the slot becoming available.[17]

The autumn tour was co-directed by Sue Parrish (then Artistic Director of the Sphinx), who had given Wolf considerable support throughout her directing debut. As Kali lacked the necessary funds to employ the original cast over the summer, it had to recast a few parts for the autumn tour:[18] Susan McGoun replaced Joanna Bacon as Eileen; Wolf played the role of Kamla, to generally mixed reviews; and Jamila Massey replaced Kusum Haider as Rajinder to positive reviews.[19] The rather complicated set design was not particularly suitable for touring, so was pared down to a simple curtain structure. Antonia Denford, who was critical of Wolf's performance, returned for *The Independent* and mourned the loss of the original set: 'Rita Wolf's original production used a striking set, full of doors—both confining and insecure. This has been replaced by a pale curtain which flattens the staging and bores the eye.'[20]

---

17 Correspondence between Tara Arts Group and Kali regarding these arrangements is found uncatalogued in the Kali archive and dates from 24 May 1990 to 5 September 1991. Rukhsana Ahmad recalls the circumstances slightly differently: Tara had to withdraw their production from the Lyric at short notice. Verma therefore offered Kali some help to ensure *Song for a Sanctuary* was produced, but also to avoid a penalty. During this period Kali employed Tara's administrator, Rita Mishra, on a part-time basis. Correspondence with Ahmad, 14 February 2009.

18 To secure Arts Council of England (ACE) funding Kali needed to confirm a certain number of tour venues. As a new company they found this very difficult, and had to stretch the originally planned spring tour to include a second autumn tour and make up the requisite number of dates [Wolf 2008].

19 Michael Arditti, 'Curtain Raiser: Song for a Sanctuary, Lyric Studio', *Evening Standard*, Tuesday 15 October 1991, p. 52.

20 Antonia Denford, 'Song for a Sanctuary: Lyric Studio, London W6', *The Independent*, Tuesday 15 October 1991.

Kali's political motivation and commitment to supporting Asian women was evidenced in its desire to extend discussion of the sensitive topics of domestic violence and child abuse beyond the performance, and to run a set of workshops scheduled to coincide with the end of the spring tour and run throughout the autumn tour. To this end, Rita Mishra (the shared administrator with Tara Arts) approached the Gulbenkian Foundation for their support and to fundraise the budgeted £5,000.[21] In the letter she stated that '[t]he workshops would be aimed at Asian women throughout England and the object would be to raise the issues of battered women within our own communities'. Members of Kali would lead the workshops, which were to be drama-based in order that the women were able to express themselves physically and vocally. Materials from these workshops would be collected and ploughed into future Kali work. A second document in the Kali Archive entitled 'Development project. Kali Theatre Co. Autumn 1991. Workshop and tour schedule October and November' refers to post-show discussions in addition to special matinee performances and morning workshops. It is notable that one of the specific functions of Kali's extra activities at Hoxton Hall, Hackney, and the Birmingham Rep was to encourage Asian audience attendance. One of Ahmad and Wolf's clear objectives for Kali was that it produce high-quality productions that would serve a new, diverse audience. To this end, Wolf used audience questionnaires to understand her audience more fully and then tailor future theatre decisions, marketing and funding applications accordingly.

In a letter dated 18 December 1991 Sue Parrish reiterated the professionalism of the two founding directors and the need to nurture Kali's development. Her letter identified Kali's political and creative identity and potential for important future work, emphasising the stories from the Asian community that need to be told and the potential of this untapped theatre audience, thereby filling 'a gap in current Arts provision'. Having confirmed the high standards and positive reception of *Song for a Sanctuary* and the administration of the company and tour, she concluded: 'I have no hesitation in recommending this company, whose work will enrich and widen the artistic community, and will bring theatre to a new audience.'[22] Kali's ability to attract support from mainstream women's theatre groups and individuals such as dramaturge Penny Gold and directors Helena Uren

---

[21] Rita Mishra, letter to Fiona Ellis, The Gulbenkian Foundation, 9 May 1991 [Kali Archive]. The proposed budget for the workshop series includes £1,000 from the Greater London Arts Association (GLAA), East Midlands Arts, West Midlands Arts and Yorkshire Arts respectively, £5,000 Arts Council proportion of grant, and £825 Sales/donations. The total calculated expenditure of £14,825 left the £5,000 deficit. It is unclear from the budget whether the income was anticipated or guaranteed.

[22] Letter from Sue Parrish, Artistic Director, the Sphinx, dated 18 December 1991 [Kali Archive].

(later Helena Bell) and Debbie Bestwick shows the company's ability to reach beyond a specifically ethnically bound vision and to aim for the highest professional standards while retaining their political integrity.

The company's accounts for the period ending 29 February 1992 state that the company faced an overall deficit of £3,210, which could be carried over to the following year. Given the high level of activity and output during the year, this was a modest deficit for a new company, which was controlled by Wolf's administrative skills and successful funding applications. After its inaugural production Kali was creatively, administratively and financially in a stable position to embark on its next phase of development.

1992–1997: building a company and nurturing new talent

In 1992, having been such a driving force behind the formation of Kali Theatre Company and the success of its first production, Rita Wolf moved to New York. Her position as Artistic Director of the company became untenable and so, by default, Rukhsana Ahmad took up the reins. Wolf remained a staunch supporter and advisor to the company, and to Ahmad in particular, and kept her place on the then board of directors alongside Ahmad, Pratibha Parma and Rawinder Randhawa.[23] Ahmad continued as Artistic Director until 2002.

In Ahmad's first year at the helm Kali commissioned a new play, *Tilak's Revenge*, from the young writer Tanika Gupta, made possible with a grant from the Calouste-Gulbenkian Foundation. In 1992 Ahmad also used her adaptation of Sa'adat Hasan Manto's short story *Kali Shalwar* as the basis for a theatre workshop, this time funded with an Arts Council Project Subsidy. However, it would be another five and a half years before Kali's next full production, *Natural World*. In the intervening time Kali created its unique identity as a company that invested in talented Asian women and actively enabled them to strive to reach their full professional potential. Rita Wolf described this professional, supportive element of Kali's remit as 'the single most important thing that we do. More important than any individual production' [Wolf 2008].

In the spring of 1994 Kali made the crucial change which ultimately defined its identity and process as a producing theatre company, which remains to this day: it organised a range of open theatre workshops, *From Idea ... to Script*, which resulted in the production of a number of early play drafts. These were then developed for a programme of rehearsed readings of new plays that were performed in autumn under the title *Dramatic*

---

23 The early Kali board consisted of nominal directors on the Companies House Register, but never met formally. Wolf and Ahmad met to decide company policy and conduct administration. Correspondence between Sarah Dadswell and Ahmad, 14 February 2009.

Encounters. This two-stage process was part of Kali's original remit for the company and had taken two years to plan and fund raise.[24] It was a practical measure that tackled the lack of Asian women in the theatre industry, especially writers, directors and stage managers. This process of training and development had the added advantage of providing Kali with a potential play to develop to full production.

Kali workshops

Ahmad organised the intensive day workshops, which were funded by the Calouste-Gulbenkian Foundation and the Foundation for Sport and Arts and took place over a six-week period from May 1994 at the Oval House, London, which contributed its space for free (**DVD** 7). They comprised a combination of structured talks from the theatre experts and time for individuals to engage in practical writing work. The writers were offered monthly script surgeries during the summer and all workshop participants could contribute to the autumn rehearsed readings.[25] The stage management workshops were coordinated by Crin Claxton, the technical manager at Oval House, with the assistance of Jennifer Ford and Jackie Grant. Rita Wolf returned from New York to run the acting workshops with Piali Ray, dancer and Artistic Director of Sampad (Birmingham-based South Asian Arts Agency)as guest director on the first day. The impressive list of tutors at the writing workshops included Vayu Naidu (writer/storyteller), Joan-Ann Maynard (Artistic Director, Black Theatre Coop), Deborah Bestwick (Artistic Director, Oval House), Winsome Pinnock (stage and television writer), Matthew Lloyd (Associate Director, Hampstead Theatre), Jatinder Verma (Artistic Director, Tara Arts Group), Tony Dinner (Dramaturge, Paines Plough) and Rukhsana Ahmad. The guest tutors used the mornings to set the day up and Ahmad then ran the afternoon sessions.[26] The list of participating writers is equally impressive and a testament to the investment of such workshops in the growing number of successful Asian women

---

[24] See 'Programme of Kali Theatre Company's Work 1992–1994', undated [Kali Archive].

[25] An outline of the workshops is given in a letter from Rukhsana Ahmad to Fiona Ellis, Calouste Gulbenkian Foundation, dated 11 June 1994. Supporting documentation gives the above list of participants. Another letter from Ahmad to Tony Craze, dated 08 August 1994, states that Claire Grove and Sita Brahmachari were also invited to join the script surgeries, with Cheryl Robson hoping to attend the final one on 9 September [Kali Archive].

[26] At this stage Ahmad and Wolf were paid only for delivering the workshops on the day (i.e. not for the previous organisation of them). Wolf returned again from New York to direct the autumn readings. Ravi Randhawa later received a very small fee for part-time administration. Correspondence with Ahmad, 14 February 2009.

writers in British theatre. The list included Preethi Manuel, Tanika Gupta, Joyoti Grech, Rahila Gupta, Seema Jena, Perminder Dhillon, Amina Osman and Sudha Bhuchar.

Although, by today's standards, scripts by Asian women with potential for professional development were relatively scarce,[27] Ahmad is clear that this was not a community initiative, but a professional strategy, run by professionals for those with existing writing experience.

Kali rehearsed readings

The rehearsed readings *Dramatic Encounters* took place over four days from 31 October to 2 November 1994 at the Tara Arts Studio, which had been donated for free (DVD 8). There were two clear objectives: to 'introduc[e] new writers to new companies and artistic directors from the smaller theatre venues which may be able to produce their work and the writers' need to learn from the process per se: the invaluable exercise of stepping off the page onto the stage' i.e. the writers were introduced to the process of staging their texts/scripts. The writers were restricted to a maximum of four actors per play as this was 'a predictable constraint in the real world of theatre productions and writers could use it as a learning experience'.[28] They would also be aware of the relatively narrow age-range of available Asian actors.[29] The process of producing the rehearsed readings was handled with as much sensitivity as the initial workshops and dramaturgical support. The writers were paired off with directors who were interested in their work and were able to develop the script before meeting the actors.[30] Each group had only one day to discuss and rehearse the reading before the public performance. Although only five of the original eight writers from the workshop were able to develop their piece to rehearsed-reading standard by the required deadline, the process from workshop to performance was highly successful. The audience consisted of all those involved in the plays and the invited representatives of small

---

[27] Penny Gold and Helena Bell both draw attention to this problem: see interviews with Sarah Dadswell, both dated 13 February 2008.

[28] Anon., Report, 'Kali Theatre Company: *Dramatic Encounters*', undated [Kali Archive].

[29] The relatively recent emergence of Asian actors to the British stage naturally led to a scarcity of capable older actors. This resulted in Asian actors frequently playing a wider personal age range than their mainstream counterparts, but also restricted writers to creating storylines with younger actors.

[30] The paired writers and directors were as follows: Joyoti Grech—Vayu Naidu; Preethi Manuel—Sita Ramamurthy; Ranika Gupta—Rita Wolf; Leena Dhingra—Helena Uren (later Bell); and Amina Osman—Joan-Ann Maynard. Stage management was by Vohrinder Dhaliwal, Casting by Rita Wolf and Co-ordinator and Dramaturg, Rukhsana Ahmad. See the above report, footnote 28.

theatre venues. The small studio environment was 'intimate and supportive' and 'energy and enthusiasm enveloped the day'. Although the writers were at an early stage, Ahmad declares that: 'it's writing in development, it's where the best writing comes from. [...] yes, it's not the best work, but it is going to get there' [Ahmad 2006].

This model of an open invitation to Asian women writers to submit script ideas for development to rehearsed reading has remained a constant of the Kali process, although it has been re-branded *Kali Shorts*. A crucial difference in the process between now and then is that under Ahmad's directorship the writers were first given an eight-week writing workshop before submitting their first drafts for development. This investment in the writers was especially important at a time when Asian women writers were relatively rare and all potential talent needed to be sensitively and professionally nurtured.

The *Dramatic Encounters* report from the Kali Archive identifies a number of valuable lessons that the company learned through the process of script development to rehearsed reading. More time for each increment of the process would have encouraged a more finished piece to present to the 'market place'. Kali also felt 'a lack of real choice when it came to finding *experienced* [sic] Asian women directors', and suggested this as a possible development for the company to explore. Under-budgeting was also an issue. Kali had insufficient funds to support the attendance of those participants who lived outside London. The second stage of the process had been made possible only through supplementary help from the Tara Arts Group and the Calouste-Gulbenkian Foundation. Script surgeries between workshop and rehearsal were therefore given on a voluntary basis. Kali's lack of charitable status had hampered its ability to raise funds and, in fact, it was only able to receive its grant from the Calouste-Gulbenkian Foundation because it was aligned with the Tara Arts Group.

Over the next three years Kali organised a number of rehearsed readings of plays in development and produced the second wave of its Asian women's theatre workshops and rehearsed readings under the title *More Dramatic Encounters*. In June 1995 the company presented a rehearsed reading of Ahmad's latest play *Meeting the Sphinx* at the Asian Drama Festival, Watermans Arts Centre, Hounslow. This was followed by rehearsed readings of two plays, which were now in development as a result of the first *Dramatic Encounters*: Joyoti Grech's *Natural World*, directed by Vayu Naidu, and Preethi Manuel's *Kurunjumalar*, directed by Helena Uren. These readings took place on 5 and 6 October 1995 at the Oval House Theatre, with Rita Wolf and Jamila Massey acting in *Kurunjumalar*. Kali's flyer for this evening (**DVD 9**) encouraged the audience to give feedback on the performances, a strategy that sought to build the relationship between audience and company and gather critical perspectives. The same autumn Ahmad submitted her application to the Paul Hamlyn Foundation for the theatre skills workshops and *More Dramatic Encounters* to be scheduled for May and November 1996 with an overall budget of £23,100.[31]

1996 was a difficult year for Kali. The company failed to raise the requisite funds for the desired *More Dramatic Encounters*. Despite their concerted efforts they secured only £8,500 of the projected £23,100 original budget.[32] The project was postponed until spring and autumn of 1997 and necessarily scaled down to within the £8,500 with the assistance of the Oval House, which again gave its space for free. The company maintained its public presence by producing a reading of Tanika Gupta's play *Ananda Sananda*, adapted from a play by Badal Sircar, *Jodi Fr Akbar* (If Only Once Again), for the Asian Theatre Festival, Watermans Art Centre, on 16 June.[33] By July, and despite this public display, Kali's next major production *Natural World* was in jeopardy, again owing to insufficient funding. The company's minutes from meetings on 16 and 24 July, together with a letter from Ahmad to the company's support group dated 11 July, raised serious questions about the production [Kali archive]. The production was originally budgeted at £43,783 but had raised only £23,483 through the Arts Council. Although an application had been made to the London Arts Board (LAB) for £9,215, Kali had over-estimated its projected income from the box office and was set for a shortfall of between £8,000 and £12,000, a disaster for a company of its size. For this reason the show was postponed until spring 1997 with venues to be re-booked.

As the company grew, so too, obviously, did the administrative workload. Although Kali was nominally operating with its original board of directors, it was Ahmad who bore the brunt of the administrative load, organised projects and produced the plays with minimal income in return; this in addition to pursuing her own successful independent writing career. Various members of the company offered their help on an ad hoc basis under the umbrella of the company's 'support group',[34] but the company's minutes for 1996 make it clear that a restructuring of the company with a more formal

---

31 See related correspondence September 1995 [Kali Archive].

32 These funds were supplied as follows: £2,000 Paul Hamlyn Foundation, £2,000 Calouste Gulbenkian Foundation and £4,500 Peggy Ramsey Foundation. See related correspondence September 1995–January 1996 [Kali Archive].

33 The minutes of the Kali meeting dated 7 May 1996 state that Indhu Rubasingham would direct the play, although this was questioned by Rukhsana Ahmad. See interview with Rukhsana Ahmad by Sarah Dadswell, 14 February 2008. The archived minutes of the meeting of 24 February 1996 state the purpose of the festival, which was organised by Hardial Rai, then director of Waterman's, was to run a '"British Asian and Indian sub-continent directors" workshop to discuss "Asian-ness" [sic] and directors' approaches and present some pieces working with actors'. Gupta's play *Ananda Sananda* could be called upon if nothing else was forthcoming from Kali.

34 See letter by Ahmad to the support group dated 11 July 1996 [Kali Archive].

advisory board to share the strategic workload and seek charitable status was needed. This would take another two years.

In the meantime, the delayed stagecraft[35] and six-week writing workshops took place at the Oval House during April and June 1997 (**DVD 10**). The calibre of tutors was impressive: Vicky Featherstone (Artistic Director, Paines Plough Theatre Company), Olusola Oyeleye (writer/director), Lin Coghlan (writer), Deborah Bestwick (Artistic Director, Oval House Theatre) and Ben Payne (Literary Manager, Birmingham Rep).[36] Six out of the ten workshop participants went on to produce scripts for the autumn rehearsed readings.[37] *More Dramatic Encounters* took place at the Oval House Studio on 30 and 31 October and 1 and 2 November in conjunction with Spread the Word (a company specialising in writing and reading development in London) and were advertised under the banner of '12 New Plays by Black & Asian Women' (**DVD 11**).[38] Kali's contribution included the following: *Relatively Sane* by Parm Kaur, directed by Anne Edyvean; *I Won't Let You Go* by Sangeeta Datta, directed by Arti Prashar; *Daag Daag Ujaala* by Shahida Omarshad, directed by Deborah Bestwick; *Today Shakuntala* by Mo Bannerjee, directed by Olusola Oyleye; *Mangos and Sacher Torte* by Bettina Gracias, directed by Helena Uren; and *The Ecstasy* by Anu Kumar, directed by Ravi Kapoor. Ahmad's report deemed the Kali plays successful in terms of delivery of script, audience attendance, post-show discussion and feedback from audience and theatre professionals involved. The list of directors reinforces Ahmad's assertion that the professionals involved did not necessarily need to be Asian, but all 'had an understanding for ethnic writing' [Ahmad 2006].

1997: *Natural World*

In 1997 Kali was finally able to stage a full-scale production of a play that had been developed through its dramaturgical process of workshop and

---

35 There is minimal archival documentation covering the actual workshops. Previous outlines of the intended workshops which were submitted with funding applications envisaged a four-week performance skills workshop co-ordinated by Rita Wolf; a weekly course over four weeks to introduce women to stage management, production and lighting skills again co-ordinated by Crin Claxton; and a short course on theatre directing run over three weekends by Helena Uren. See 'Outline of the Theatre Skills Programme 1996' [Kali Archive].

36 Information taken from letter from Rukhsana Ahmad to workshop participants, 22 April 1997 [Kali Archive].

37 Rukhsana Ahmad, 'Report Writers' Workshops and Rehearsed Readings', undated but sent to Calouste Gulbenkian Foundation and The Paul Hamlyn Foundation with accompanying letter dated 17 November 1997. Also Get that play wright?, undated, but sample scripts requested by 20 April 1997 [Kali Archive].

38 Press Release 'Kali Theatre & Spread the Word present 12 New Plays by Black & Asian Women', 30 October–9 November, Thurs–Sun 8 p.m. [Kali Archive].

rehearsed reading. Joyoti Grech's *Natural World* had been in development with Kali since its first set of writing workshops in May 1994. Various people had been involved in its development, including Ahmad as dramaturge and Vayu Naidu as director of the rehearsed reading in 1995. However, it was Anne Edyvean, who had previously directed Grech's first radio play in 1995 as part of BBC Radio 4's Bite Festival, who now directed the full-scale production. According to *Natural World*'s programme (**DVD 12**), Grech had been writing since 1988, was a member of the AWWC and a performance poet with Apples and Snakes.[39] She had also participated in workshops with Tamasha and Talawa Theatre Companies.

Natural World is a coming of age story in which the fate of best friends Benita and Laura Lee hang in the balance as they take stock of their single-parent existence and explore levels of love that run contrary to the natural order as prescribed in their forthcoming biology A level.[40] Benita's Bengali mother, Radhika, died of cancer but returns in dream sequences to guide Benita and her Italian father, Beppe, through Benita's transitional phase. As the story unfolds Laura Lee's mother walks out on her and her baby sister. The situation is resolved, at least for the time being, as Benita and Laura Lee realise their sexual desire for one another and rather than move down to her newly discovered Bengali family in London, Benita moves in with Laura Lee and Martin, a mutual friend who has been thrown out of his home.

According to Wolf and Ahmad, the production had a poetic, lyrical quality. The production was beautiful, very simple and clean and 'centred around the relationship between the two women, and was not sensational in any way' [Wolf 2008 and Ahmad 2006]. Carla Eve Amie's set design combined with Crin Claxton's lighting to create a dreamlike quality using mirrors and slides. This surreal, dreamlike quality was also reflected in the marketing flyers and programme, which featured layering of liquid-like negative photographic images of a flower, a woman's smiling portrait and architectural drawings in shades of yellow, turquoise and deep burgundy (**DVD 12–13**). Charles Godfrey-Faussett's review for *TimeOut* acknowledges the neat casting as the characters doubled up: Nina Wadia as Benita/Angie, Nathalie Armin as Laura Lee/Radhika and Ravin Ganatra as Beppe/ Martin. He also praises the 'sure-handed direction'. However, with the play's frequent use of Italian and Bengali he declares that it is 'Grech's carefully constructed multilingual script and her acute ear for dialogue that

---

39 Grech worked with groups including Artists for Palestine, ANC, Asian Dub Foundation and Survivors Poets and her writings of various genres were published in a number of anthologies. See programme to *Natural World*, Kali Theatre Company, 1997, p. 5 [Kali section, Salidaa Archive, Brunel University].

40 The unpublished script of *Natural World* is housed in the Salidaa Archive, University of Brunel.

provide the most satisfying moments'. Although he feels that the play might be better suited to radio, he praises the Oval House theatre for 'pay[ing] rewarding attention to minority interests'.[41] The somewhat patronising tone aside, what is most notable is Godfrey-Faussett's glossing over the subject matter, what he terms '[e]ighteen-year old Asian lesbians from single-parent families'. Although this is a play about love 'first love, family love, lost love', as the programme states, it was a brave decision for Kali to produce a play with openly lesbian content. While Kali strives to develop and challenge its audience in parallel with its company, in 1997 gay issues were a taboo subject among large sections of the Asian community. That Kali's audience was predominantly female-orientated in its first decade would make it generally more willing to explore subject matter traditionally deemed taboo. However, it should be noted that the marketing for this production was carefully managed to avoid explicit allusions to lesbianism.

Kali had experienced great difficulty in raising funds for *Natural World* and had already expended much energy in booking, then rebooking, tour venues. When the production finally became financially viable, with a grant from the Arts Council, Ahmad approached Tara Arts to help manage the tour. *Natural World* was therefore produced and tour managed by Tara, and premiered at the Oval House on 20 February before embarking on a national tour.[42]

Natural World established Kali's profile as a company that invested in new writing and was evidence for future investors that it could deliver a full-scale production. The successful tour also encouraged the directors to maintain the company, although Ahmad had no wish to continue with sole responsibility for production. Wolf therefore sought the advice of Tony Craze (writer, former Director of Soho Theatre Company and Theatre Writing Associate to the LAB), who championed new writing initiatives. He encouraged Ahmad to set up a board of trustees to create a more formal and dependable structure to make company decisions and take responsibility, which she did. Motivated by Craze's offer to join the board himself, Ahmad approached a number of people already associated with the company, including Penny Gold, Helena Uren, Rena Sodhi (specialist in TIE (theatre in education), and Planning and Development Officer for South Eastern Arts Board), Preethi Manuel (writer and performer, former coordinator of the AWWC), Kamila Zahno (accountant and member of the AWWC, specialist

---

41 Charles Godfrey-Faussett, 'Natural World', Oval House (Fringe), *TimeOut*, 26 February–5 March 1997.

42 The tour dates were as follows: 20–23 February, 27 February–2 March and 6–9 March 1997, Oval House, London; 25 February, Theatre in the Mill, University of Bradford; 5 March, The Gantry, Southampton; 13–15 March, Leicester Haymarket Theatre (Studio); 25–29 March, Tara Arts Studio, London; 4–5 April, The Drum, Birmingham, (presents at the Library Theatre); 7 April, Redgrave Theatre, Bristol; and 11 April 1997, Hawth Theatre, Crawley.

in small businesses) and, of course, Rita Wolf. The board was formalised and the following year the company acquired charitable status.[43]

1999: *Love Comes in at the Window …*

Kali's next full production came in the form of the double bill *Love Comes in at the Window*, incorporating *The Ecstasy* by Anu Kumar and *Black Shalwar* by Rukhsana Ahmad, the latter an adaptation from the short story *Kali Shalwar* by Saadat Hasan Manto. *The Ecstasy* was new writing that had been fully developed through the Kali process. Ahmad's adaptation had originally been commissioned by Tara Arts, but had been cancelled at the last minute owing to the female cast member's illness. The play had then been used as a basis for a Kali workshop in 1992.[44] It was only when *The Ecstasy* was deemed too short to secure a national tour that Helena Uren suggested they expand to a double-bill with a second short piece and approached Ahmad for one of her plays. With Uren as dramaturge, and then director of the double-bill, Ahmad reworked the play [Ahmad 2008].

According to the programme, '*The Ecstasy* was inspired by John Donne's poem of the same name, which tells of the "interanimation" of souls' (**DVD 14**). It is the story of chance encounters of three people whose interactions help them to process their pasts and resolve their immediate futures. Jackie, played by Adele Salem, is the vulnerable yet quirky and often humorous white working-class northern older mum, who has responded to ex-accountant Amit's (Royce Ullah) advert for a life model to pose for his new sculpture. But Amit finds Jackie's neediness and attachment to him increasingly annoying, especially when he develops a homosexual relationship with the embryologist Sanjay (Ashvin Kumar Joshi). The action is naturalistic and takes place in Amit's flat/studio, which is adorned with his paintings of various religious iconic figures. The emphasis is on the intimacies shared through this process of painting and the parallel unravelling and negotiating of problematic personal histories. The denouement comes when all three gather to celebrate Amit's birthday at his flat. When the men leave for the restaurant Jackie dissolves into an alcohol-driven crisis as she grieves for the death of her nineteen-year-old son. The men return to find her in a heap on the floor, smeared with clay. It turns out that Amit's mother died in childbirth, which is why he always

---

43 Registered Charity Index Report, Charity Commission. Registration date of Kali as a charity is 28 September 1998 [Kali Archive].

44 In an application to the Arts Council of Great Britain for a Development Subsidy dated 29 May 1991 Wolf states Kali's wish to workshop two short plays, *Black Shalwar* and *A New Constitution*, as a double-bill to celebrate the original writer Manto. The original intention was to have a cast of five doubling for both plays, a set design flexible enough to accommodate both plays, and a musical director to focus on *Black Shalwar* [Kali Archive].

felt compromised by Jackie. In the final scenes Sanjay has replaced Jackie as Amit's model, and Jackie is enchanted to discover Amit's finished sculpture, depicting her sitting at peace with flowers emanating from her stomach.[45]

Ahmad's project report acknowledged the pleasing mix of both mainstream and Asian audiences, as well as a good mix of ages and genders.[46] The reviews rightly praised Salem's performance, which was compelling, yet surprisingly subtle.[47] Her character was more complex and far more convincing than that of the two male characters, whose on-stage relationship seemed rather superficial and unconnected. Her character also has some wonderful lines, including her love for men with curly hair—'it brings out the boy in a man'—and the list of cakes she made for her son, which she recites as she descends into crisis:

> I can make things too Amit, like cakes. Been making cakes for years. Can make cakes with my eyes shut. Nineteen boy's birthday cakes; this will be the twentieth. Twenty boy's birthdays: smarty cakes, Doughal cakes, car cakes, football cakes, Kevin bloody Keagan cakes. (**DVD 15**)

The Ecstasy featured full nudity of both the Jackie and Sanjay characters in the course of their separate modelling, which was alluded to in the marketing for the regional venues to avoid causing offence. It also featured male embracing and kissing. As Helena Uren later admitted, it was, given the Asian audience, a brave if not rash decision to include the nudity, even if the male reviewer from *The Stage* commented on its sensitive delivery in which 'such is the nature of the subject, one barely notices the nudity' [Bell 2008].[48] Uren had attended life drawing classes and researched the topic for this play, so had couched the nudity firmly in terms of the painterly process. That said, full nudity and homosexuality were potentially very challenging aspects of the play for some members of the Asian audience. In comparison, both elements are absent from the mediated form of mainstream Indian films.[49] Anu Kumar had insisted that a white actress take the role of Jackie

---

45 The script is not published. This commentary is based on an audio-visual recording of the double-bill *Love Comes in at the Window* ..., kindly lent by Rukhsana Ahmad.

46 Rukhsana Ahmad, *Project Report:* Love Comes in at the Window ..., submitted with letter to Jo Hemmant, London Arts Board, 18 June 1999 [Kali Archive].

47 See, for example, the *TimeOut* review [n.d.] [Kali Archive].

48 See also Nick Awde, 'Oval House (Downstairs): Love Comes in at the Window', *The Stage*, 18 March 1999.

49 As *The Ecstasy* was a play produced in the UK, not India, it was therefore performed in the context of British audiences and followed Kali's aims of producing new plays for new audiences. However, in 1999 the majority of British South Asians would not have been theatre-goers, but many would have been cinema-goers. One

[Bell 2008]. Most probably, this decision served the purposes of the play in terms of aesthetics and dramaturgy, but it also avoided the multiple potential problems of having a young Asian woman in that role.

Although the central theme of both plays was 'love and loss', which had been an alternate title for the double-bill, it was courageous of Kali to support the development of Kumar's play, which dealt with challenging topics in both form and content. It is also a credit to the Kali audience that they too supported such a challenging play.

The second play of the double-bill, *Black Shalwar*, featured the same actors and the same set design, albeit adapted, by Sophia Lovell Smith, thereby reinforcing the intertextuality between the plays and foregrounding their mutual themes of love and loss. This doubling was the result of budgetary restraints but also directorial choice.[50] In fact, the doubling of Adele Salem in what Nigel Reynolds of *The Daily Telegraph* termed 'cross-racial casting' drew positive attention to the play, but also challenged the audience.[51] As stated in the performance programme, Adele Salem was of bi-racial origin, with an English mother and Afghani father. She played a white working-class northern mum in *The Ecstasy* and an Indian prostitute, Sultana, in *Black Shalwar*. The characters' mutual wish to be industrious and independent, even if they were vulnerable, found themselves in adverse circumstances and longing for lost loves, underpinned the theatrical challenge of the racial dualism.

With the exception of the ending, Ahmad's adaptation of *Black Shalwar* is faithful to Manto's original short story. It tells the story of prostitute Sultana, whose trade thrives on the presence of the British 'gora' army in Ambala. She falls in love with Khuda Buksh (Royce Ullah), who finds pleasure and a source of funding in her arms (**DVD 16**). But when Buksh forces a move to Delhi so he can follow his guru, Sultana forfeits her clientele. Buksh slowly pawns her wares to pay his way, abandoning Sultana in favour of long nights with his guru in search of enlightenment. Lonely and poverty-stricken Sultana turns to Shankar (Ashvin-Kumar Joshi), a playful character who reveals little, yet manages to trick Sultana into giving her services for free. With Moharram (the Shi'ite month of mourning) fast

---

could argue that those experiencing British Asian-led theatre for the first time may have taken their reference points from film (where even the depiction of a romantic kiss is rare) and would therefore have been quite surprised, if not shocked, when faced with on-stage unmediated full nudity and homosexuality.

50 Documentation in the Kali Archive suggests a pared down contribution from funders as follows: ACE £28,000, ACE new commissions £1,750, LAB production fund £13,200, giving a subtotal of £42,950. As the budget documentation is undated it is impossible to confirm if this was the actual or projected budget. *Love Comes in at the Window*, Kali Budget [Kali Archive].

51 Nigel Reynolds, 'Racial Casting No Black and White', *The Daily Telegraph*, 20 February 1999.

approaching, Sultana is desperate to renew her wardrobe with a new black *shalwar* (shawl). Shankar comes to Sultana's aid and promises to supply her with a new *shalwar* in exchange for her silver earrings. Finally, on the morning of the first day of Moharram, an exhausted Shankar delivers the beautiful black *shalwar* to Sultana. Sultana is delighted, until she meets her friend Mukhtar, who is wearing her silver earrings. They silently acknowledge the exchange of each other's possessions and their mutual relationship with the charming gigolo Shankar. This dramatic realisation comprises the conclusion of Manto's original short story. In Ahmad's adaptation, however, Sultana regains a degree of control and hope for an independent future. Rather than waiting for Khuda Buksh, who has left Delhi to follow his guru, or placing her faith in Shankar, she decides to return to Ambala to recapture her former successful life.

Once again it was the central female character and Adele Salem's performance that carried the play. Although the script was overly reliant on lengthy monologues more suited to radio and which occasionally compromised the play's actual theatricality, Ahmad's script included some comic, playful dialogue between Sultana and Shankar. Lovell Smith's set design, which had been created on a shoe-string budget and which director Uren exploited to full effect, provided an ideal environment for such playfulness. The set consisted of five arched panels with criss-cross girded ironwork. In *The Ecstasy* Lovell Smith had covered the arches with paintings and used them in a naturalistic way to provide the backdrop to the studio, which encompassed the whole stage space. However, in *Black Shalwar* the revealed, girded arches contributed to a sense of the exotic, luxurious atmosphere of 1940s colonial India and the intimacy of a prostitute's boudoir with balconies overlooking the street. Two half-arches were placed downstage right, a central full arch centre stage with a single bed was placed at a diagonal to the archway, and the other two half-arches were positioned upstage left. This allowed Uren copious flexibility and permutations for her characters to move from room to room, and from street to balcony. The set remained static throughout, with only minor changes to accessories, and the bed was sumptuously covered in materials of various deep colours and textures. The overall look was slightly stark but dramatic, akin to the German Expressionist tone with striking visual images that Uren was seeking. This aesthetic was reinforced by Salem's almost caricatured range of heavily made-up facial expressions (reminiscent of Indian dance theatre), hand movements and posture.

The overall tone of the play was more romantic than the original short story, and made more so by the use of music, especially *qawalis* (sung Urdu poetry, which was very popular with the older generation), and uncomplicated lighting. This was a simple tale, but with strong political undertones, where the author fully appreciated the plight of a female who trades her independence for love only to be left stranded. There were no value judgements about Sultana's status as a prostitute, a point emphasised by Uren's directing of the silent comic scenes between prostitute and client, and beautifully acted by Joshi (**DVD 17**).

Ahmad's appreciation of Manto is reflected in her extensive four-page analysis of his writing included in the programme. In it she states that Manto 'is undoubtedly the most translated Urdu fiction writer of our times'. Although *Black Shalwar* was not the new writing usually championed by Kali it was used strategically to support *The Ecstasy* and secure the national tour. Also, at a time when Kali's core audience demographic consisted of young–middle-aged Asian women, Manto's popularity with the older Asian generation would have secured higher audience numbers and encouraged audience crossover.

As Ahmad acknowledged in her report, *Love Comes in at the Window* was '[i]n many ways [...] the most successful show [Kali] have delivered as a company'. It played at fourteen venues and audience figures are stated to have been 'gratifying', in the region of '65% in about 90% of the venues'.[52] Ahmad referred to negative feedback regarding the pronunciation of some Urdu names. However, she counters such criticisms in line with Kali's overall agenda for authentic work by Asians as follows: 'Tolerance for voices and accents is part of our agenda for change as a company; and so is the attempt to slowly engineer shifts in traditional attitudes.' In other words, Kali were also concerned with the acceptance of Asians on the British stage, regardless of their accent.

Without doubt, the successful tour of *Love Comes in at the Window* reaffirmed Kali's profile as a company that could deliver a professional production and target new audiences. The double-bill was Kali's most ambitious production to date and, as such, put enormous demands on the company and its resources. In addition, Kali had scheduled a two-day theatre training day in the middle of the tour, which brought together five of Kali's writers with five members of United Scenographers. The workshop was led by Penny Gold for Kali and Julie Matthews from United Scenographers and its purpose was to allow the participants the chance 'to explore the imaginative impact of colour, sound and smell and to investigate the way we use space, movement and words'.[53] Up to this point Kali's administrative

---

52 Ahmad, *Project Report:* Love Comes in at the Window, The tour venues and dates were as follows: 4–14 March 1999, Oval House, London; 17 March, The Mill Arts Centre, Banbury; 20 March, Harrow Arts Centre; 24 March, 21 South Street Arts Centre, Reading; 26 March, The Chipping Norton Theatre, Chipping Norton; 1 April, Maltings Arts Centre, St Albans; 7 April, Watermans Arts Centre; 9 April, The Bull, Barnet, London; 10 April, The Gantry, Southampton; 17 April, Bowen West Theatre, Bedford; 19 April, Darlington Arts Centre; 20–21 April Live Theatre, Newcastle Upon Tyne; 23 April, Queen Elizabeth Hall, Bristol; and 24 April Hawth Theatre, Crawley.

53 Penny Gold, *Report on: United Scenographers/Kali Workshop, 10th and 11th*

work had been carried out at Ahmad's home. The company's volume of work was expanding, however, and it had relied on Tara Arts to produce and tour manage *The Natural World* and *Love Comes in at the Window*; it was quite clear that, if Kali was to continue producing and touring full-scale productions and deliver writing in development programmes, the company would need a full-time administrator, office space and greater financial stability. The next phase of the company was, therefore, concerned not only with its artistic output but also the procurement of revenue-funded status, which would guarantee financial stability on a rolling three-year basis and allow for more extensive planning and development.

Approaching the Millennium: *Meri Kahani* and *River on Fire*

Following the success of *Love Comes in at the Window* Kali set out to expand the scale of both their productions (which they now wished to deliver annually) and their outreach programme.[54] Not only was the focus on outreach or community work in line with Kali's aim to improve access to theatre for Asian women but it was also increasingly a requirement of the funding bodies that Kali's work be seen to serve 'its' community.[55] The community project came in the form of *Meri Kahani* (*My Story*) and was a collaboration with Southall Black Sisters (SBS), a not-for-profit organisation which supports Black (Asian and Afro-Caribbean) women, especially in the fight against domestic violence. SBS was in search of a project to support its 'survivors' group and, through Rahila Gupta, Ahmad offered a theatre project that was envisaged as 'an important record of oral history-as-drama that will raise awareness of the issues around domestic violence for audiences and participants'.[56] The idea was for members of SBS to reflect on their own personal histories and participate in writing workshops with writers associated with Kali. The SBS women would tell their stories to the writers, who would then shape the material into a short play. These plays

---

April 1999, 26 April 1999 [Kali Archive]. Participants from Kali were Bettina Gracias, Parm Kaur, Afshan Malik, Meiling Jin and Veronique Christie.

54 In her application to London Arts Board for funding towards *Love Comes in at the Window*, under the sub-section 2g) 'The Significance of this project for Kali', Rukhsana Ahmad noted 'Over the years we have worked steadily and with determination on training initiatives to prove that Asian women have as much talent and potential as any other group of writers. Now we wish to raise our profile and establish our presence by producing a play every year.' Application with covering letter to Helen Carter, dated 20 May 1998 [Kali Archive].

55 Many Asian theatre practitioners have commented on the changing requirements of funding bodies and the need for the theatre companies to be seen to be serving their own communities. See [Ahmad 2006] and Jatinder Verma, 'Subversive Cultures in Thatcher's Decade', *Contemporary Theatre Review*, 16:3 (2006), pp. 366–80.

56 Anon., but presumably by Rukhsana Ahmad, description of 'Project: *Meri Kahani: My Story*'. Undated, but c.1999 [Kali Archive].

would later be presented in dramatic form to a larger, mixed community audience. The aims for the SBS participants were to 'help women get in touch with their own creativity, but also to bring to them an understanding of drama and how it is constructed—hopefully making them feel it is within reach both as an art form and as a profession'. The role of the Kali writers was to receive the 'experiences sensitively and help [the] subjects achieve a distance from them'. The writers would have 'to grapple with the technical problem of dramatising the stories without diluting their truth'.[57]

Following an exploratory meeting with SBS, Ahmad realised that the workshops would have to be multi-lingual and, owing to the mixed ability of the group, would have to be varied enough to engage women 'who had not done anything remotely like drama before'.[58] Only two members of the group, Freda Obado and Bobbie Wasson, had previous experience of drama, as a drama teacher and in amateur theatre respectively. After the initial meetings between the participating SBS members and Kali writers, Ahmad led two weekends of all-day workshops (3, 4, 10 and 11 June 2000) with guest tutors and actors. Ahmad found it necessary to include the actors at this early stage because it would have been too difficult for the participants to cope with her usual style of writing workshop, which was quite writing-orientated. The Kali writers included Parm Kaur, Yasmin Khan, Manjinder Virk, Bettina Gracias, Kam Dhenjan and Parminder Sekhon. SBS participants included Fiaz Ghaus, Samia Khan, Fayeeza Hanoush, Norma Lloyd, Joginder Kaur, Bobbie Wasson, Freda Obado and Rahila Gupta. Ahmad encouraged the participants to use whichever language came most naturally, which was generally one of Urdu, English, Punjabi or Hindi, a range of languages that Ahmad spoke and that was also covered by the cohort of Kali participants.[59] The workshops were followed by a three-week development period for writing at home. During this period script surgeries were held at SBS on Wednesday afternoons and informally by telephone or face-to-face sessions. Contributing dramaturges included Ahmad, Penny Gold and actor/director Parminder Sekhon. Finally, the rehearsal period afforded each writer half a day to work with a director and up to four actors to read the play aloud. During this preparatory stage the SBS participants had access to rehearsals but were not obliged to attend. The work was then

---

57 See Anon., project description *Meri Kahani*.

58 Rukhsana Ahmad, *Meri Kahani: Writing Workshops Final Report*, archival document submitted to Michael Holland, PUSH, with letter dated 21 November 2000 [Kali Archive].

59 Other personnel for the project included: directors—Helena Uren, Shakeela Maan, Rita Wolf and Parminder Sekhon; administrators Sophia Akbar (Kali), Pragna Patel and Anita Johal (SBS); performers—Seema Bowri, Deni Frances (who also ran the acting workshop), Ntin Ganatra, Shivani Ghai, Harmage Singh Kalirai, Parminder Sekhon, Norma Lloyd and Bobbie Wasson; readers—Fayeezah Hanoush and Samia Khan. See Anon., '*Meri Kahani*: Personnel', undated [Kali Archive].

presented to the community audience at Watermans, which gave its space free of charge (**DVD 18**).

It is quite astonishing that Ahmad managed to coordinate the entire project on a budget of c.£2,500 awarded by the Millennium Festival Fund, a testament to the commitment and goodwill the company engendered in their working relationships.[60] In addition to being a thoroughly rewarding experience for all concerned, Ahmad, Penny Gold and Helena Uren all agree that the level of writing among the SBS participants was surprisingly high. For Gold what was most fascinating was that although 'none of them started out with the notion of "I want to be a playwright" [...] one or two of the pieces seemed [to her] to have as much power and talent behind them as the work of people who were consciously aspiring to be playwrights' [Gold 2008]. Ahmad recognised 'the kind of presumption that the middle class has, that [...] we have the skills, therefore, we are the better writers is completely [...] out of the window because the best writers were actually in the languages' [Ahmad 2006]. The process of reliving their tragic life experiences before seeing a version of them played out on stage was at times, understandably, a traumatising experience for the SBS participants. SBS therefore provided a counsellor, Anita Johal, to support the women during these difficult moments, which also allowed the others to maintain some distance and continue their work. Despite the tears and sadness, Ahmad wrote in her report that 'there was also a great deal of laughter and fun',[61] an element reflected in the final pieces that Uren described as so 'uplifting', 'interesting', and 'warm' [Bell 2008]. The realisation of the hidden strength of women's creativity was empowering for all concerned.

The entire project had been an overwhelming success and energised many participants to continue the work and explore the themes further. SBS was so taken with the response from their participants and the demand for more workshops that they approached Kali to run a second series. So in 2002, and having raised nearly £28,000 from a combination of the Regional Arts Lottery Programme (through LAB), Baring Foundation, Lloyds TSB and Watermans Arts Centre, Ahmad organised an expanded eight-week programme *Meri Kahani: Meri Duniya* (My Story: My World), which built on lessons learned from *Meri Kahani* 2000 and culminated in full rehearsed readings at Watermans Art Centre (**DVD 19**).[62]

The success of *Meri Kahani* and Kali's ability to attract substantial funds to run a second series of the community workshops is evidence of Kali's rising

---

60 Rita Wolf stated that it is this goodwill and commitment to develop and maintain positive relationships that has contributed to Kali's longevity over the years [Wolf 2008].

61 This and next quotation, Ahmad, '*Meri Kahani:* Writing Workshop'.

62 A DVD copy of *Meri Kahani: Meri Duniya* is housed in the Kali Archive. No recorded materials exist of *Meri Kahani* 2000.

profile as a theatre company that could be relied upon to deliver professional programmes that fully engaged with the Black and Asian communities, encouraged new talent to prosper and, all importantly, stayed within budget. By 2000 this professional recognition in the community sector was seen as a prerequisite for any theatre company wishing to apply for a National Touring Contract from ACE and fixed-term funding from LAB. Kali's success with *Meri Kahani* and their next large full-scale production, *River on Fire*, would therefore place them in a strong position for application.

River on Fire

As with *Song for a Sanctuary*, Rukhsana Ahmad's *River on Fire* experienced a considerable developmental period. It began life as an original radio drama *Urnful of Ashes*, commissioned by BBC Radio 4. It was then commissioned for the stage by Bill Alexander, the Artistic Director of the Birmingham Rep. However, despite Alexander's dramaturgical investment in the play, he eventually decided against producing it to full-scale production in favour of Briony Lavery's *Frozen*. In 1999, having produced a number of smaller plays by new writers, Kali now required a more substantial piece that would consolidate its public profile, attract a broader audience and establish a presence with a network of theatres that would buy this and hopefully future Kali productions. So, with *River on Fire* already in development and Helena Uren keen to direct it, and an absence of any other viable Kali play that would be ready in time for 2000, it seemed an ideal time for Kali to produce Ahmad's play. *River on Fire* commenced with a three-week run at London's Lyric Studio, Hammersmith, in the autumn of 2000, before continuing with a national tour in the spring of 2001.

The idea for *River on Fire* came from Ahmad's observation of the acute dilemma of religious ritual after death faced by families of mixed faith. The decisions taken to favour one particular faith could have traumatic and divisive effects on the remaining, grieving relatives. Linking the contemporary with the historical, Ahmad transposed this predicament to the Mughal court of Akbar the Great, a king who has assumed almost mythological status as India's greatest secular ruler.[63] He is famous for having taken wives of different religions to promote religious and social harmony. Ahmad, who was primarily interested in exploring the battle of faith versus secularism, and the relationship of the state to the individual, wished to explore how this 'empowering of the citizens' ethic actually worked in practice. She therefore mapped onto this factual history the probable dilemma of what happens when the rebellious son of a Muslim king and Hindu wife dies. Is the mother's religious identity honoured and

---

63 *River on Fire* is currently unpublished, but a copy of the script is lodged with the Salidaa Archive, University of Brunel.

the son cremated, or will the imperial power insist on a Muslim burial? Will the public display of imperial Muslim ritual dominate the private need of a Hindu ritual for a grieving mother? As Ahmad developed the play, she saw the possibilities of a parallel with Sophocles' *Antigone* and created the Shola character. This tale from Akbar's court, set in Delhi and Fatehpur Sikri, was the basis for the radio play *Urnful of Ashes*. The radio production featured the storyteller Vayu Naidu, who led the listener into the scenes, and newly commissioned music.[64]

In 1992, having secured her Radio 4 commission, Ahmad spent some time in India researching her play. During this time India erupted in a swathe of communal riots that started on 6 December 1992 and spread across the country (and then to Bangladesh and Pakistan) in reaction to the demolition by Hindu extremists of the Babri Mosque in Ayodhya, believed to be the birthplace of the Hindu king Ram. The Bombay riots raged over the course of the next four months and culminated in a wave of ten bombs that ripped through the city. According to the *River on Fire* programme the death toll for Bombay during this period was 784, with 4,679 injured, and tens of thousands fleeing the city. Of the riot victims, 60–67% were Muslims, who constituted 15% of the city's population.[65] At the same time, and in a coincidental parallel with her narrative for *River on Fire*, the radical feminist writer and scriptwriter Ismat Chughtai died. Although born a Muslim, in her will Chughtai requested to be buried at sea. However, this rite is only legally available to those who have actually died at sea. On learning this, her grandson (whose father was a Hindu) had her body cremated, a ritual usually associated with Hinduism. In the atmosphere of the communal riots this act, which Ahmad notes 'may have been a purely secular act which failed to see the importance of the ritual', upset Chughtai's Muslim supporters and brief 'controversy raged in the newspapers'.[66] The event of the riots in particular affected Ahmad's understanding of the relationship between faith and secularism and of appropriation of ritual symbolism by individuals, communities and the state, which influenced the development of *River on Fire* (DVD 20).

The result of these combined influences on the development of *River on Fire* was a play of complex construction, in which multiple narratives explored the private and public symbolism of faith rituals and the balance of state versus individual power. The reference to *Antigone* set in Mughal times is now transposed to a Bollywood film, scripted by Seema, a well-known scriptwriter and radical, and directed by Waheed. Seema's daughter Kiran

---

[64] Dramaturgical information supplied by Rukhsana Ahmad, 15 December 2008 and 14 February 2009.

[65] The play's programme cites the source of these statistics as the *Times of India*.

[66] Brief details of Chugtai's cremation and ensuing controversy are given in the programme of *River on Fire* (DVD 20).

has arrived from London to play the role of Shola, the daughter of Akbar's Hindu wife and sister to his now dead son, Deepak. For Ahmad, this transposition to a modern setting avoided the problem of representing an historical period in a 'language that makes it immediate' [Ahmad 2008].

This discussion of historical faith on film is set within a more pressing family drama in which life begins to imitate art. *River on Fire* opens with Seema dying in a Bombay hospital, as the riots rage on the street. Following her principle of 'Why should your birth determine your faith?' Seema has explored a number of religions in the course of her life. As a result she has a Hindu daughter in Bombay, Zara, from her first marriage, and two children, Kiran and Bobby, from her Muslim marriage, which she has spent in London, where the two children were raised. By the time she reaches her deathbed she is an atheist, which she wryly describes as 'just a wee bit scary right now! But I've left it too late to worry about it—I reckon. We shall see how it goes!'[67] Having slipped into a coma, Seema dies before being able to speak to her children Kiran and Bobby or express her wishes for the disposal of her body. What ensues is a major family rupture as Zara's husband Ashok, a senior member of the local assembly, convinces her to take her right as the oldest child and bury Seema according to Hindu customs, which she prepares to do without consulting her siblings. On seeing her mother's body prepared for cremation Kiran is outraged and declares that Seema:

> liked Muslim burials—for their simplicity ['white shroud; cotton, bleached, un-stitched. Absolutely no jewellery, and no make-up']—and equality—you have the same for everyone, men and women, rich and poor. It's the one thing she said she admired about our faith.[68]

Kiran and Bobby feel obliged to attend their mother's Hindu funeral, but in an act of sacrilege chant their own Muslim prayers. This offends Ashok, who punches Bobby, knocking him unconscious and landing him in hospital.

The plot thickens as Kiran becomes aware of the link between the Hindu politician Ashok and his company Fair Homes Plc, which is not only responsible for the mass slum clearances but has invested in the film that Kiran is working on. She claims her mother's script is being bastardised, with extremes of fanaticism replacing a discussion of secularism to serve the right-wing Hindu investors. Not able to protect her mother's physical body, Kiran sets out to protect her reputation and agrees to address the memorial meeting that the *Awaaz*, an extremist Muslim group, has organised to honour her mother. En route, however, she changes her mind, persuaded by Bobby, the rational scientist, that their mother would not want her name to

67 *River on Fire*, Act 1, scene I, by Rukhsana Ahmad. Draft script with directorial edits [Kali Archive].

68 Act 1, scene v.

be used to fuel the sectarian warring parties. In a cruel twist of fate, Zara, who had secretly come to protect her siblings, is captured by members of the Muslim group and is identified as a Hindu. Zara and Bobby rush to her aid, but it is too late, she is killed by a lone sniper.

Although she dies in the opening scene, Seema remains on stage throughout the play as a ghost narrator, who addresses the audience directly. Dressed in her pyjamas, she follows the action with the audience and then offers her own insightful take on the scenes in a series of monologues. As she pines for her children, this once radical protestor for human rights is now powerless to help them negotiate their way through these traumatic dilemmas. Her monologues are often an ironic commentary on the proceedings, particularly where Ashok and the film are concerned. For example, before her funeral in the opening scene of Act 2 she declares:

> Ashok got his way with my remains. And, just as he'd planned, as the husband of the oldest daughter, and a practising Hindu, it was *his* privilege to light the pyre. I must admit, it's a bit difficult to object when you're dead, so I said nothing.[69]

For Ahmad, Seema's monologues functioned as a means to 'pace out the emotional journey and the action' in the rather 'dense and complex accretion of themes and stories'.[70] The commentaries communicate details of the multiple narratives, but also express sincere compassion for her children: 'Amma …! Amma …! That cry goes straight to my heart! I hear you both—so very clearly—but I cannot see my way out of this! Who do I comfort first—and how?'[71] When Bobby is recovering in hospital she visits him in a dream, trying to encourage him to look beyond his rational mental boundaries for other answers to his dilemmas.

The role of Seema was played by Shelley King, a classically trained actor. In Ahmad's research for the play she had seen a version of *Antigone* by Tara Arts, directed by Janet Steel, with King in the leading role. Ahmad's Seema was not directly written for King. However, once cast for the role, Ahmad saw her 'incredible facility with the lines, [and] her monologues grew in volume and frequency at the cost of the Akbar story'.[72] King's portrayal of the mother was strongly praised across the all the reviews. As Helena Bell explained, the character of Seema functioned as a negotiator for the audience. She was onstage throughout in a kind of purgatory, observing with the audience, as if she was one of them, but at the same time the audience knew 'she was somewhere else as well'. Her pyjamas meant that 'there was

---

69 Act 2, scene i.
70 Correspondence with Ahmad, 14 February 2009.
71 Act 2, scene i.
72 Correspondence with Ahmad, 14 February 2009.

something quite vulnerable and kind of cosy about her in a way. But yet we know she was dead. So it was quite odd, but it was quirky' [Bell 2008].

River on Fire fulfilled Kali's aim in that it delivered a large-scale production, incorporating major themes, which mixed the historical with the contemporary. The set was, again, designed by Sophia Lovell Smith (**DVD 21**). It was a clean, simple design that comprised a wide raised platform with a choice of steps leading up to it. A three-arch and single-arch structure was mounted on the raised platform, with a second single arch positioned stage left. Minimal furniture represented domestic settings. The set was fixed and props were brought on for particular scenes, including the hospital scenes, which took place in front of the raised platform. Although some reviewers found the raised platform cumbersome, Bell thought it worked well and could be used to great advantage for the Bollywood scenes, as if separating them to a different reality. Although the film's original intention was to tell the historical story of Akbar's rule, the scenes were light-hearted and ironic, evoking the Bollywood genre. They lent a comic contrast to the heavier, more classical tone of the other aspects of the play and included the requisite choreographed kitsch Bollywood dances with sexed-up traditional *kathakali*. Penny Gold likens the film's light-hearted scenes in tone and function to the Mechanicals in *A Midsummer Night's Dream*. Borrowing from a well-known story from Akbar's court, one scene depicts the film's characters blindfolded and instructed to touch an object and describe it. It turns out to be an elephant, which has been alternately offering its rump and legs for stroking. There is much farce as Mitthoo, the long-suffering costume designer, dons an elephant costume in lieu of the actual elephant. The audience loved this scene, which provoked much laughter.

Light and sound were also crucial to the set design. Drawing on Ahmad's experience in radio drama and use of monologues, Uren decided to explore sound and create a kind of soundscape, which was created by Ansuman Biswas. This was complemented by dramatic lighting in the style of Russian epic or German Piscator, designed by Flick Ansell. So, for example, the second act begins with the funeral scene, which took place on the raised platform. A cyclorama was placed behind it with light projected onto it, so that when the audience returned after the interval they were met by the scene of the cast in mourning, wearing white, against a massive backdrop of pink-red. As the chanting began, the red backdrop was a reminder of the on-going riots.

River on Fire featured a very strong cast of well-known British Asian actors, which was another indicator of its larger scale. The three-week opening run at the Lyric Studio from 31 October to 18 November 2000 included Ravi Aujla as Waheed (film director); Lyndham Gregory as Ashok and Raj Dada (who played the role of Akbar in the film); Shiv Grewal as Bobby Siddiqui and Mitthoo; Shelley King as Seema Siddiqui; Parminder K. Nagra as Kiran Siddiqui and Parminder Sekhon as Zara Metha; other minor roles were played by members of the cast. With the exception of Patrick

Marmion's review for *The Evening Standard*, which was quite scathing about Ahmad's intellectual and artistic approach to the text, Uren's inadequacy as a director and the cast's whispering in the wings, the reviews were generally very positive.[73] Aleks Sierz, writing for the *Tribune*, concluded: 'Deftly staged by Kali Theatre Company, it is full of passion and dignity. While the debates about belief and faith are clear and compelling, the play also bravely grapples with big spiritual ideas about what becomes of us when we die.'[74] Nick Awde, writing for *The Stage*, praised the performances, directing and script, but his suggestion that 'things would really gel more smoothly if this were a novel since there is far too much detail jostling for centre stage' is a recognition of the complexity and scope of the multiple narratives at play.[75]

It echoes the sentiments of some that Ahmad's stage plays risk compromising the theatricality of performance with her need to include a high level of detail, often delivered in long monologues—a dramaturgy more suited to radio than stage. However, *River on Fire* demonstrates the subtlety of a writer who always places the plots of her plays in the broader meta-political and historical narratives.

The run at the Lyric was overwhelmingly successful. Boosted by positive reviews in mainstream and Asian media (it was 'Pick of the Week' in *Eastern Eye magazine*, 10 November 2000), the show sold out in its final week. In spring 2001 the show toured to seven venues outside London, including those which had taken previous Kali productions, such as The Hawth (Crawley), The Gantry (Southampton), the Unity Theatre (Liverpool) and Live Theatre (Newcastle-Upon-Tyne), but also other established venues with national reputations for staging small to mid-scale (and in some cases large-scale) productions, including Leicester Haymarket, Derby Playhouse and Midlands Arts Centre (MAC) (Birmingham). Unlike previous Kali tours, *River on Fire* secured more than one night in each venue, which helped to establish the company's presence with local audiences. There was also a partial change of cast. Shelley King, Ravi Aujla and Lyndham Gregory remained and were joined by Sumitra Bhagat as Zara, Rina Mahoney as Kiran and Sanjit Sil as Bobby Mitthoo.

Audience numbers varied significantly during the spring tour. Shelley King noted that performances were cancelled for two nights at Leicester, where marketing had been all but nonexistent. The production report to ACE explained that Kali had an existing profile in London, particularly within the Asian communities, which was yet to be established elsewhere. In addition, the positive reviews from the London run coincided with the Lyric's 'experienced marketing department who were able to work well with

---

73 Parick Marmion, 'In the Shadow of Sophocles', *Evening Standard*, 6 November 2000, p. 69.

74 Aleks Sierz, 'Bravely Bollywood', *Tribune*, 24 November 2000.

75 Nick Awde, 'River on Fire', *The Stage*, 16 November 2000.

our marketing manager', Suman Bhuchar. For example, the Lyric linked Kali's production to another British Asian play, *Hijra*, by Ash Kotak, that was playing at the Bush Theatre, London, and offered a 10% discount on *Hijra* if booking to see *River on Fire*. Bhuchar herself had extensive experience in marketing Asian-led theatre and, having been responsible for the Tamasha Theatre Company's larger audience numbers, was engaged by Kali to promote *River on Fire* and *Love comes in at the window* ... External factors also influenced poor audiences outside London. A major earthquake in North India coincided with tours to Leicester and Derby, and a high proportion of Leicester's population had links with the geographical centre of the earthquake. The consequential low turn-out was a phenomenon that had affected other Asian shows. In addition, illness in Leicester Haymarket's marketing department during the critical lead-in period left no time for later detailed marketing. By contrast, the performance at the MAC was sold out, where 'promoters SAMPAD have a good organisation and an established profile within the Asian community'.[76]

It is fair to say that *River on Fire* did represent what Helena Bell describes as 'moving up a notch'. This production had originally been conceived on a grander scale than previous Kali plays, possibly because it had been originally commissioned for the stage by the Birmingham Rep. During its long development it had received the LAB award for top Diverse Acts New Script in 1999. It was later short-listed for the Susan Smith Blackburn prize. For the first time, the company had raised enough funds to produce the show with high production values themselves and to employ a strong cast and full production team. This level of professionalism is reflected in the play's substantial programme, which not only showed the commercial glossiness of a confident company but was also full of useful information relating to the play's many themes (**DVD 20**).

Another reason for the success of *River on Fire* and the general running of the company during this busy period was the level of experience and eye for detail that a number of individuals contributed. Ahmad organised most of the set-up and carried out the administration of the London run, with solid support from Helena Bell. Someone at the Independent Theatre Company (ITC) drew up the contracts, and Susannah Croft, a professional tour booker, arranged many of the tour venues. At the end of the Lyric run of *River on Fire* Christopher Corner, a freelance arts project manager, was given a temporary appointment as administrator. Corner had extensive experience in theatre administration and had helped project manage Kali's recent endeavours. By 2000 Kali was juggling a number of major projects including *River on Fire*, *Meri Kahani*, rehearsed readings

[76] Rukhsana Ahmad and Kamila Zahno, *Arts Council of England National Touring Programme, Kali Theatre Company*, River on Fire *Grant Ref 3–414: Final Report*, undated but attached to letter to Isobel Hawson, dated 18 June 2001 [Kali Archive].

and the usual workshops and development of new work, including the next show for full production, *Singh Tangos*, by Bettina Gracias. For the past five years Ahmad had been bending under the strain of her administrative and artistic responsibility at Kali, even when the pressure had been eased with short-term administrative appointments. Corner's input was therefore particularly helpful and is evidenced in the business plans and funding applications in the Kali archive from around this time.

The successful projects of *Meri Kahani* and *River on Fire* represent the maturation of a company that reflected the character and objectives of its Artistic Director. Both projects were politically motivated and rooted in a specific set of cultural and historical circumstances. In early 2002 Rukhsana Ahmad received notice of Kali's successful application to two large sources of funding:[77] a National Touring Contract from ACE 2002/3–2004/5, and LAB fixed-term funding. In its contract dated 8 March 2001, ACE ear-marked £50,000 for 2002/3 and £70,000 for 2003/4 for Kali and advised them to budget for a 'standstill grant' in 2004/5. In preparation for becoming a fixed-term funded organisation Kali had secured a Regional Arts Lottery Programme award of £15,000, which it used to contract Corner to act as project manager and draw up a three-year business plan, including a fundraising strategy to seek supplementary income to support special projects. The company also commissioned a new website and invested in office equipment and audio-visual equipment to start documenting its work.

The new three-year funding enabled the company to plan its future activities with confidence, aiming for the larger-scale productions like *River on Fire* and more substantial regional and London tours, thereby raising its national profile. In December 2002 Rukhsana Ahmad stepped down and Janet Steel was appointed full-time Artistic Director. The new funding also enabled the company to employ Corner on a part-time basis to provide the administrative stability essential to the Artistic Director. Both remain in post at the time of writing. At the same time Tony Craze, who had been a very active chair for the board for the previous five years, also stepped down to be replaced by Kamila Zahno. Since 2002, under Steel's directorship, Kali has delivered at least one full-scale national touring production each year and has also maintained its investment in new writing by Asian women, script development and community projects. In November 2006 Kali celebrated its fifteenth anniversary with a week-long festival at the Soho Theatre, *Asian Women Talk Back*. It comprised three full-length plays, four rehearsed readings and *20/20*, which Steel described as a 'tapestry of snippets from twenty women writers' to 'point the way'.[78]
[SJD]

---

77 Correspondence between Sarah Dadswell and Ahmad, 14 February 2009.

78 Janet Steel, 'Asian Women Talk Back', festival programme, Soho Theatre, 14–25 November 2006.

9

Man Mela

from 1989 to 2001

The history of Man Mela is that of a continuing set of initiatives in the presentation and performance of poetry, live theatre and new writing, and involvement in education, and it has been sustained jointly by Dominic Rai as director and facilitator and Caroline Goffin as administrator.[1]

Rai grew up in Handsworth, Birmingham, completing a business training course and pulling out of an art course at Bournville Colllege after a year. His inclination was to visual art, photography and poetry, and with Colin Gabdon (of Steel Pulse) and Faud Khan he collaborated on a small series of exhibitions around Birmingham. He began to attend some mime and drama workshops at the weekend with Adrian de Redman, joined the amateur Birmingham Cooperative Theatre under the director Coleman Kelly, and performed in a production of Debra Levy's *To Be Somebody* for the company Dark Movers within the Black community. A key moment came when he saw the Tara Arts production *Chilli in Yor Eyes* at the Triangle in Birmingham in 1984, which was the first play on Asian life in Britain that he had come across, and by responding to an audition call in *The Stage* he found himself one of the two new performers (with Ajaykumar) taken on for Tara's new TIE (theatre in education) company in 1985. Two of his closest contacts there were the actor Nizwar Karanj and Rohmana Mahmoud, the TIE administrator, with whom he could talk in Urdu, with which he had a strong family connection beyond Punjabi and English. Rai was from a Punjabi–Christian community, and the bible was translated into Urdu first of the South Asian languages, while his father came from a village which was well known for its Urdu poets.

Of Tara's three TIE productions in 1985, all of which explored aspects of colonial history and oppression and exploitation, the most influential on Rai was *Sepoy's Salt, Captain's Malt*, scripted by Rukhsana Ahmad from

---

1 The Man Mela documentation is held by Goffin. There is a good set of images and associated commentary for a substantial period of activity in the Salidaa on-line archive, www.salidaa.org.uk, which also includes a short outline history of Man Mela and Dominic Rai, with biographical elements.

English-language translations of letters by soldiers from the sub-continent kept in the India Records Library. Rai was developing an interest in writing and reading Urdu, and Shobana Mahmoud, Rohmana's elder sister, was Head of the Urdu collection at that time. In visiting the archive, Rai found an immediate connection with this material from the First World War, which offered the possibility of 'dynamic characters on stage' drawn from 'real people' instead of the re-created colonial figures of the first two TIE plays.[2] The letters were in the archive as a result of the British army's censoring process, which saw some of them withdrawn and never sent, and Rohmana was instrumental in bringing in Ahmad from the Asian Women's Writing Collective (AWWC), who was commissioned to write a play.

By this time, Rai had felt rather at odds with the Tara company itself, and became the stage manager for the tour, eventually leaving Tara early in 1986. He worked subsequently for the Watford Palace TIE company during 1987–88, and in early 1989 won a £1,500 commission from Tara to develop an idea called *Portraits*, in a group of commissions which included the play-reading of *Untouchable* by Kristine Landon-Smith and Sudha Bhuchar, which became Tamasha's first production. *Portraits* ran for three nights at the Tara Centre in Earlsfield, with Amber Lone as stage manager and four actors, and very bare staging. It included an element from the material in the India Records Library drafted into a monologue from an Indian soldier on the western front, and closely resembled the later production of *Asian Voices* in 1994, which carried a few minor adjustments. *Portraits* was subsequently taken to a large event at Greenford Community School in 1990, as Rai recalls.

At this point, Rai 'stepped out of theatre', as he puts it, and enrolled part-time on a film production course at Goldsmiths College in Lewisham. Through contacts with the Lewisham Arts Service he organised an evening course as an introduction to Hindi and Urdu through music and art at the Ackroyd Centre in Forest Hill in the spring of 1993. He soon took the class to see a production of Lorca's *Yerma* in Punjabi by Neelam Man Singh Chowdhry's The Company, at the Tricycle theatre in Kilburn. Although The Company came from India, the performance in Punjabi made a strong connection for Rai with his own life and experience in Birmingham, 'where Punjabi was very much part of our normal Brummie-speak', and he felt inspired to return to the material of *Portraits*. This was remounted as *Asian Voices* for three performances in Lewisham and Southwark in October 1993, as part of the Black History Month, with a mixed cast of Asian and Afro-Caribbean actors, followed by several workshops in schools, which were now informed by his further work in TIE with the Watford-based company. The show came back for eight performances at the Oval House in January–February 1994, and for four performances at the Tara Centre in

---

2 Dominic Rai interviewed by Graham Ley, Exeter, 12 December 2007.

February. The cast was Rai, Rezaul Kabir, whom Rai had met at Tara and who had performed in Tara's *The Government Inspector*, Rachel Chatterjee and John Lloyd-Stephenson, and the seven scenes had interludes of poetry sung by Kanan Bala Kapur (**DVD 1–6**).

The short pieces that comprise *Asian Voices*, and *Portraits* before it, range from monologues by the First World War soldier and a westernised maharajah to scenes involving several characters. These include an exchange between Madan Lal Dhingra and the judge and a reporter at his sentencing to death in 1909 for shooting and killing an aide to the Secretary of State for India; a short sequence of scenes about the strike by Asian women workers at Grunwick in 1976; a dialogue between two schoolchildren about Salman Rushdie, reflecting on the reaction to Rushdie's novel *The Satanic Verses*, published in the autumn of 1989; a parody of the first Asian family to be shown in a television advert; and a mini-drama about the overwhelming expectations that are to be loaded on an Asian baby, from parents to schoolteacher to employer to marriage. What Rai is clearly realising and dramatising is almost the shock of Asians actually taking voice, in the voices that articulate the baby's experience for him; in the soldier who speaks directly to us of his feelings and suffering, because he may have been denied their expression in his censored letters; in the stereotyped family of the advert coming into life; in the children's naive but sincere version of the debate about Rushdie; in the oppressed and bullied women workers at Grunwick; and in the revolutionary's alternative vision of what justice is between India and Britain. There is, in this respect, a profound consistency and a particular view of what a British Asian theatrical presentation and performance should be, or is bound to be, in the cultural circumstances and historical background of Asians in Britain.[3]

With *Asian Voices*, Man Mela was in existence, and Caroline Goffin, who had come as a student to the Introduction to Hindi and Urdu course in Lewisham, was involved from the beginning, establishing a role as an administrator. A number of opportunities began to develop at the same time, and the first of them was *We Sinful Women*, which was a performance of contemporary Urdu poetry from Pakistan drawn from a translated collection by Rukhsana Ahmad. Shobana and Romana Mahmoud 'had been collecting these poems and had suggested that they could be put into an anthology', and Ahmad was contacted to translate and edit the collection [Rai 2007].[4] Rai's family included published poets from earlier in the twentieth century, and his father was also an Urdu poet, so he felt a close connection to the initiative and worked with Samia Malik in shaping it for performance. In looking back, he feels that it answered 'one of my gripes about British Asian

3 The script is held by the Man Mela administrator, Caroline Goffin.

4 *We Sinful Women: Contemporary Feminist Urdu Poetry*, ed. and trans. Rukhsana Ahmad (London: Women's Press, 1991).

theatre', namely 'where is the Pakistani voice, where is the Muslim voice on stage?' It was performed bilingually, with music, and 'generally there was a pattern that the English was spoken and the Urdu was sung', which he felt was suited to a potentially broad audience [Rai 2007]. The two earliest pilot performances took place in the Lewisham Theatre Studio on 10 March 1994, and involved Samia and Afshan Malik as singers and performers. It was revived the following year for three performances in March 1995 funded by the London Arts Board (LAB), and for a short tour funded by the Arts Council of Great Britain (ACGB) to Portsmouth, Birmingham, Oldham and venues in London in April and May. On that tour the performers were Samia and Afshan Mailik, Kulwinder Kaur and Kanan Bala Kapoor (DVD 9–12).

At this time, Rai also began to be invited to develop work in relation to mental illness and to the lives of Asian elders, and began to look closely at sexuality in two projects, for which the scripts exist. The first, *Romeo and Ram*, was part of a showcase event in Lewisham in the autumn of 1994, 'a gay love story set within the Asian community' as Rai describes it, a cameo-piece conjoining two iconic figures in an unexpected and tragic relationship, as it also conjoins Shakespearean with contemporary English and with Punjabi. It was a masked performance, with songs, mime, movement and dances, with allusions to the 'Hindi buddy movie' [Rai 2007]. Its development was associated with workshops held at the Oval House on the theme of forbidden love in June 1994, looking at Jyoti Patel and Jez Simons's play *Prem* and work in progress by Parminder Chadha, with Arti Prashar and Rezaul Kabir among the performers (DVD 13–15).[5]

The second project in a hectic period of activity was a commission from BHASEL (Black HIV and Aids South East London), which was aimed at 'young people or adolescents', and so picked up on Rai's established skills in TIE. The devised piece, called *The Dangers of Common Sense*, proved to be 'too strong for BHASEL, too explicit', but Rai kept his commitment to it and it was able to tour to colleges and youth centres in London two years later, during November and December 1996 (DVD 16–17). The production worked through a combination of Bhangra dancing scenes and representations of spoof TV shows, with explicit physical displays of sex and discussions either conveying information about risk or playing comically with condoms, through the medium of the character Rubber Girl.[6] Here she is interviewed by the hosts of a TV show:

DEV: You seem to be trying to change attitudes towards sex. Is that fair comment?

RUBBER GIRL: My message is that you don't have to have penetrative

[5] The script of *Romeo and Ram* is held by Caroline Goffin for Man Mela.

[6] Both the script and a video recording of a performance are held by Caroline Goffin for Man Mela.

sex to enjoy yourself. You can suck, lick, rub, touch. Rubba-dub can do some amazing things with whipped cream. Always remember, use a condom.

SARITA: I can see from here that you have brought in quite a variety. All these condoms, femidoms, poppadoms.

RUBBER GIRL: Yeah, Sarita man, we've got strawberry, chocolate, lime, dime, *gulab jamon*, extra strong, extra long ... and if the heat's rising the hot and spicy is the one for you. But if you're gonna get it together at night, then *Sarita milan ki raat*, or for you young girls out there, there's gold ones that's coordinated because it matches your bangles. But remember, always carry them around with you—but don't eat them if you're hungry! If you're an independent woman of the nineties like me, then use femidoms, because you have to remember it's your choice. Don't just leave it up to the man. Get strong. Get independent. It's as easy as the flick of the wrist.

On 10 October 1996 *Kya Haal Hai* (*How Are You Keeping?*) was performed at the Camberwell Day Centre in Hindi/Urdu for World Mental Health Day and as part of an Asian elders' event in Southwark. It was later given an English-language performance at the Oval House on 27 March 1997. The play was the end result of a long process of involvement with issues of mental health in Southwark, and with contact with Asian elders and agencies in the London borough, which had started in 1994. The final piece was 'about the pressures of living on an estate in Bermondsey for an elderly couple who might have young family', and the portions of a script that are available contain a series of scenes about the inability of a frail father to continue to run his shop after suffering a heart attack, and the difficulties his family face.[7]

In contrast to this sequence of commissions that followed the launch of the company, *Azadi: The Story of Freedom, fifty years of independent writing* was a return by Rai to his commitment to the presentation of South Asian literature. The occasion was the fiftieth anniversary of independence, and the material was chosen and developed for performance by the initial cast, Mina Anwar, Arti Prashar and the playwright Shamsuddin Agha, and the dramaturg Liz Ingrams, with Rai directing, Gerald Wells designing and Baluji Srivastav providing the music. It featured extracts from novels and short stories with poetry and slides of sculpture, providing what was

7 Some short scenes from the script of *Kya Haal Hai* are available from Caroline Goffin. A DVD, with the title 'Showcase 1993–1997', was produced by Man Mela, containing short clips from *Asian Voices*, *Romeo and Ram*, *We Sinful Women*, *The Dangers of Common Sense* and *Kya Haal Hai*.

effectively a multi-media production, but one which was essentially designed to celebrate and display the variety of experiences expressed in the material. It played first in September and October 1997 in a range of London venues, including the Clocktower in Croydon, the Bull in Barnet, the Dominion Community Centre in Southall and the Albany Arts Centre in Deptford, where Man Mela had taken an office in the spring of 1997. It was revived for a tour in April–June 1998 to venues in Haslingden, Accrington and Nelson in Lancashire, Ludlow, Ilkley, Bradford Library, arts centres in Reading, Doncaster, Swansea and Southampton and the Hawth in Crawley. For the revival the performers were Razia Ayub, a regular Man Mela performer, Riz Meedin and Qasim Shaheen, and some changes to the contents saw the introduction of extracts from two recent British Asian plays, *Oh Sweet Sita* by Ravi Kapoor and *East Is East* by Ayub Khan Din, providing a stronger accent on British Asian and contemporary diaspora writers (DVD 18–26).

Azadi was a direct development, in both commitment and style of presentation, from *We Sinful Women*, and of Rai's founding conception of giving performance to Asian voices. It also connected the past with the present, and with *Across the Black Waters* Rai returned to the searing experience of Indian soldiers in northern France in the First World War. But on this occasion—that of the commemoration of armistice—he chose to work that through a celebration of the writing of Mulk Raj Anand, from whose novel of that title the show was created, through a process of devising around the selection of scenes from the novel, in which Gerald Wells played a significant role as assistant director. The play opened at the Imperial War Museum on 21 July 1998 and subsequently toured to London venues for twenty performances in October and November that year, including the Hawth in Crawley (DVD 27–33). But it was notable for the degree of integration that Goffin and Rai achieved with other institutions involved in the armistice commemoration. There were two short runs at the National Army Museum in Chelsea in that period, with an accent on schools, a symposium at the Imperial War Museum, and events at the Albany in Deptford as part of Black History Month in Lewisham, including contact with the Commonwealth War Graves Commission offering help in locating the war graves of relatives (DVD 34). The performance also integrated readings of letters from the India Records Library with which Rai had started his work. The production was designed once again by Wells, with music from Baluji Srivastan, and the actors were Vincent Ebrahim, Sarah Carpenter, Qasim Kazmi and Laura Whittard.

The choice of Anand led on to *Untouchable Century*, in which Rai formed cameos from a number of Anand's novels and writings into another presentational performance centred on voices drawn from the novels. Rai adopted an extract from the Hindi translation by students at the National School of Drama in Delhi that had been directed by Kristine Landon-Smith, and a scene from his own production of *Across the Black Waters*. There were also extracts from *Conversations in Bloomsbury*, featuring Virginia Woolf with Anand, *The Private Life of an Indian Prince* and *Little Plays of Mahatma Gandhi*, and the performers were Razia Ayub and Dev Sagoo. The production, with music by Baluji Srivastav, opened at the Albany on 19 July 1999 and played at the Drum in Birmingham on 21 July, going forward to a short tour to Glasgow, Brighton and the Drum in October and November 1999.

The Cornershop was a major initiative in new writing that Rai undertook with the Hawth in Crawley. Man Mela had been founded on dramaturgical skills, with Rai himself adapting and scripting Asian voices in *Portraits* and moving on into the creation of short, issue-based plays. Dramaturgy on the work of others had also appeared early, with the workshop on Jyoti Patel and Jez Simons's *Prem* at the Oval House in 1994, in which a play that had originally dissected a young Hindu–Muslim love affair was adapted to an Asian and Afro-Caribbean love affair.[8] During 1996 Rai had taken a placement in the script department at the National Theatre, under Jack Bradley, reading and evaluating ten to fifteen scripts a month. The placement had ended in January 1997, and in the spring of that year Man Mela took an office at the Albany Arts Centre in Deptford, Lewisham, with Rai soon starting a continuing series of workshops called 'Write Now' to develop new writing. So when the Hawth opened in Crawley in June 1998, dramaturgy was a direct path forward from the workshops given there by Rai on 'Asian Audience Development for Drama' between August 1998 and January 1999, put together with three-year funding from the Arts Council. In the second half of 1998, Rai also took both *Azadi* and *Across the Dark Waters* to the Hawth.

Rai chose to develop the work of three writers, two of whom were gaining experience in the growing comedy circuit for Asian performers, Ashok Patel and Rav Mantel; the third writer was Yasmin Khan. Rai came across Patel and Mantel at Watermans, not through his work at the National Theatre, and invited Patel on to his 'Write Now' workshops at the Albany. Khan herself

> had not done any writing before, except she had a good ... she was very gobby. And I'd met her a year or two before and she used to tell me stories and I just thought well, Yas, look, no more, you've got to start writing.
>
> [Rai 2007]

---

[8] *Prem* was originally performed by Sudha Bhuchar and Dhirendra at the Battersea Arts Centre in June 1988, directed by James Macdonald in a British Petroleum (BP) Young Directors festival. It was later toured by the same performers in a linked production by Asian Cooperative Theatre (ACT), *Jawaani*, in November and December 1988: see the section above on ACT.

Cathy Westbrook, Arts Officer at the Hawth, offered Rai a commission of £3,000 for the project. The chosen theme was the cornershop, which had become the focus for the concern for the elderly in *Kya Haal Hai*, with the children debating the possibly conflicting claims of career and duty. Rai worked with the writers from autumn 1998, and all three succeeded in building their plays in this setting of the shop, with Khan opting to transform hers into one selling fabrics. All three plays exploited the setting, much as in *Kya Haal Hai*, to examine core relationships—familial and sexual—in the material circumstances of earning a living. The set for the eventual opening at the Hawth for 23–25 March 2000, although spare, remained the same throughout the trilogy with minor adjustments, allowing the plays to function as connected explorations; it was designed by Paul Waring. In all three plays the aftermath of the death of a parent added poignancy and tension to the relationships between the living, and the contradiction to expectations about marriage was a major component in all, with violence leading to trauma in the second and tragedy in the third. Dramaturgically, *The Cornershop* achieved a remarkable unity, in a consistent and almost relentless study of versions of confinement in a thoroughly familiar, almost iconic, if not stereotypical, socio-economic setting.[9] The performers at the Hawth were Ashrat Mayat, Hari Sajjan, Shawani Gai, Mamta Anand and Hassani Shapi (DVD 35–38). *Wish* by Ravi Mangat is the lightest in tone, with Satnam visited by voices and discovering strange powers as he sentimentally asserts the continuing value of his father Mohan's shop even after the death of his mother. The shop, it seems, has a transforming power that may bring wishes to fulfilment, in contrast to the conventional assumption that for a second generation it will act to do just the reverse. Satnam is empowered by it, and when the doctor is brought in to analyse his supposed condition, he entrances her into a vision of wish-fulfilment. On his father's prompting, she is convinced that he is hearing voices, but he turns this idea back towards her.

SATNAM: Relax Doc. You're looking for something that's not even there. Why don't you look for something that you always wanted?
DOCTOR: What?
SATNAM: You don't want to be a doctor anymore, do you?
DOCTOR: Why do you say that?
SATNAM: Because you've helped people for so long, and now you just want something for yourself, don't you?
DOCTOR: Of course, everyone wants something, don't they?

---

9 The scripts for *The Cornershop* are held by Caroline Goffin for Man Mela, and there is a video recording of a full performance.

SATNAM: Yeah, but you never had the time for even finding yourself the love of a good man ... did you doctor?
MOHAN: Satnam! Don't be rude.
SATNAM: The minute you stepped in here, I knew what you really wanted from life.

SATNAM starts to play with the light that the DOCTOR was holding.

DOCTOR: Satnam, I really don't know what you are talking about. (To MOHAN) I'm sorry, I can't really do anything here. You need to consult someone else.

The DOCTOR and MOHAN turn towards the door.

SATNAM: Birds flying over warm seas. Watching your children play on the golden sand of a Caribbean beach. Sharing the warmth of the sun with a man who has filled your every wish.

The DOCTOR slowly turns around to SATNAM.

SATNAM: (continued) Running your own bar in the West Indies. Now, tell me doctor, that's what you wish for.
MOHAN: Satnam, stop your nonsense.
DOCTOR: (to SATNAM) How ... how do you know that?
SATNAM: I told you. The minute you stepped through the doors of the shop ... I knew. The hardest thing to do is to achieve a wish because a wish is something that people believe they cannot have.

[Ravi Mangat *Wish*: scene 7] (DVD 39)

If the influence of the comedy sketch is never far from the surface in *Wish*, in Ashok Patel's *Jeevan Saathi* (*Life's Partner*) the tone is ominous from the outset. The play is haunted by the shop-owner's brother, Nathu, who is devastated when his sons marry two English girls. He suspects his niece Meena of having an affair with her flatmate Sheela, whom he calls a half-caste, and the play builds inexorably to his violent confrontation with and attack on Sheela. The play includes a short scene with an elderly white man in the shop reminiscing about his wartime service with Indian soldiers, in which Rai's influence is obvious, and the setting is split between the flat shared by the women and the shop. Although the beating of Sheela by Nathu occupies the climax of the drama and determines its aftermath in the court scene in which he is sentenced to a prison term, the effects of the pressure are felt even before then in the women's relationship.

(The studio. MEENA is distraught. SHEELA is holding up a piece of paper.)

SHEELA: What the fuck is this?

(MEENA remains silent)

SHEELA: Lesbian Gujerati female seeks gay Gujerati male for marriage of convenience. Both families happy and both lives facilitated with discretion and sensitivity.

(SHEELA looks at MEENA in disbelief.)

SHEELA: What the hell is this?
MEENA: It could be the answer for us.
SHEELA: If this is the answer, what's the fucking question?
MEENA: Look, I could marry a gay Asian man. The families would be happy, and we could have our separate lives. Don't you see, Sheela? We could be together.
SHEELA: Together! You call that being together?

(Beat. SHEELA is distraught.)

SHEELA: Are you saying we can't be together, unless you get married?

(SHEELA crumples up the piece of paper and throws it at MEENA.)

SHEELA: Are you going to let them treat us like shit?
[Ashok Patel *Jeevan Saathi*: scene 8] (**DVD 40**)

In the trial, Meena defends her uncle as a man who always tried to do the best thing and 'must have lost control in a moment of madness'. In the final scene of the play she cannot find the will to go away with Sheela.

In previous work, Rai's concern with British Asian youth experience had been directly with sexuality, with gay love facing violence and murder in *Romeo and Ram*, and with a comic but explicit encounter with sexual activity in *The Dangers of Common Sense*. In *Reshaam* (*Silk*), Yasmin Khan takes as her catalyst the theme that had shaped the work on the adaptation of *Prem* with which Rai had been involved, a relationship between an Asian young woman and an Afro-Caribbean man which has resulted in pregnancy. In Khan's play, the tension is not in the relationship but in the reaction in the young woman's family, in which a grandfather embittered by the suicide of his son is haunting the son's wife as well as her daughter. Rai was undoubtedly interested in giving voice in performance to those from communities of a Pakistani origin, to redress an imbalance he saw in British Asian theatre and cultural expression. As in Patel's play, in which a specifically Gujerati identity is the subject, the threat and violent reaction does not come from the surviving parent, here Samina's mother Zora, but from a male relative with conventional assumptions who is himself emotionally disturbed by loss. While Patel's play shows the act of violence but stops short of ultimate tragedy, Khan avoids the moment of violence itself but leads inexorably through to tragedy. In the final scene, Samina lies in her bedroom strangled with a strip of fabric by her grandfather, who is squatting on the floor and 'clutching a picture frame with the photo of his son and is rocking back and forth'. The mother, Zora, who has herself lived partly in a dream world of communication with her dead husband, is first heard howling, and then laments the loss of her daughter:

> ZORA: (crying and sobbing) Oh my baby …
> Meri jaan …
> You've left me …
> Oh Allah Ji, why me?
> Why do I have to go through all this hurt and pain?
> As if we haven't suffered enough.
> Is there never going to be any peace in my life?
> Oh my baby.
> Why you?
> Look at you lying here asleep.
> Dreaming.
> Oh Allah Ji, Allah Ji why?
> She was just a child.
> Why didn't you stop him? Allah Ji, tell me, why did you not stop him?
> Allah Ji, please give me my baby back …
> [Yasmin Khan *Reshaam*: scene 6] (DVD 41)

In the final confrontation, there is no reconciliation possible between mother and grandfather, with the son's photograph held up as a symbol of the tortured loyalties that divide them.

The Cornershop went on tour from March to April 2001, taking in arts centres in southern England, Bristol, Birmingham and Scotland; the performers for the tour were Shapi, Pia Khan, Veejay Kaur, Georgie Hayes and Saiked Ahamed. Some years later, after her play *Bells* had been produced by Kali, Khan attested in a newspaper article that her own mother had been the victim of an honour murder.[10] Rai has continued to develop and mount initiatives as Man Mela, but none has repeated the scale of live theatre embraced in that production.
[GL]

---

10 *Mail on Sunday*, 9 September 2007.

10

Watermans

from 1992 to 2000

In April 1992 Hardial Rai was appointed Cultural Development Officer at the Watermans Arts Centre in Brentford in the London borough of Hounslow, which had opened in 1984. The post was a response by Mary Allen, the current artistic director of Watermans, to local lobbying, and reflected a limited shift of attention away from the more affluent east of the catchment towards the west and Southall. Rai had considerable experience with local communities and audiences from his work with Hounslow Arts Cooperative (HAC) in the early 1980s, an initiative which he had led until the mid-1980s. He resisted pressure to make Watermans into the venue for established Asian-led companies, since he felt that this would detract from their integration into other London venues, but also because he had a clear commitment that rapidly became a firm strategy:

> I wanted to create a new body of work which had a local agenda, local voice, and work that was at that time—and still is now—under the radar of the funders. So basically work that you would now classify as audience development work.[1]

From the beginning he had a minimal budget of £5,000 a year, and was given a Friday and a Sunday night once a month. For the Friday nights, in the foyer, he programmed Bhangra, drawing on his experience with the music and the leading groups:

> For about a year and a half to two years we had a very successful Friday-night Bhangra culture going on there, bringing in five hundred people once a month who then started discovering Watermans. Then, when they were there, we started giving them the comedy and the language theatre.
>
> [Rai 2008][2]

---

1 Hardial Rai, interviewed by Graham Ley, Exeter, 19 May 2008.

2 (DVD 1–2) All the materials cited in this survey and reproduced in the accompanying DVD are in the possession of Hardial Rai.

The comedy came partly from the satirical sketches that had been a hallmark of HAC; that was reflected in the enduring brand name *One Nation Under a Groove … Innit*, which lasted throughout the 1990s at Watermans.[3] The former HAC performers Poulomi Desai, Neran Persaud and Parv Bancil came forward as the Sycophantic Sponge Bunch, and were joined by Nitin Sawhney and Sanjeev Bhaskar as the Secret Asians, with other acts by Ravinder Gill (formerly of HAC), Nina Wadia and Jeff Mirza. These shows occupied the one Sunday evening a month, with an open-mike slot for new comedians, and became a scouting stage for radio and television, drawing second- and third-generation audiences and the young Asian professional kids, as Rai describes them. In 1993 Rai decided to use £4,000 of his annual budget to provide Equity rates for two weeks' development of material by Desai, Persaud, Bancil, Sawhney, Bhaskar and Wadia, which sustained the work (**DVD** 3).

In the 1980s Rai had attempted to set up a contemporary Punjabi-language theatre in Southall, and the other strand of his policy at Watermans pursued that idea, bringing together a number of small amateur groups and their leading figures to suggest to them the formation of a company that would operate from Watermans, exploiting the Sunday evening slot in alternation with the comedy. Punjabi Kalamunch was directed by Arjun Rayait, and they started with *Dhesi Mundah Vilaiti Kurri*, a family comedy with a daughter, a cheating boyfriend and an arranged marriage with a husband from India. This ran over a period of Sunday evenings during 1992–93, since the cast was not professionally engaged, bringing in audiences that included the parents of those who were coming to the comedy. This strand of work continued throughout the 1990s, with productions coming back in revivals, including *Dhesi Mundah …* and the later *Chutkara*, also written and directed by Rayait, about an alcoholic and abusive husband and domestic violence, which was first performed at the second Asian Drama Festival at Watermans in June 1996 (**DVD** 4–5).

Rai's policy at this time was 'for and by', by British Asian practitioners for British Asian audiences, and it was funded by box-office receipts covering costs, with the strategic deployment of that annual £5,000. Watermans had been transformed by new, diverse Asian audiences responding to different elements of the programming, and a 'space' had been created extraordinarily at the margins of a venue that was beginning to look like an Asian performing arts centre. This increasing confidence and profile within Watermans led to an application for £20,000 to the London Arts Board (LAB), which was awarded under the London Collaborations scheme, for a performance of the Punjabi love-story *Sohni Mahiwal* on and by the River Thames at the Watermans site, which took place 11–14 August 1994. The funding brought

---

3 *One Nation Under a Groove* was the title of a comedy-sketch show by HAC in 1984–85: see the section on HAC above.

in leading professionals to work alongside local community performers: the jazz musicians Gary Crosby and Keith Waithe, the multi-media and sound-sculptor Paul Burwell, the Kathak dancer and choreographer Alpana Sengupta and Harmage Singh Kalirai as the director. The narrator was Tuup, and the Thames was standing in for the River Chenab, one of the five rivers of the Punjab, with performances timed to fit in with the flow of the tides. The production, with its funding and prominent professional practitioners, caught the imagination of some of the national press as well as the local newspapers, notably *The Independent*, which published two previews (DVD 6–10).[4] A third draft of the script, dated 17 June 1994, carries precise cues for music and dance with evocative indications of the spectacle, alongside the words of the narrator, the only scripted figure. This section is from the opening:

> *Prelude*
> Through the windows of the foyer of the Watermans Arts Centre, looking out onto the river, we see a typical setting of an Indian village by the banks of the River Thames.
> A variety of village life activities, and some abstract images of Indian life are seen.
>
> We see on the opposite bank, coloured tin foil wrapped around stranded rocks, to form images of icons. Saris and other offerings can be seen displayed on the branches of trees.
> (*these must be colourful, so as to be seen from a long distance*)
>
> Some dummies and/or cut-outs of women working, carrying baskets, washing clothes, carrying water in pots, cooking and some washing themselves, are seen floating or fixed in certain positions in the river. They are in various postures above and halfway in the water, showing their status in society and work.
> On some of them sari material is dressed around them, and is flying in the wind.
> (*this is created more as an abstract fashion*)
>
> Giant water lilies in different sizes and colours are seen floating on the river. Three or four Dancers are seen, each placed in the middle of the lilies, standing in a dance posture, as statuettes, facing the Arts Centre.

---

4 Dolly Dhingra, 'Indian Summer: Brentford's Riverside Enjoys Punjabi Finery', *The Independent*, 9 August 1994; Robert Maycock, 'On Classical Music', *The Independent*, 10 August 1994.

Intro.
[*Music*] We hear the sound of a conch. It is played from the courtyard balcony.
Cue 1 : For the Audience to gather around the wall.
The Audience enters onto the upper walkway (*the roof*), from the reception area (*possible ticket office*) past the Studio.
[*Music*] Second sound of the conch.
Cue 2 : For coloured smoke.
Appearing from either or both the dummies and the lilies, creating a misty effect.
Cue 3 : For the Dancers to dance. They begin halfway through the smoke. The Dancers are relating different part of the story of Sohni Mahiwal, to each other and the audience.
[*Music*] Third sound of the conch.
Cue 3 : For the Shehnai players.
[*Music* played is of a wedding procession, sadness and happiness at the same time.]

The music is heard and seen coming from the far bank of the river.

A couple of Indian boats are making their way through this smoky atmosphere.

[*Sohni Mahiwal*, script in the possession of Hardial Rai, p. 1]

In 1995, Rai once again took the step of investing £4,000 of his budget in a single initiative, which itself formed part of an Asian drama festival that he organised, with Watermans hosting Neelam Mansingh Chowdhry's The Company from the Punjab as part of the London International Festival of Theatre and Feroz Khan's Hindi production of *Saalgirah*, starring the Bollywood actor Anupam Kher. Funding and sponsorship were already in place for these two productions, and Rai's money went to two and a half weeks of rehearsals for Parv Bancil's *Ungrateful Dead*, which then ran for three weeks. A run of this length was unprecedented for Rai at Watermans, and apart from the fact that the standard bookings were going down, which he attributes to competition from a dynamic programme at the Lyric Studio, Hammersmith, there was also his bravado in taking on Wimbledon:

> I remember this conversation because there was a staff meeting and the director said 'Well, yes, how about the Asian theatre festival going in the week of Wimbledon?' And everybody looked at me, because I don't think she realised what she said. I said 'Oh, yes, great!', and I told her I always miss Wimbledon, I never watch Wimbledon, you

> know that would be good ... But you see that was the culture of Watermans ... so that was why we took that slot.
>
> [Rai 2008]

Bancil's *Ungrateful Dead* related to his earlier scripts for HAC such as *Kings*, offering a bleak view of young lives based on an awareness of the culture of Southall's gangs, and Rai knew there was a degree of risk involved:

> We knew that we were going to be playing with fire a bit there. And we did; some gang members came in one night into the theatre during the performance—I don't know where the security was on that day—and took a fire extinguisher and threw it on the stage. They were just very offended that we were doing something on them without consulting, or that sort of thing. But Parv knew all of them in the first instance, so he wrote from that anyway.
>
> [Rai 2008]

In fact, Bancil's play has a domestic orientation rather than a bias towards the streets, the external location being an expressionist graveyard in a direct carry-forward from *Kings*, the central group as much a father and his son and daughter-in-law as the violent life and connections of the son outside the home. The dead are in mind throughout the play, haunting the father's conscience and consciousness and waiting in the graveyard, and failed or unrealised sexual relationships cannot distract from a compulsion towards the Sikh warrior identity, as criminal violence and suspected betrayal lead grimly towards ritualised combat and revenge at the conclusion. The language is aggressively colloquial, but the flow of dialogue and the exchanges themselves are slightly removed from a naturalistic tone, as if all the characters are experiencing the kind of futility and lack of communication that occurs in dreams. Rai directed the play and Bancil took the lead as Billu, with Brij Mohan as his father Hargeet, Parminder Sekhon as his wife Surinder, Neran Persaud as his friend Ash, Krishna Kumari as Ash's sister Kiran and Ameet Channa as Mota. Music for the production was supplied by the Asian indie band Huge Baby (**DVD 11**).

Parminder Sekhon had been one of the performers in *Ungrateful Dead*, and after attending a play-reading at Tara Arts of *Kali Salwar* (*Black Shalwar*), her powerful Punjabi-language adaptation of the Manto story, Rai undertook to promote the Mehtab Theatre production. It was directed by Harmage Singh Kalirai, with Sekhon as the prostitute Sultana and Tony Singh Thind as her partner, and was performed in Punjabi. With support from the London Borough Grants Committee, the LAB and the Arts Council it went on to tour extensively, opening at the Oval House on 7 March 1996, taking in a women's only matinee at Watermans and moving on to the Midlands Arts Centre (MAC) in Birmingham and theatre venues in Reading, Bradford, Glasgow and Leicester later in March and in April; the tour was renewed in October 1996, taking in community venues in Derby, Nottingham, Bristol, Birmingham, Greenwich, Coventry, Hounslow and Preston. Sekhon had encountered Manto's writing through Rukhsana Ahmad at the Asian Women's Writing Collective (AWWC), and had worked at a women's refuge in Birmingham, and she and Rai had a shared belief in the value and directness of working and performing in the UK's second most-spoken language (**DVD 12–13**). Their collaboration continued with productions of Sekhon's ten-minute solo performance *Madhuri I Love You*, dramatising a young girl's obsession with the Bollywood star Madhuri Dixit, and the play she wrote with Shakila Maan, *Not Just an Asian Babe*. The script was developed at Watermans with support from the LAB and the dramaturg Sita Brahmachari, and the Mehtab Theatre production was designed by Kevina Khan, who had designed *Ungrateful Dead* and would co-design *Papa Was a Bus Conductor*. It was directed by James Neale-Kennerley and opened at the Arts Depot in April 1997, moving to Etcetera in Camden from late May to mid-June, and returning in the autumn for a ten-day run at Watermans in September 1997. The play is naturalistic and episodic in structure, centering on the predatory, bisexual nature of club-owner Saquib, his relationships with his toy-boy Roshini and Julie, the girl he keeps, and her relationship with the newcomer Nasreen. The dialogue is bilingual, but predominantly in English, blunt, bleak and as harsh as the environment it anatomises, with ambition the driving force in those exploited from one form of sexual commodification to another, either live or for video or film. The performers were Madhav Sharma as Saquib, Sekhon as Julie, Anisha Charania as Nasreen and Pravesh Kumar as Rohini (**DVD 14–15**). Rai's final collaboration as a programmer with Sekhon was to be *Sweet Like Burfi*, a celebration of South Asian lesbian, gay, bisexual and transgendered art in a festival of film, photography, dance and performance (featuring *Madhuri I Love You*), which ran at Watermans 17–20 February 2000 (**DVD 16–19**).

The success of the 1995 Asian Drama Festival led to a second festival in 1996, once again in the same June slot, on this occasion supported through the Arts Council's New Collaborations Fund as well as the LAB (**DVD 20–21**). There were several constituents, including a revival of Bancil's *Bad Company* (first performed by HAC), the first production of *Chutkara* by Punjabi Kalamunch and comedy from the Secret Asians, but the primary justification for the Arts Council funding was *Dogs of Desire*, which Rai describes:

> My main work there was a very risky *Dogs of Desire* that was set in the underground car park of Watermans, which is very dark, a very dodgy area of the building. We set that as our stage ... there were six stages in a circle, and each stage had different work going on.

> We had *qawwali* singers and Fundamental, who are a hip-hop Asian band. We had spoken-word artists, and the first ever internet-based work happening in London took place there, where there was a live internet feed to a porn site in which Ravinder Gill was a performer, and he changed his gender in costume, and converses on the internet.
>
> [Rai 2008]

Apart from Gill and Fundamental, the programme lists the film-maker Shakila Maan, the poet and singer Kalvinder Khaur Kinder, Abdul Kadir Durvesh, who led the Shehnai players in *Sohni Madiwal*, and performance artists Mash and Tamami Yamudhi from Tokyo, with the dancers Amina Begum and Multi Patel. The performance is described there as exploring 'sexuality, ritual, "deviance", and identity', and as 'a collision of live music—fusing western rhythms with oriental sounds such as Qawwali—dance, theatre, inter-active action paintings, performance poetry and an internet performance'. The description continues:

> Surrounding the audience in a pentagonal stage area various ritualised performances are taking place without words or commentary:
> A woman explores her body and sexuality.
> A man transforms himself into a woman.
> An unseen man plays out a sexual fantasy—a performance in text only with an unknown lover on the internet—
> The conversation text only is projected on to a screen for the audience to follow and is witnessed by all netizens who by chance have logged on that night.
> A woman tells her story in verse which we do not hear because of the music until the final moment when there is dark, silence and only her voice ...
> *Dogs of Desire* is exploring new arenas for performance. It is investigating the nature of live performance within an evolving new technological culture which is not reliant on live presence.
>
> [*Dogs of Desire*, programme, back page (DVD 22–23)]

In conceiving and developing the piece, Rai had Ajaykumar as his main collaborator, who through his company International Arts (1992 forwards) had formed established connections with performers in India and Japan.

The continuing *One Nation* strand of comedy, alongside club nights of music and dance, was a mainstay, and there had been one successful attempt to make a more coherent and thematic show out of it, *Love Hurts*, which had run for a week. But in the autumn of 1996 Harmage Singh Kalirai directed a script by Parv Bancil, *Papa Was a Bus Conductor*, which was based on the style of satirical comedy performed by the Sycophantic Sponge Bunch and shaped as a 'kind of farce', with Bollywood as a prominent reference. The play is not, like *Love Hurts* and the later comic productions *Arrange That Marriage* and *Don't Look at My Sister … Innit!*, a thematic set of sketches. It exists as a constant satirical and farcical scenario in the domestic setting of Papa and his family: a wife, twin boys (supposedly separated Siamese twins) and a daughter. The idea of a plot is satirised too, with a minimal flashback to Papa's arrival in the UK looking for a career as an actor, the only decisive action being Papa's disgruntled desertion of the home to return dressed as his sister from India, Auntie Pinki. The tone is set by the set, with a bus-conductor's uniform hanging in the living room and a portrait of Adolf Hitler. Papa believes Hitler is in fact Winston Churchill, having gathered this from a skinhead with whom he first shared lodgings, whose name he took to be Nancy-boy. So he uses Enoch Powell's 'rivers of blood speech' as a text from which to teach his children English, and the satire savages the image of the submissive, conformist, culturally assimilating Asian family and the stereotypical portrayals of its generational conflicts. Here Papa converses with his daughter Wanna:

> WANNA: I'll do what I want. You're humiliating me, Pa. I'll never be the same again. I want to go to University to get a degree.
>
> PAPA: Degree? What use is that when you are cooking the dinner and dropping babies?
>
> WANNA: But daddy gee … I want to have a career of my own, that's why I want a degree. Not to get married to some hard-up Paki.
>
> PAPA: My child, when you are a little older and a little wiser, you'll realise that this is just a phase you are going through. You have to understand, my lub, that there are not many samosas in the sea of oil that we call life.
>
> WANNA: Oh no.
>
> PAPA: I've brought you up as best as I can, keeping you locked up in a cage, keeping you safe from the evil world, choosing your friends for you. I feel content with my good work. There's no fear of you going out with bad boys and taking drugs and getting pregnant is there?
>
> [*Papa Was a Bus Conductor*, Act 1, scene 1][5]

Constantly interlaced with the satire is the purely farcical, as in this moment when all suspect that the knock at the door must mean the electricity man:

5 The script in the possession of Parv Bancil is the revised version for the later production in 2000.

All run around and put on hats and false beards then hide. PA *puts on his and a northern accent.*

PAPA: There's nowt int'ere pal. There's non-o' them Pakistanis ere like so bug off.

Moment. PA *cautiously peers through the window. He jumps back with fright.*

PAPA: We are deaded. It is the Tee Wee licence man.

All fall to their knees and pray in silence. Long moment. PA *checks again. It appears the stranger has gone.*

PAPA: Relax.

[*Papa Was a Bus Conductor*, Act 1, scene 1]

When Auntie Pinki arrives by kicking in the front door in Act 3, she is inevitably not the ideal Bollywood character—'Alright you miserable bunch of cunts! I'm your sweet little Auntie Pinki from India'—and displays an immediate control of the vernacular: 'I'm Pa's long lost sister. In his last moments, the old tosser asked me to come to England to sort you lot out. So ere I am.' But the satire turns from Bollywood to closer to home in the final disrobing, as Papa reverts to himself and reveals that he lost his job as a bus conductor many years ago and instead realised his ambition to be an actor.

PAPA: I became the bus conductor on all the two-bit tee-wee shows that were ever made. It was me ... I ruined the respectability of your generation. Yes, I'm the Paki who sold out.

HARBUJHAN: Were you the waiter with that pathetic accent in all those cheesy sit-coms?

PAPA: Forgive me son.

HARB *breaks down.*

AZIZ: Were you the Paki who played the wictim in all the crappy soap operas and screen-one dramas?

PAPA: I was ...

WANNA: Were you the Asian women who were forever being beaten up by the cruel Asian men for wanting to be free?

PAPA: I can explain ...

[*Papa Was a Bus Conductor*, Act 3]

Bancil and Persaud acted the brothers, Gill performed as Papa and in drag as Auntie Pinki, and Rai placed the show in the small studio upstairs at the Oval for a further two weeks on top of one at Watermans, so creating the three-week run that he felt to be standard to attract critics, and it was appeciatively reviewed in *Time Out*.[6] It was later revived in a revised version, going to the Edinburgh Festival in August 2000 and playing at Watermans, Haymarket Leicester, Warwick Arts Centre, Lyric Hammersmith and the Green Room Manchester in November 2000–January 2001 (DVD 24–27). The play is particularly interesting because it carries the qualities of a large amount of ephemeral comic work from *One Nation*—and specifically from the former HAC performers who continued at Watermans as the Sycophantic Sponge Bunch—for which there are no scripts, and indicates the contrast that there was between that kind of comedy and the work of Sawhney and Bhaskar as the Secret Asians (DVD 28), which led into the broadcast style of *Goodness Gracious Me.*

The initiatives that had begun at Watermans had gathered strength from additional exposure in venues in London and on tour, and the culmination of that process of producing came in early 1997 with 'Making Ladoos', essentially a package of work in a festival of Asian arts and culture that coincided with the fiftieth anniversary of independence in the sub-continent. It took placed at the Bull in Barnet, north London, from March to April 1997, and featured comedy drawn from the Watermans sets, South Asian dance (with Nahid Siddiqui's company), music (including Nitin Sawhney, who also appeared with Bhaskar under comedy in Secret Asians), children's shows (from the Half Moon and Tara Arts), fabric and fine arts in the gallery, and theatre. Ajaykumar led a community performance of the traditional Gujarati comedy *Bhavani Bhavai*, Tara Arts brought *Oh Sweet Sita*, and *Not Just an Asian Babe* ran for three nights. The festival also featured *Papa's Third Wedding*, the launch production of Shivam Theatre, a Gujarati-language company led by Kiran Purohit, which Rai saw as a parallel to the initiative of Punjabi Kalamunch (DVD 29–32). Purohit taught drama at the Bharatiya Vidya Bhavan in London, and he had worked for Verma at Tara Arts on the Gujarati *bhavai* form, which had become central to Tara's performance skills by the early 1990s. He had approached Rai, and Rai had helped him put together an application for funding to the Arts Council of England (ACE) for £14,000, which was awarded. Rai's approach to the definition of the company was consistent with his reasons for wanting to establish and support Punjabi Kalamunch.

> The same development model that we gave to Punjabi Kalamunch we gave to Shivam. The condition I gave Kiran was this, that there's a lot of work coming from Gujarat, from India in Gujarati theatre, and I said I'm not interested in India. If you want to create something new

---

6 Charley Godfrey-Faucett, *TimeOut*, 23–30 October 1996.

> it has to be stories from here. And in fact it's still the only company that works in Gujarati writing from here.
>
> [Rai 2008]

In 1997 Rai also chose to respond to the fiftieth anniversary of independence by thinking about those states and regions that were still contested, including the Punjab. Ajaykumar had already worked in India with Lokendra Arambam, director of the experimental Forum for Laboratory Theatres of Manipur, and the commission for Watermans followed to a degree the performance concept for *Sohni Mahiwal*, involving the river and the waterside. Tiken Singh, the musical director, and Arambam were brought to the UK to work with British Asian actors, whose individual performances alluding to shamanistic ritual served as a prelude in spaces of the Arts Centre itself before the production itself, which involved twelve male actors from Manipur. *Macbeth—Stage of Blood* was an adaptation from Shakespeare by the playwright Somorendra Arambam, and drew much media and press attention, with a floating stage with a combat- and trance-driven, torch-lit display that drew diversely on animistic beliefs (seven witches representing the seven traditional evil spirits) and the Manipur martial art Thang Ta. The production ran 20–24 August 1997 (DVD 33–34).[7]

1998 proved to be the year of comedy, with *Arrange That Marriage* and *Don't Look at My Sister ... Innit!*, which Rai partly saw as money-spinners for other, less popular, work. The shows were directly from the established long-running *One Nation* comic brand, and were conceived in that vein by Persaud and Rai, with *Arrange That Marriage* crafted and written by Bhaskar, Ravi Mangat and Ashok Patel, with further contributions from Sody Kahlon and Jeff Mirza. It was directed by Persaud and designed by Kevina Khan, and the performers were originally Gurpreet Bhatti, Bindya Solanki, Ajay Chhabra and Ameet Chana, with Chana replaced by Pravesh Kumar. It opened in February 1998 with a run at Watermans and other London venues, but returned for a national tour in the autumn of 1998 (taking in the MAC in Birmingham, Bloomsbury Theatre London, Warwick Arts Centre, Alhambra Theatre Bradford, Haymarket Leicester and the Green Room Manchester) and came back again early in 1999 (DVD 35–36). The structure relied on the thematic, linking approach that had been used for *Love Hurts*, sweeping through every sociological caricature attached to its theme to the thumping accompaniment of Bollywood songs, including turning a stereotypical revulsion to an arranged marriage on its head: 'a lot of costume changes, a lot of sketches, a lot of characters', as Rai puts it. The companion production, *Don't Look at My Sister ... Innit!*, was

---

[7] Reviews by Jeremy Kingston, *The Times*, and by Garth Cartwright, *The Guardian*, both of 22 August 1997.

lavishly sponsored by Benson and Hedges to the tune of £90,000, and consequently was able to go to the Edinburgh Festival from 8 to 28 August 1998 after opening in early June at Watermans and touring to Warwick Arts Centre, Gravesend, the Drum in Birmingham, Guildhall Theatre Derby, Gantry Southampton and Luton; it was then placed in the Bloomsbury Theatre in London in early October, and later revived in 1999. The script was by Mangat, Kahlon and Mirza, and was developed over about three months, with writers paid by the scene or sketch, with the understanding that sketches would be worked and changed in rehearsal. The performers were Seema Bowri, Raj Ghatak, Ameet Chana and Paven Virk, and it was directed once again by Persaud (**DVD 37–39**).

In 1997 the Conservative government was replaced by Labour, which as part of its image began promoting the phrase 'Cool Britannia', which implicitly had a multicultural element to it. Bancil's *Made In England* was conceived in that atmosphere, on an invitation in late 1997 from the director of the Red Room, Lisa Goldman, to contribute a short piece to a collection of plays in the 'Seeing Red' season at the Battersea Arts Centre, which took place in July 1998. Discussions with Rai led to a commission for a fuller script, to be directed by Goldman, and Rai saw the successful comedy runs in 1998 as a means to finance the production. Bancil took a simple scenario—a group of friends falling out, here members of a punk and post-punk band—and built into it his underlying concerns about the presence of British Asians in British culture, and the danger of selling out. These had been criticisms he had voiced to Rai about the commercialisation of the satirical comedy of the *One Nation …* brand for the 1998 shows, and they were brought to a head by his observation of the scene after Labour's victory.

> 1997 saw the height of the Asian underground music scene. But by 1998, it seemed to have run its course and hit a brick wall. Where once there was unity with the Asian music makers and the supportive clubbers, I began to sense the music makers beginning to bow down to the temptations of the interested record companies and the selling of souls began.[8]

His particular target was the desertion of a vernacular sound in favour of the cultivation and marketing of an ethnic, Hindi-music amalgam which he felt had no basis in any facet of the contemporary British culture to which second-generation Asians in the UK belonged. So in the play the younger Asian band-member, Bally Dingra, changes his name to Billy India and

---

8 Parv Bancil, preface to *Made in England*, in *Black and Asian Plays Anthology*, ed. Cheryl Robson (London: Aurora Metro Press, 2000), p. 90. Extracts quoted below from the playscript refer to this edition of the play.

takes up the sitar, achieving the great if momentary commercial success which had always been awaiting the Death Row sound. The band includes the Anglo-Saxon Mick and Kes, a British Asian, both in their late thirties, and by making Kes a tattooer Bancil is able to play with images and their significance, both carried but also etched onto and into the skin of whatever colour. For Bancil, the band has contested the slogan 'there ain't no black in the Union Jack' by its very presence as much as with its lyrics, and as such has asserted the vital truth that of that generation all were 'made in England'. The Union Jack they had at gigs had that slogan sprayed on it, and it went elsewhere:

> MICK: This thing was with me at West Ham on Saturday afternoons and then behind us at our gigs on Saturday nights. 'Made in England.' That used to wind people up no end. Especially when they saw you.
>
> KES: A Paki made in England. They didn't get the joke.
>
> *Made in England*, Act 1, p. 94

Not that Mick himself was not caught up with the skinhead culture that tried to own punk, but the band persisted within those contradictions because those contradictions were the reality of the lived life and the music scene. For Bally, self-transformed into Billy India and interviewed by the young British Asian journalist Cheryl in Los Angeles, the new story is about self-realisation:

> CHERYL: It's a happening time in England for music. It's the first time British Asian acts like yours are getting a fair go. Do you think it's just the flavour of the month or something more than that?
>
> BALLY: I'm not a "British Asian" act. I'm a musician. The fact that I'm brown doesn't come into it. It's a changing time in Britain. People are more open to different music styles. My success is just a sign of the times.
>
> CHERYL: But other British Asian acts haven't quite achieved the success that you've had ...
>
> BALLY: That's because I'm a musician. I'm an artist.
>
> CHERYL: But do you think you'll open doors for other Asian ...
>
> BALLY: Fuck other Asians! It's not about whether you're black, brown or blue. It's about talent.
>
> [*Made in England*, Act 2, p. 108]

Made in England previewed at the Bull in Barnet, London, in mid-October 1998, opened at Watermans for a short run 21–24 October, and then transferred to the Etcetera Theatre in Camden from 27 October to 15

November. The performers were Shahid Ahmed as Bally Dingra, Ravinder Gill as Kes, Natalie Tin as Cheryl and Tony Taylor as Mick (**DVD 40–45**).

In the final years of Rai's tenure at Watermans, the emphasis in new work shifted to dance conceived in the UK context, with two seasons of 'Two Brown Feet' in 1999 and 2000, with Angika coming into being for the first of these and reappearing for the second. Concerns about the management at Watermans brought the Arts Centre into the Stabilization programme of the Arts Council. Rai found himself offered his old job under new terms, significantly placed under marketing in the proposed structure, and despite arguing during an extended consultation period that the conditions had long existed for a producing house. The building closed in November 2000, and he left in March 2001.

[GL]

11

Peshkar Productions

Peshkar began life in 1991 as a community-based theatre project in Oldham, Lancashire. Aziz Zeria, Arts Officer at Oldham Leisure Services, had conceived the idea of a theatre project with the potential to develop skills across the arts. This, in turn, would promote artistic expression and encourage social cohesion of the local South Asian population. The term Peshkar means a presenter in Urdu, or, in musical terms, a 'particular kind of rhythmic composition': so, in this case, the presentation of 'particular compositions in theatre'.[1] Zeria had a keen understanding of the cultural and artistic heritage and needs of the local South Asian population. Having moved to the Cheetham area of Manchester from Mombasa as a boy in the 1970s, he had experienced the house-based *mehfils* of his parents' generation, participated in the first Asian youth clubs and been inspired by the experience of singing with members of his youth club at the Royal Albert Hall, London, as part of the national Asian Youth Festival.[2] In the pursuit of a musical career he enrolled as the first South Asian at Dartington College of Arts, Devon, where he also received formal training in key theatre-making skills, including musical composition, movement, voice work and the principle of *Gesamtkunstwerk*. A short spell of teaching at the Commonwealth Institute, London, was followed by further music study for two and a half years in India, sponsored by the British Council. On his return to England, Zeria changed direction and decided to move into arts management. Before taking up the position at Oldham Borough Council he worked as an Arts Development Officer in Manchester with the remit to expand minority arts. One of his many projects included a writing workshop, for which he engaged Lem Sissay. From this evolved what Zeria describes as the first, if relatively short-lived, Asian theatre company, Ajka, which was run by Saquib Deshmukh Mohammad and Razia Mohammad at the Abraham Moss Centre.[3]

---

1 Interview with Shashi Mohandas and Aziz Zeria by Sarah Dadswell, 16 October 2007.

2 The Asian Youth Festivals are discussed in 'Actors Unlimited', in this book.

3 According to Zeria (interview with Sarah Dadswell, 17 October 2007), Saqib

With this wealth of personal and professional experience behind him, Zeria was in an excellent position to respond to the artistic needs of Oldham's local South Asians. He set up a lunchtime drama group at a local school with Nigel Soni, a specialist in voice work. Its purpose was to facilitate Asian arts development, although non-Asian children also attended the classes. It proved to be very popular and Zeria began to explore ways of expanding the activity.

In the autumn of 1991 Zeria met Basir Sultan Kazmi at Oldham's Diwali celebrations. Kazmi, son of a well-known poet, Nasir Kazmi, was visiting from Lahore, Pakistan, and studying for an MPhil at the University of Manchester. Having learned that Basir Sultan Kazmi wrote poetry and plays, he immediately suggested they work together. The outcome was a series of weekly drama and creative writing workshops led by Kazmi and writer Kakoli Thompson, originally from Calcutta.

Kazmi had already tapped into the UK *mushaira* [poetry recital] network, which he describes as 'organised, lively, [with] full participation of women, even children. So *mushairas* here were, and still are, more like social gatherings where people listen to poetry as well.'[4] In a bid to create the same informal and mixed social environment, Kazmi and Zeria's aim was for the workshops to be as accessible and inclusive as possible. Although they were primarily aimed at the South Asian communities, which were principally of Pakistani, Bangladeshi and Punjabi descent, anyone was welcome. The drama club was therefore held 1–3 p.m. on Sundays from 19 January 1992 at Breeze Hill School Theatre, Salem, Oldham; Sunday was the only day when a working family might have some free time. Those who did decide to come out on a Sunday were therefore generally very committed to the work.

The drama club was initially scheduled for ten to twelve weeks. The advert for the workshop printed in the programme for the later Peshkar production *New Horizons* (**DVD 1**) stated the following:

> The workshop will provide a forum for playwriting skills, acting, stage setting, lighting and technical work.
> It is hoped that the drama club will produce a play to be performed during Eid Mela in April.
> The drama club will cater for all Asian languages as well as English.[5]

One of the participants, Abdul Malik Ahad, was seventeen at the time.

---

and Razia Mohammad were strongly influenced by Lem Sissay and the style of the American Black Movement. Ajka was politicised and provocative and dealt with contemporary issues.

4 This and further references to Kazmi are from an interview with Basir Sultan Kazmi by Sarah Dadswell, Manchester, 17 October 2007.

5 Programme for *New Horizons*, Peshkar, scripted by Basir Sultan Kazmi, 1992.

He was working as a translator/interpreter for Oldham Borough Council and would later become its Bangladeshi Arts Officer. Ahad was impressed by the end goal of the group, producing a performance created through dialogue and exploration of one another's ideas in a welcoming environment:

> It was more like a coming together of people who had, you know, similar ideas. [...] it was a case of okay we were told what the aims and objectives of it were. Okay it's fun, but at the same time there should be an outcome at the end. So we all gave our ideas [...].[6]

Kazmi and Thompson led group discussions, improvisations and exercises that led to plot development and the creation of a number of skits. People of all ages attended, including Shashi Mohandas and his six-year-old daughter Karuna. Mohandas valued this social time with his daughter. Not only was it a place for her to make friends outside school, but it was 'quality time spent together, because we could talk about other things, rather than just the home and the family'.[7] Mohandas would also bring food and refreshments for all, which had been cooked in his home.

Zeria was on hand throughout this process as facilitator between the communities and the workshop providers, a role which Ahad, Mohandas, Kazmi and others found essential to the overall success of the project. He organised two more arts groups with the aim of developing a range of Asian arts and building capacity of talent and professionalism within the Asian communities: a music group was led by himself and Praful Chanda and a dance class was led by Minoo Lord. The adverts for these classes (also printed in the 1992 *New Horizons* programme) underlined both the professionalism of the tutors and the accessibility to all people of all backgrounds and levels of experience. The adverts read as follows:

> MUSIC GROUP
> It is for you if you like Bhangra, Qawali, Ghazals, film songs or Bangla folk music. Aziz Zeria, Praful Chanda (professional musician) will lead the workshops. Tuition will be provided on voice, harmonium and tabla. There will be opportunities to learn non-Asian instruments from time to time. We shall also put on regular shows.
> Western instrument players also very welcome.
> No experience necessary.
> Venue: Werneth Park Music Room, from Wednesday 22nd January 1992, 6–8 p.m.

---

6 This and further references to Ahad are from an interview with Abdul Malik Ahad and Aziz Zeria by Sarah Dadswell, Manchester, 17 October 2007.

7 This and further references to Mohandas are from an interview with Shashi Mohandas by Sarah Dadswell, Oldham, 16 October 2007.

DANCE CLASS
MINOO LORD, from New Delhi, will lead the dance classes. She has studied all styles of dance from a number of great dance masters in India and holds a degree in Kathak style. She has given performances in India, Japan, Spain and the UK.
Her classes are open to all and will be held every week from Tuesday 4th February, Werneth Park Music Room, 6–8 p.m.

These classes combined to create the first production, a collection of skits titled *Eid Mubarak* (*Happy Eid*), which was programmed in April 1992, during Ramadan, at Oldham Theatre Workshop. The performance drew on the participants' experiences of Eid and what it meant to them, whether they were Muslim and Asian or not, as the group was multi-ethnic and multi-denominational. This and the following Peshkar productions were also multi-lingual. A mixture of Asian languages (Urdu, Hindi, Bengali and Bangla) was interspersed with English in each skit, enabling the audience to follow the meaning. The link with Oldham Theatre Workshop was highly significant and indicative of Zeria's ambitions for Peshkar and the local Asian population. Oldham Theatre Workshop was not previously considered open to Asians and enjoyed a reputation for developing actors for the popular television soap opera *Coronation Street*. Zeria wanted to embrace this professionalism and encourage Asians to see the Workshop as a possible pathway to success for themselves, but was also keen for the Asian performance to be received in equally professional terms. In addition, he stated that the local authorities had been leaning on Oldham Theatre Workshop to act more inclusively and demonstrate their diversity. Ahad recalls the good audience turnout, which was 'one hundred percent white', because the Asian families were generally at home breaking the Ramadan fast. The production also clearly bolstered the participants' own self-confidence. Ahad, who was a member of the Asian Youth Movement, not only appreciated the life skills learned through the experience (such as the voice and posture work with Soni), but understood 'the nature of self-help in migrant or newly migrant communities' in which 'if they don't help themselves no-one else will help them'. He understood Zeria's insistence that it was for all the participants to make this arts initiative work, to gain the support of the Council, Oldham Theatre Workshop and other local authorities.

The next two productions *Robot 420* and *New Horizons* fulfilled Zeria's vision to drive the Peshkar project 'step by step into producing its own work, and also developing higher standards as it went on [...]. An essential ingredient of that was to have a team that was professional and competent, who could actually provide that support to the young people of the community who were part of it. And that worked.'[8] Both productions

8 Aziz Zeria, taken from interview with Abdul Malik Ahad.

were devised, multi-lingual and again scripted by Kazmi. Mohandas explained that '4–20' in Hindi, Gujurati and Urdu means a 'thug', so the performance included a 'small showcase of how a robot can be dodgy'. The production was initially played in Werneth Park with an audience of fifty to sixty, but then filled the Werneth Park Music Rooms.

New Horizons was produced on a bigger scale (**DVD 1–2**). Based on his contribution to the development of Asian theatre in the North West, Kazmi had been given a Writer-in-Residence award by the North West Playwrights Workshops. *New Horizons* was scripted by Kazmi and produced by Peshkar, but now engaged Ajaykumar as director, Shobna Gulati and Minoo Lord as choreographers and Megumi Kawaminami and Alnoor Mitha as set designers. Zeria remained musical director. The programme also credits a nine-member technical team. The genre and theme of the play are described in the programme as follows:

> It communicates through a series of stories the struggles and anxieties of the Indian, Pakistani, Bangladeshi and English communities and celebrates their lives, hopes and aspirations.
>
> The four, sometimes disparate communities come together, led by their young people to challenge such issues as racism, migration, integration and cultural identity. It is this unity of purpose and vision that enables the community to both cherish the old and make an impact on the new Britain of today.

If this sounds a little utopian, the printed play's synopsis cites the catalyst for the action as: 'The joyous celebration of Eid is violently interrupted by a racist attack: Bina, a young Hindu woman is raped and murdered.' Three DVD excerpts of the play communicate the wide range of material covered in *New Horizons*, from the murder of the Hindu girl to a protest speech to rally the Asian community and various dances that take place in an Asian community space. These include both community and professional dancers and, in so doing, make some suggestion about the diversity of Asian culture in the UK (**DVD 3–5**). The set was fixed with minimal props and a bare stage. The musicians, who were present for the duration of the play, were seated on a fixed podium in front of the backdrop; they play almost continually throughout. The cast also remained on-stage.

New Horizons premiered at Oldham Sixth Form College on 29 November 1992 and then toured to the NIA Centre, Manchester, on 6 December 1992. The performance was complemented by a special guest appearance of renowned tabla player Ustad Faiyaz Khan, who accompanied Kathak dancer Minoo Lord. This mixed programme would therefore be as attractive to the older generation as the younger. The play toured during the following year to Oldham Coliseum, Bolton Octagon and Manchester's Contact Theatre.

Zeria's ambitions for Peshkar and its strategy for developing creative and sustainable financial capacity while remaining true to its community roots was stated in the *New Horizons* programme: 'As part of the Arts 2000 strategy, it is hoped that Peshkar will become an independent professional company by 1994, the Year of [Manchester City of] Drama. However, the community aspect will remain its priority, as will its training programme, through intense workshops and programming policy.'

In fact, Peshkar finally achieved this desired independence as a theatre company in 1998 with funding from the European Regional Development Fund. This followed a two-year preparation period by Zeria and included the creation of a board of directors in 1997, initially chaired by Shashi Mohandas, and the appointment of an administrator in order to qualify for Company Status and draw up a constitution. The intervening years had witnessed an expansion and continued investment in the professional creative team. Peshkar produced three productions: *Chapati & Chips* in 1994, scripted by Kazmi and directed by experienced theatre-practitioner Harmage Singh Kalirai; *Jaago Get Real* in 1995, written by Parv Bancil and also directed by Kalirai; and *Tricked Me Yaar!* in 1996, written by Adam Strickson and directed by Sazzadur Rahman.

Chapati & Chips was Peshkar's contribution to Manchester's City of Drama Festival. Zeria was on the board of the City of Drama, but it had been a tussle to persuade the organisers to include Peshkar. Peshkar did not yet exist as an independent theatre company and, owing to its main source of funding, was understandably perceived as an Oldham Borough Council-based community arts project. This community perception clashed with the City of Drama's desired projection of a festival of internationally renowned theatre companies. For Zeria, not only did Peshkar aspire to the highest professional standards possible, but its very existence bolstered Manchester's diversity-profile in the arts. *Chapati & Chips* had been adapted by Maggie Willet from the novel by Almas Khan, and was semi-bilingual. The narrative followed the new male Asian migrants of the late 1950s–1960s, who worked in factories and the cotton mills and lived in shared houses of up to twelve or more people, even sharing the beds according to their work shifts. Shashi Mohandas played a character who feeds the men in the house and then begins to cater for the canteen in the mill. In time, his family arrive and he opens the first Asian restaurant. Along the way his character encounters the usual racism of the times and then broader prejudice as he is now in competition with other restaurants. Social boundaries gradually break down and his younger brother marries a white girl. The 'chapatis' become symbolic of the older generation, the 'chips' of the younger generation, both served up at the restaurant. According to Mohandas and Zeria, there was still no other provision for Asian theatre at that time, and the production toured Manchester's Nia Centre, Oldham Coliseum and Bolton Octagon as before.

For the next two plays Peshkar ventured further afield and commissioned other writers to deliver scripts. Thus Parv Bancil, a writer associated with Hounslow Arts Cooperative (HAC) and Watermans Art Centre, wrote a play about real-life modern-day issues related to Asian youth that caused tension between the younger and the older generations: drug use, smoking, clubbing and relationships. The youths are forced to lead double lives and hide the perceived undesirable elements of their lives from their elders. Mohandas remembers that it was only when he came to participate in *Jaago Get Real* that he 'realised how much swearing they used to do in the school and colleges [...] but not at home'. Bancil was introduced to Peshkar through Kalirai, who returned as director.

Tricked Me Yaar! is testament to Peshkar's process and its success in developing young talent to a professional standard. All previous plays had included actors of all ages, from five years old upwards. *Tricked Me Yaar!* was a strategy to focus specifically on youth theatre. It was commissioned by Peshkar's youth theatre wing, Ayna (meaning mirror), which was run as a separate entity by Sazzadur Rahman. Rahman had come to Peshkar as a boy and had developed as an actor and theatre practitioner through the workshops and productions, just as Zeria and other founder members had intended. So, following its usual strategy of bringing in professionals, Peshkar, through Ayna, commissioned Adam Strickson of Rochdale-based Chol Theatre to write the play. The result was a trilingual play (English, Punjabi and Bangla) based on the lives of British Asians in Oldham. The earlier traditional music was replaced with rap and contemporary references.

Until this point Oldham Borough Council had provided Zeria with a generous investment for this community-based level of arts. Zeria, however, had been complementing this income with private sponsorship and the box office takings from the concerts of well-known Asian artists, which he had been programming at venues across Oldham. Although this enabled him to pay all the professionals who contributed to Peshkar, he felt that it was time for the company to realise its full potential. In 1998, after a two-year preparatory period, Zeria was successful in securing the European funding that enabled Peshkar to pursue its own identity as an independent theatre company. In the same year Zeria left his post at the Council. During this period Oldham Borough Council had also been undergoing extensive restructuring of its own organisation. Leisure Services were now merged with Education, which prompted a number of cuts in Leisure Services, including the Asian Officers' posts and support assistants. Zeria's key position was therefore not replaced. Although Oldham Borough Council ceased to fund Peshkar projects directly, it continued to support the company through the provision of office space, a policy which the Council continues to implement at the time of writing.

The first Artistic Director of the newly independent Peshkar was Sazzadur Rahman. Rahman had received his training in performing arts through

Peshkar and Oldham College,[9] followed by one year at the Liverpool Institute for Performing Arts.[10] He then took the title role of *King Lear* with Chol Theatre, which was a professional contract and included an international tour. He also set up the youth theatre company Ayna. After *Tricked Me Yaar!* in 1996 Peshkar was relatively dormant. It continued with its workshops and outreach programme with various local schools, which was a condition of some of its funders,[11] and its performances of *Masala Girls*. Masala Girls was a female dance theatre group run by Shobna Gulati under the Peshkar umbrella. Gulati had been a key figure in the Peshkar professional team from the outset. She wrote skits and choreographed movement and dance for this group, who performed locally and in North West venues. Rahman married the resources he had at his disposal from Ayna with the access and networks built up by Peshkar. He started his post in December 1999 with only his salary covered. By the time he left in 2006 Peshkar was financing five full-time staff and, according to Rahman, had delivered a number of projects whose accumulated budgets totalled more than £4 million.

Rahman was highly motivated to increase capacity and establish Peshkar's national profile. To achieve this he set out to broaden the range of work presented under Peshkar to include: professional theatre; continuing the youth theatre; providing training and development for the Asian community in the arts; and organising festivals and conferences to pool ideas to explore future strategies to support the development of British Asian participation in the arts. Peshkar's first production under Rahman was a joint commission with Oldham Coliseum to Adam Strickson for *A Beautiful Violin*, which was directed by Ian Bloomfield and toured to theatres in Yorkshire and the North West and some national venues in 2002. It signalled a move to higher production values and the use of a fully professional team, including the actors. The play was marketed as 'a tragic love story from the rivers and jungles of East Bengal'. According to a review by Dominic Rai it was a two-hour production with a mixed cast of eight, including two musicians, presented in *jathra*-style, 'a folk form from Bengal and Bangladesh using contemporary and folk music' (DVD 6–9).[12] During the two-year research

---

9 This and further references to Rahman are from an interview with Sazzadur Rahman by Sarah Dadswell, Oldham, 18 October 2007.

10 Rahman left the course early because he felt that, having learned so much through his activities with Peshkar and Oldham College, the Liverpool Institute for Performing Arts was not offering him anything new.

11 Mohandas cites funding given by British Telecom for outreach work on voice projection and elocution—a particularly useful service for the Asian and British Asian youth who may have been struggling with their accents and diction.

12 This and previous quotation by Dominic Rai, 'The Beautiful Violin: Peshkar Down South', a review of the performance at the Nuffield Theatre, Southampton, http://www.asiangigs.com/violin.htm.

and development period Strickson and Rahman travelled to Bangladesh, the first time Rahman had returned since his departure as an eleven-year-old eleven years previously—an element reflected in the story's theme of lost childhood.

The production was a success and was nominated for the *Manchester Evening News* Best New Play Award. It undoubtedly bolstered Peshkar's successful application to the Arts Council of England (ACE) for a national touring programme grant, which the company was awarded in 2003. This was a considerable achievement for such a young company. It also fulfilled the conditions of the existing European funding grant to secure matched funding. Rahman's confidence and the direction of the company is reflected in the following statement which was published on Peshkar's website:

> Our work is about expressing the urban attitude coming from the British South Asian perspective, creating small ripples that have a large impact in the wider society. We are at the beginning of a new era and will continue to play a lead role in the South Asian arts arena as a leading creative and cultural powerhouse for the British South Asian community. We aim to position ourselves at the centre of a new network of high-quality culturally diverse arts, artists, organisations and venues.[13]

Throughout Rahman's time at Peshkar the company produced at least one major production a year. In 2002 Shobna Gulati wrote and choreographed the comedy skits of the *Masala Girls* for Manchester's Green Room (DVD 10).[14] The same year the company was given a 'Pride in Oldham' award for its 'outstanding multicultural and multilingual work'.[15] The next major production, *Just Before the Rain*, was based on testimonies taken from those who experienced the riots that took place in Oldham in May 2001. It was co-written by members of Peshkar, Zaheda Choudhury, Aklakur Rahmun, Anjub Ali, Mahmood Ali and Shahena Choudhury, who had direct experience of the riots as they lived in Oldham, and directed by Ian Bloomfield. It incorporated music and choreography which reflected the tension and sense of threat that was central to the play's narrative.[16] The stark, minimalist stage design consisted of a number of chairs and a pile of

---

13 http://www.artscouncil.org.uk/media/uploads/documents/publications/php8oHvzK.pdf.

14 See the anonymous review 'Peshkar Production's Masala Girls—The Green Room', 1 October 2002 http://www.theasiannews.co.uk/entertainment/s/480/480464_peshkar_productions_masala_girls__the_green_room.html.

15 'Peshkar Perform for Unity', *At Home In Europe: News for the North West Objective 2 and 3 Community Initiative Programmes*, vol. 2:1 (2004), p. 5, http://www.eurofundingnw.org.uk/downloads/At_Home_October.pdf.

16 Recollection of production by Graham Ley.

rubble and made good use of lighting to communicate atmosphere. All five cast members were dressed in black with mid-length leather jackets (**DVD 11–12**). In accordance with the ACE national touring programme conditions, *Just Before the Rain* secured a national tour in 2003, which included venues in Manchester, Cardiff, Bradford, London and Newcastle.

In 2004 the *Masala Girls* returned for a touring production of *The Wedding*, this time co-written and choreographed by ex-Peshkar participants Perveen Hussain and Sri Sarker. Other Peshkar performance activity this year included an Indian and Bangladeshi contribution to the cultural programme of the Commonwealth Games in the form of street theatre. In partnership with Tara Arts and Oldham Coliseum, Peshkar organised the Kala Festival, a one-week festival of British Asian arts programmed across Oldham venues. It incorporated a two-day conference, 'Islam and the Arts', which included contributions by high-profile speakers including Tariq Ali. Reiterating its founding principles, in 2004 Peshkar also launched a performing arts training scheme for 16- to 25-year-olds in partnership with Bolton Octagon, Contact Theatre and the Oldham Coliseum. The participants worked alongside professionals for twelve weeks and created a piece of theatre which was performed in December 2004 in all three venues. The aim of the scheme, as Rahman has written, was to develop creative skills among young British Asians, but also increase infrastructure and audience capacity in the North West.[17]

The final major production under Rahman was *In God We Trust*, written by a new writer, Manchester-based Avaes Mohammed, and directed by Rahman. This story, with a cast of three, explores the relationship of two male inmates of Camp X-Ray in Guantanamo Bay, who find sanctuary in their faith as a means to survive the degradation and violence of their daily lives: a popular theme in British Asian theatre at this time (**DVD 13**). The play featured on- and off-stage scenes of torture and humiliation by the female guard, mostly delivered with a view to securing a confession of membership of a terrorist cell in the UK. The set, designed by Emma Wee, consisted of a central wire cage with lookout platform encircled with barbed wire on top. Towards the end of the play the off-stage voice of Tariq, who had injected witty comments into the proceedings, went ominously silent. Three cage walls representing the prisoner's cells were hinged to this central cage. The lack of privacy in the prison reinforced the exposure and vulnerability of its prisoners. Music was supplied by Jaydev Mistry. The play toured nationally across venues in the north of England and Chester, Crawley and Birmingham. *In God We Trust* coincided with Rahman's award in 2005 of a Clore Fellowship, a prestigious award run by the government's

---

[17] See discussion of Rahman's experience with Peshkar by Charles Leadbeater, *Britain's Creativity Challenge*, Creative and Cultural Skills, http://www.creative-choices.co.uk/upload/pdf/Creativity_Challenge.pdf [accessed 2 February 2009].

Department of Culture, Media and Sport, which recognises the potential of entrepreneurial candidates with experience in their given field and provides the opportunity to extend their training within a high-profile environment. Having completed the Fellowship Rahman returned to Peshkar, but was disillusioned by what he perceived as a ceiling to the Asian community's success in the British theatre system. 'We do amazing, fantastic work with minimum resources', declares Rahman, 'yet we have to prove so [many] things to these buggers. And yet we are left like that.'[18] So, in 2006, having achieved his initial goals for Peshkar and increased its creative and financial capacity, in addition to a continued commitment to the local British Asian communities and training in the arts, Rahman stepped down from his post as Artistic Director.

The most recent era of Peshkar began in 2007 with the appointment of its present Artistic Director, Jim Johnson. Johnson came to Peshkar from his post as head of the outreach team at the Gateway Theatre, Chester. Following his drama degree, he qualified as a teacher and also worked in community theatre. He was familiar with Peshkar's work under Rahman and perceived its potential for further development.[19] It was 'the opportunity to lead a company dedicated to new writing' with Peshkar recognised as a 'stomping ground for developing new Asian writers' that really attracted Johnson to the post. His original remit from the board was not an artistic director's brief, but a restructuring of the organisation and long-term strategic planning. Part of this strategy was a rebranding initiative that included the mission statement: 'Pushing the boundaries of young British-Asian theatre'. Although the existing European funding required Peshkar to focus on the 16- to 21-year age range, Johnson explained how 'beyond that we've got plans to develop a proper dedicated British Asian youth theatre. But again with an intercultural focus. So it's for, by, and with the support of anybody interested in the young British Asian experience.' This reflects the mixed racial participation within the company. At the heart of the mission statement are 'core values of participation, inspiration, progression and enterprise'. For Johnson this is not necessarily a change of direction from earlier eras of Peshkar, but rather an explicit statement that announces its identity.

Part of Johnson's strategy has been to employ an in-house dramaturge and associate writer, Tajinder Singh Hayer. Hayer, from Bradford, had developed as a playwright through a Black and Asian writers group set up

---

[18] Quotation taken from interview with Rahman. For a fuller description of his dilemma see Leadbeater, *Britain's Creativity Challenge*, Creative and Cultural Skills, http://www.creative-choices.co.uk/upload/pdf/Creativity_Challenge.pdf [accessed 2 February 2009].

[19] This and further references to Johnson or Tajinder Singh Hayer are from an interview with Jim Johnson and Tajinder Singh Hayer by Sarah Dadswell, Oldham, 16 October 2007.

through the BBC's Northern Exposure programme at the West Yorkshire Playhouse, where his first play, *Players*, was produced in 2005. He therefore hopes the role he now has with Peshkar will provide a similar support for Oldham-based young writers. Another key person is Sophia Rashid, who runs a female group, Hamara Ayna, which operates under the Peshkar umbrella. Rashid is local to Oldham and invests a significant amount of time in direct outreach work, including visiting the homes of some of her group members to talk to their families about the work that Peshkar and Hamara Ayna do to enlist their support for the group. Other key figures are Vicky Bell, education manager and a project manager, and two additional Asian arts workers.

This most recent phase in Peshkar's history has enjoyed a strong start, with three new productions in 2007: *Hip Hoperatic*, a large-scale site-specific production, written by Hayer, directed by Rashid and performed by Latte (Local Asian Theatre Touring Enterprise), Peshkar's 16+ youth group; the one-woman show *Dance without Movement*, by Rashid, directed by Johnson and performed by Poppy Jhakra in local venues; and *Tales from Number 10*, written and directed by Rashid and performed by Hamara Ayna at Number 10's Café. In 2008 *Dance without Movement* (**DVD 14**) played at the Edinburgh Fringe Festival and *Hip Hoperatic* was remounted at the Oldham Festival with Latte and Emerge, Peshkar's 11–15 group. The new writing continued with *Passengers* by Hayer, directed by Bell and performed by Latte at Oldham Coliseum (**DVD 15**); *Fugee* by Abi Morgan, directed by Bell as part of the National Theatre's Connections series and performed by Emerge and Latte at Salford's Lowry and returning to Breeze Hill Schools, the site of Peshkar's first ever workshops in Oldham in 1992; *Bring it! New writing showcase*, directed by Johnson at Oldham; *Towards Tomorrow*, written by Conor Ibrahiem, Randeep Kaur Assi, Sophia Ali and Tajinder Singh Hayer, directed by Johnson and performed in local venues; and *Siege*, by Hayer, directed by John Doona and performed by the Cheshire County Youth Theatre, Latte and Chorlton High School students. *Towards Tomorrow* is the verbatim theatre output of an oral history project, 'Unclaimed', with local first-generation South Asians, which sought to document the contributors' stories of migration to the UK.

Clearly, this new phase of Peshkar has enjoyed a prolific start and has sought to harness the energy and creativity of its new production team and the potential of the different age groups resident in the Oldham area. With the new theatre groups and collaborations now firmly established, the company is pursuing Peshkar's long-term objective of engaging with the community and supporting the development of new theatre practitioners. [SJD]

12

Asian Theatre School

The Asian Theatre School was set up by Red Ladder Theatre Company, based in Leeds, in collaboration with the Theatre in the Mill at Bradford University. The background lay in Red Ladder's outreach work and touring to youth centres and its commitment to training. In 1996 an application was made to the Foundation for Sport and the Arts, and in a document accompanying that application the company outlined the specific context:

> We are continually being contacted by Arts/Media organisations for advice and information about Black and Asian artists and have become a resource for the area. However despite having many contacts ourselves we are acutely aware of how difficult it is to recruit Asian artists and administrative staff. This highlighted the need for creating training opportunities for Asian Young People who are grossly under-represented in the Arts in general.
>
> Our current tour *Kaahini* by local writer Maya Chowdhry continued to highlight the lack of regional personnel with performers and freelance artists coming primarily from London.
>
> In response to this Red Ladder initiated a series of Black/Asian women traineeships in Stage Management and Arts Administration. Recruitment was difficult which indicated that greater investment was required to generate interest in the Arts. It became clear that there was a need to create an environment which would nurture and develop cultural expression and creativity, hence the Asian Theatre School project.

The document goes on to propose 'a week-long skills-based theatre school for Asian young people', based on workshops 'on a number of aspects of Theatre Craft': 'The training week will examine the language of theatre, starting from the basics of using space and techniques and finishing with an opportunity to combine newly acquired skills.'[1]

---

1 Undated document from Red Ladder Theatre Company, Leeds, probably from

A facsimile of the application to the Foundation for Sport and the Arts, sent by Kate Chapman at the Theatre in the Mill to Red Ladder (22 November 1996), also exists. Chapman was the Fellow in Theatre at the Mill, and her application adds that the 'long-term aim is to see young Asian people from Bradford/N. Yorks go on to become performers, directors and theatre practitioners'. The numbers envisaged were fifteen to twenty, and the funding requested was £8,883, in which there was a comparable emphasis on fees for visiting practitioners and on publicity. A provisional schedule was attached for five days of workshops, above the names of Chapman and Kully Thiarai, as Artistic Director of Red Ladder, who would also lead some of the sessions. These were to start with static images in space (Day 1), then movement and communication (Day 2), voice work (Day 3), writing and dialogue 'led by a practitioner experienced in using styles rooted in South Asian culture and applying them to contemporary theatre' (Day 4), and a final day putting together 'the layers of theatrical language which have been introduced during the week'.[2]

According to Red Ladder Reports which exist for the Asian Theatre School in 1997 and 1998, there were twenty participants during 21–25 July 1997 and ten during 20–24 July 1998. Invited tutors for 1997 were Nitin Ganatra, Nandita Ghose, David Mishra, Ravinder Gill and Maya Chowdhry, while for 1998 they were Faroque Khan, Akintayo Akinbode and Ajay India; Chapman and Thiarai led sessions in both years. In 1997, a performance was excluded from the plan to keep the focus on training; but in 1998 a week's residency to devise a performance, open to participants from both years, followed in October. The show, called *Masala Nights*, looked to Halloween and Diwali for inspiration, and involved music and movement as well as drama (**DVD 2–7**). In 2000, the New Asian Theatre School was launched for a projected three-year period. Wendy Harris, the Artistic Director at Red Ladder, and Andrew Loretto, Fellow at the Theatre in the Mill, were joined by Milan Lad, Asian Performing Arts Development Officer at Bradford Theatres. An application to Yorkshire Arts for funding, including an outline budget for the three years, exists, with the covering letter to David Brown dated 10 January 2000 (**DVD 8**). For 2000, registration cards were printed (**DVD 9–11**), and workshops in April and July were followed by a week of training sessions in August, involving Akinbode and Khan again, with Ashmeed Soyhee on writing, Manjinder Virk on drama and Balbir Singh on dance. There were

1996, headed 'Asian Theatre School' (**DVD 1**). All documentation quoted or cited in this section is held in the archive of the Asian Theatre School, now Freedom Studios, in Bradford.

2 Facsimile of application to Foundation for Sport and the Arts by Kate Chapman. The fax is dated 22 November 1996, but the application states 30 April 1996 as the date by which Chapman wanted to know the Foundation's response. The facsimile is too faint for reproduction.

eighteen participants, with eleven going on in the following year to devise a short piece—directed by Mark Hollander—during weekly workshops from February 2001 forwards for performance in April, in the initiative *Storyscape*. Later that year, workshops were held on a weekend in June and for the standard week in July.[3]

In January 2002 Madani Younis was appointed director of the Asian Theatre School, in a move that was not originally anticipated in the three-year plan. Yet his brief was thoroughly recognisable: he was to run weekly workshops and to 'create a forty-minute piece of theatre that should be devised, and had to play for two nights at the Theatre in the Mill in August'.[4] The workshops were held on Tuesday evenings, and Younis recalls that at the first session he led there were only seven people. The numbers built to around forty, with an age range from fifteen to forty, and soon there was a waiting list. The idea of weekly workshops had been tried with the lead-in to *Storyscape*, but in addition Milan Lad was running a drama group called Sapna on Tuesday evenings at the Alhambra Theatre studio. Wakas Zamurad recalls that these workshops led forwards to a devised piece called *Trust Me, It's All About the Money*, directed by Iain Bloomfield, during 2001.[5] As he remembers it, the group closed because the funding was cut, and some of the Sapna members who had been on the Asian Theatre School now moved across to Younis's weekly workshops.[6] Zamurad is forthright about the feel of the work from the beginning.

> Initially with Sapna you'd turn up on the Tuesday, do some warm-ups, lots of improvisations, and then you went home and there was nothing really to think about. With the Asian Theatre School it was very different. You came in, you had an idea of where you wanted to be, and it was really the start of a development process ... It really did open up numerous doors for me, and just gave me a better understanding of theatre, of the arts, of creativity, of directing, of writing, of performing, and just allowed me to hone my own skills.
>
> [Zamurad 2007]

What is clear from the testimonies is that there was an extraordinary acceleration in the pace of the work, the identification with it and the sense of direction. A theme for the resultant performance had to be chosen, and Younis opened that up to the group, as Zamurad recalls.

---

3 There is a report for April 2000–April 2001 up to the contribution to *Storyscape* in the archive, which notes Kamini Gupta on mask-making and Ivan Stott on music; but there is no report on the 2001 summer sessions.

4 Madani Younis, interviewed by Graham Ley, Leeds, 18 July 2003.

5 Bloomfield was Head of Outreach at Bradford Theatres from 1997 to 2001.

6 Wakas Zamurad, interviewed by Graham Ley, Bradford, 13 November 2007.

> So there were lots of ideas bandied about and the Bradford riots had just happened the year before. And it was why don't we do a piece about Bradford, rather than have some London company doing it who haven't actually lived the event as people who are in Bradford have? Surely our story counts for a lot more, and we can give the nuances of what happened, rather than people generalising and stereotyping? And that's why people really started throwing their passion in, because it was about us ...
>
> [Zamurad 2007]

Shaida Chaudhury, who had joined the group, came from Keighley, but she also notes how close the issue was.[7]

> I worked in a school and some of our students had been present, and so when police stuck up posters around the school of 'Do you recognise male A, B, C?' some of them were our students, they were people we knew from Keighley as well. So it obviously affected a lot of people. It was a very brave issue to tackle.
>
> [Choudhury 2007]

Zamurad recalls the hurt about the press coverage of the riots, and the sense conveyed that 'we were all hooligans who were burning cars and smashing up buildings'.

> Whereas everybody else could turn round and go 'poor Bradford', we were the residents who had to deal with the aftermath of the Bradford riots, we had to deal with being looked at suspiciously by the police, by the white community, with people not sure of who took part and who didn't. And being Asian and male really didn't help at all. It was a chance to redress it, and say 'Actually, not all of us are like that, not all of us agree.'
>
> [Zamurad 2007]

The riots took place on 7–8 July 2001, and resulted in 200 custodial sentences totalling over 600 years; some were reduced on appeal. Many people were injured, including approximately 300 police officers. There had been other riots earlier in the summer in Oldham on 26 May and in Burnley on 23–24 June.

The process that created *Streets of Rage* was partly dependent on Younis's background. He had taken a degree in film studies at Southampton University, but then went to the MPhil in Playwriting at Birmingham University after being introduced to scriptwork at Southampton on one

---

7 Shaida Choudhury, interviewed by Graham Ley, Bradford, 13 November 2007.

course unit taught by the playwright Seamus Finnegan, who remained a mentor. He was uncomfortable at Birmingham, feeling isolated as an Asian, but he developed a script there about the pregnancy of a young British Asian woman who is torn between her former lover and the man she now wants to marry. Yet it was Finnegan who had introduced him to the black American playwright Lorraine Hansberry and *A Raisin in the Sun*, and on Finnegan's course at Southampton he had written a monologue which Finnegan prized. During his work for the Birmingham MPhil, the Birmingham-based Asian arts organisation Sampad had given him the opportunity to lead drama workshops, and for Sampad he directed *Harvest* by Manjula Padmanabhan in September 2001. So Younis had a strong sense of script development and experience of scripting and directing from the start, and it was his decision to turn to script-making skills in the process.

From February to May the devising and training for *Streets of Rage* continued on Tuesday evenings, and from May to June the play began to form. In order to facilitate that, he established a smaller group of about ten who met on Thursday evenings to brainstorm, and took those ideas to the next Tuesday's full-group workshop. In June Younis wrote the play, and in July the group went into three weeks of rehearsals at the Theatre in the Mill, working with those who were free during the day, and with others in the evenings, and all at weekends. Younis had a methodical approach—'someone once said to me that seventy-five per cent of writing is in the planning, and twenty-five per cent is the writing: and I live by that rule'—and he believes that 'it is characters that make good scripts'. He and the group had three months 'to flush out these characters'.

> For each of the characters in *Streets of Rage* I'd write a monologue, and discover rhythms of how these characters speak ... So on my wall I'd have fifteen or whatever character monologues, and then I'd put that into a structure of how their narrative would work in terms of the broader picture.
>
> [Younis 2003]

He did this by having the group ask all the characters the same question about what happened in the riots, and both he and Zamurad remember the arcs of marker pen connecting and linking characters across the wall on which the monologues were hung. The participants in the Thursday meeting would brainstorm ideas, and on Tuesdays groups would work on characters, or on scenarios for those characters, and later on scenes. The first reading of the script for rehearsals was deflating, until Younis realised that his actors were not trained to do sight-reading. His pragmatic approach was to control the performance demands by allowing each character only six scenes. The whole was woven together by Younis and the associate director Sarah Brigham, after difficult casting decisions, giving fourteen characters named roles and allowing for a substantial choreographed involvement for the rest of the group.

In May Younis had negotiated a slot for the production at the West Yorkshire Playhouse in addition to that already fixed for the Theatre in the Mill, and granted the theme he was able to create a great deal of advance interest in the regional papers. The riots had been a traumatic experience, renewing a history of serious disturbance in the city, and the research had been able to draw on a network of contacts existent in the group itself, including those who might not otherwise have spoken about their experiences.[8] The police eventually allowed interviews to be held, but only over the telephone. Younis was fascinated diversely by how a crisis of this sort created spokesmen out of figures in the Asian community, and how taxi drivers were often the best witnesses. He also travelled well outside the Bradford area, taking workshops in schools in Huddersfield and Halifax, because he believed that the perceptions of Bradford and of the riots from outside were important: Huddersfield is only forty minutes away, but 'in the space of forty minutes stories had just exploded into street tales, almost into myths' [Younis 2003]. In an advance interview for the *Bradford Telegraph and Argus*, Younis was concerned to point out that the performance was not a celebration of rioting.

> The only thing I can stress is that the piece does not in any way incite or support rioting, it's not about Bradford riots part two. In no way are we justifying what the rioters did because even now we're still struggling to understand what they were fighting for, if anything. We are not defending anything that took place. In many ways the piece is holding up its own community and asking questions of it.[9]

The production was designed by Leslie Travers, who worked with a long white bench on casters and a backdrop covered with graffiti to create different locales for the action (**DVD 12–18**). The riots themselves appeared as back-projection of the media coverage, and then as live events in the choreography of the ensemble. The script itself is a cleverly crafted network of scenes and relationships, interspersed with parallel cameos of speakers in different situations and short monologues, operating to Younis's scheme

---

8 There had been disturbances in Bradford earlier in 2001, in April, but more serious clashes occurred 10–12 June 1995.

9 Madani Younis in conversation with Ian Midgley, *Bradford Telegraph and Argus*, 16 August 2002, on the opening night of the two-day run at the Theatre in the Mill, Bradford. Further features appeared in the *Bradford Telegraph* for 20 July 2002, the *Yorkshire Post* for 16 August 2002, and the *Yorkshire Post* for 6 September 2002, on the opening of the two-day run at the West Yorkshire Playhouse, Leeds. The play was also reviewed in the *Bradford Telegraph* on 17 August 2002, by Rosey Hamilton.

of six scenes per character. At the centre is the dysfunctional Hussain family, in which two parents speak to each other only through their sons, with one of the sons, Irfan, constantly in trouble with the police, for whom his brother Rizwan works. The tension between them is palpable, because Rizwan has good reason to believe that his brother's reputation is blocking his attempts at promotion. Alongside them are the Chaudhary son and daughter, Nadeem and Nadia, coping with an alcoholic father desolate at the loss of his wife, and a take-away that no longer functions successfully as a business. Into this strained but sensitive portrayal of family life the threat of a British National Party march and the news of its cancellation gradually seep, followed by a growing awareness of the incidents that combine to form the rioting. Yet the climax of the play is occupied by the suicide of Nadia, who has never recovered from her mother's death, leaving a sense of the desolation of personal lives in front of public chaos. The most unsparing portrait is reserved for the would-be reporter, who will torture any event into a sharp news story.[10]

Streets of Rage was generated from the energies and experience of the group with an immediacy for both group members and their regional audience that was likely to be unrepeatable, yet continuity was essential in order to retain momentum. While writing *Streets of Rage* Younis had become aware of the case of Christopher Allder, a former soldier who had died from injuries while in police custody, and was drawn into researching deaths in custody. This became the theme that he put to the group for its work on development, and he knew that it stretched beyond the Asian community to the experiences of many thousands of families throughout the UK of all ethnicities. Other members of the group were involved in the research, and Shaida Choudhury went to Burnley with Younis to interview Janet Allder, Christopher's youngest sister, for a whole day. Both were strongly affected by the experience, and by the frustration that family members would feel, and the struggle for justice.

> You can't say anything consoling, what can you say? They've been to court and a judge has cleared these officers of manslaughter. What can one possibly say? I could say you'll get the justice you deserve, but they've been there, they've done it, and they haven't.
>
> [Younis 2003]

Younis started the group process in the autumn of 2002, before the break that the School had until January, with a showing of the film *Injustice*, which had been banned by Channel Four, about deaths in police custody. From that point, the group knew that this would be the theme, and early in

[10] The riots of 2001 were later to be the subject of a television drama by Neil Biswas, *Bradford Riots*, broadcast on 4 May 2006 on Channel Four.

2003 Younis was 'running around the country meeting civil rights workers, families, and those who had been affected, like friends'. He asked David Blunkett, then Home Secretary, for an interview, wrote to Diane Abbott and Paul Boateng and contacted Inquest, the organisation that deals primarily with this issue. He went to Feltham Prison to follow up on the case of Zahid Mubarek and spoke to the governor, but had his scheduled meeting with inmates cancelled when he asked the governor for a response to the statement by the Director General of the Prison Service that the prison service was institutionally racist.[11] The emergent sense gained from the research was not just that the incidents were horrific, but 'what the families went through was horrific on another level, just because of the inhumanity in how they were treated, the lack of respect they were given by the system'. So the families became the subject of the devising process, and the group was given an insight into their lives.

> All our research was filmed, so I could feed that back to the group. They've seen all my interviews that I had with families and friends, so they were always kept in the loop, in that any information I had was shared.
>
> [Younis 2003]

This permitted a similar development process to that for *Streets of Rage*, with the difference that the raw material lay in 'the case studies and the types of people'. Younis was bound by the advice that, if he wished to tour, then an hour and ten minutes would be his maximum running time, and by the knowledge that in order to tour his cast had to be smaller.

> With *Streets*, we had interest from everywhere to bring the show to them. But with a cast of thirty, and a set as big as we had, economically we just couldn't realise that, because we would be making a loss of about a grand each time …
>
> So I knew that if we wanted to do this piece, it had to be smaller in order for it to go to those venues I believed it deserved to go to.
>
> [Younis 2003]

These were the practical constraints, and from families the subject came down to a family, extending to the best friend of the deceased and the civil rights worker, creating a cast of six for a play with the title *Silent Cry*. Red Ladder advised taking on a dramaturg, who was Andrea Earl,

---

11 The case of Zahid Mubarek, who was assaulted by his cellmate and died from the injuries in March 2001, was later dramatised by Tanika Gupta in *Gladiator Games*, using the methods of what had come to be known as verbatim theatre. It opened in autumn 2005.

whose play *Aftermath* had been on the experience of families after one of their members had been put in prison. The schedule was set earlier in the year, with *Silent Cry* opening at the Bradford Alhambra on 9 and 10 May 2003, and then going on a regional tour to the Hub in Sheffield, Loca in Batley, the Square Chapel in Halifax and the Nidderdale festival for single performances in June and early July, and finishing with a run of five nights at the West Yorkshire Playhouse. The design was by Leslie Travers and the music by Ivan Stott, with choreography by Jason James. *Silent Cry* was jointly directed by Younis and Sarah Brigham, and Wakas Zamurad was brought in as Assistant Director, in a distinct development of the training programme. The cast was Lubna Shuja, Rafique Butt, Kashif Khan, Lena Kaur, Asif Khan and Shaida Chaudhury, and there was significant advance coverage in the regional newspapers (**DVD 19–21**). Members of the families involved in the research, including Janet Allder, came to the performance and took part in the after-show discussion (**DVD 22–28**).

The play examines the lives of the family of a charismatic young man, Arif Ahmed, seven months after he had died in police custody. The script is much more evenly based on dialogue than *Streets*, with the occasional monologue or speech to an imagined audience, and some structural features are similar. The sensitive portayal of individual lives in motion, affected by a common situation, is very strong; the charismatic figure of the son proves to have been involved in crime; the parents, Bashir and Safia, are to an extent divided from each other; and cynicism attaches itself as readily here to Nina, the support worker from Fight for Justice, as it did to the journalist in *Streets*. Above all, the threatening shadow of the police looms large in both plays, with sons particularly at risk, here fatally. The dramaturgy subtly supports our sense of the increased isolation of individual responses to a trauma of loss, most dangerously registered on the younger brother Nadeem, who turns to violence once he discovers that his idolised brother was making money from ringers, welded remakes of crashed cars. The dialogue acutely serves to emphasise that all the characters are left in their own worlds, with perhaps only the women of the family progressing, the wife of Arif, Noreen, finding consolation in religion, and his mother eventually taking up the struggle after great reluctance. If the climax is represented by the revelation about Arif, and Nadeem's violent response to it, lighter touches give the play a particular quality, with father and son for once choosing to smoke in the garden at the same time, despite the stigma that each knows is attached to it.

> (NADEEM is sat on his own. He holds back the tears and walks outside into the garden to have a cigarette. BASHIR, unaware of what has happened, walks into the garden and lights up a cigarette. They share a moment as they realise what the other is doing. It is

a somewhat bizarre Father and Son moment. They continue to smoke.)

BASHIR: Busy night.
NADEEM: Yeah.
BASHIR: (Notices the necklace.) He used to wear that when he/
NADEEM: Played cricket I know.
BASHIR: I gave that to him on his first match. I told him I wore it when I scored my first century/
NADEEM: I didn't know you played?
BASHIR: Oh no I never played cricket. I left that to your uncles/
NADEEM: But you told him/
BASHIR: He was feeling nervous. I thought it would help him play better.
NADEEM: Yeah, it did the trick.

[*Silent Cry*: scene 12][12]

At the West Yorkshire Playhouse there was an after-show discussion every evening, and on the Friday night of the run Jatinder Verma of Tara Arts was joined by Isobel Hawson from the central office of the Arts Council of England (ACE), and by a representative from the Lyric Theatre in Hammersmith. Other potential venues had also been invited, and the Lyric registered strong interest, while the ACE encouraged a touring application. The production had from the outset been conceived for touring, to reach a wider regional audience, and this permitted Younis's strategy for a national tour. The application for £60,000–70,000 was successful, and there was a five-week rehearsal schedule at the Theatre in the Mill. The policy of auditioning within the company for the regional tour was completely opened for the national tour, with performers from the Asian Theatre School also included, and after auditions Kashif Khan was retained to play Nadeem. The production opened at the Theatre in the Mill on 15–16 September 2004, and toured for six weeks to York, the Midlands Arts Centre (MAC) in Birmingham, Contact in Manchester, Batley, Rotherham, the Phoenix Arts Centre in Leicester, Barbican in Plymouth, the Lyric in Hammersmith, the Sherman in Cardiff, Unity Theatre in Liverpool and the Oldham Coliseum.

Immediately after the regional tour of *Silent Cry* work began on an initiative of new writing within the group, which culminated in the production of eight fifteen-minute plays by group members in a season called *Street Voices*. Four plays were performed on each of the three nights, capped by longer scripts by Younis, Verma and the playwright Neil Biswas. The production was presented at the Theatre in the Mill, West

---

12 Madani Younis, *Silent Cry* (London: Oberon Books, 2004), p. 55. The rehearsal script, which differs in minor respects, is held in the archive by Freedom Studios.

Yorkshire Playhouse and Contact Theatre, Manchester, in July 2004, and it coincided with a second initiative, 'Contacting the World', funded by the British Council, in which the Asian Theatre School was linked with Al Sajer Theatre in Damascus (**DVD 29–30**). The aim here was compare and experience convictions and working methods, and Younis and Zamurad, who was by now an administrative assistant to the group, travelled to Damascus early in 2004 and worked with the company there.

Drawing on her work as a counsellor at a Keighley school, Shaida Chaudhury wrote one of the plays, *Ring O Ring O Roses*, that came through to production in *Street Voices*:

> I worked in a high school for five years, with a lot of young, white girls who were involved in third-party abuse, where they were being groomed.
>
> [Chaudhury 2007]

The girls were as young as eleven and the youths involved were in their twenties, although boys in the school who were cousins and brothers were involved at age fifteen. Once the scripting opportunity arose Chaudhury 'didn't have to think about anything else', because she felt that 'the characters were all around me, and it was just the most natural thing for me to have written'. Schools were invited to attend the performances:

> I just felt that even if one person ... whether it was the school or just generally the public, even if it affected just one person, for them to see the signs and see the pattern, whether it was their own daughter or somebody else's daughter, I felt that it needed to be addressed ...
>
> [Chaudhury 2007]

The spare naturalism of Chaudhury's unsettling play stood alongside a solo performance piece, *Beyond Skin*, written and performed by Bhavini Raval, a choreographed duologue, *Equal*, by Prakswr Missttry, and an atmospheric study of two Asian men in a hospital ward, *The Window*, by Lubna Shuja; other scripts were *China Calls* by Imran Hamid, *Him, Them and Me* by Asif Khan, *Summers End* by Mohammed Irfan and *A Tortured Soul* by Duggal Ram. The longer script by Younis, *Freeworld*, came out of the relationship with Al Sajer Theatre (**DVD 31–36**). After the visit of Younis and Zamurad to Damascus, communication proceeded as intended by internet and webcam, but the script was developed by the group. Zamurad recalls being struck by the oppressive atmosphere in Damascus, 'knowing that the secret police were around you continuously and just not being able to say anything that was out of order'. But both politics and religion were discussed in private, and 'how terrorism was seen by the wider community and just what that means' brought members of both companies together during the exchange. Not all of the Asian Theatre School were Muslims, but the majority were: they wanted to make 'a point of saying just because we are Muslims we are not terrorists', and to tackle the theme of 'scapegoating other countries, and just scapegoating in general' [Zamurad 2007]. The internet exchanges, which were part of the planned development, embraced images of food and sustenance, and stories from both regions, Bradford and Damascus, while the webcam permitted reciprocal views of rehearsals in progress. Both Al Sajer and the Asian Theatre School were to work to an hour's length, and they decided during the meetings in Damascus to set their plays on a roof, with six characters.

Freeworld was set in 2024, with a number of individuals marooned on the roof of a block of flats in Bradford, awaiting a food-drop, and it opens as a new person clambers into view and collapses. They are short of water, and there is a baby who is clearly suffering, but the play reveals its own background more effectively than the relationships on the roof, with terrorism and supposedly anti-terrorist wars now widespread. The principal vehicle for this grim panorama is the experience of the new arrival, who is, it seems, a military deserter. A further dimension is added by a character who insists on recording everything on camera, who is reminscent of the journalist in *Streets* and the alienating mechanism of the media. The play offers a bleak picture of a future urban landscape, but seems inconclusive in working through largely unexceptional dialogue to connect its chosen characters and their situation with the wider, overwhelming themes that stand out from it: water shortage, the fostering of militarism in apparent response to terrorism, and mediatised paralysis. It was performed by Aliyah Bhatti, Ayeshah Arif, Duggal Ram, Kashif Khan, Lena Kaur and Mohammed Irfan, and directed by Younis with Zamurad and Bhavini Raval (**DVD 37**). The design doubled for the short plays in *Street Voices*, using only three twelve-foot benches of adjustable height, with lighting and sound creating specific environments. *Freeworld* was produced back-to-back with Al Sajer's related play, which was in Arabic, in the season 'Contacting the World', alongside five other pairings of British companies with companies from Nigeria, Pakistan, Bangladesh, Malaysia and Jordan. The season played at the Contact Theatre in Manchester in late July 2004. got to here

Projected work for 2005 was founded on a grant from Audiences Yorkshire of £15,000, but it tied Younis and the group into making a show for their partner, West Yorkshire Playhouse, the scale of which prevented the possibility of touring. In the event, the conduct of this collaboration was unsatisfactory, with misunderstandings and disagreements about costing, and over the same period some disillusion with the relationship with Theatre in the Mill also set in. Office space at the Theatre in the Mill had been promised, and some preparations were made, but eventually the idea fell through, and Younis came to the conclusion that the Asian Theatre School was not really considered an integral part of the operations at the University of Bradford. There can be little doubt that these experiences broke what had been an extended period of the Asian Theatre School working to a relatively stable brief, and led to the period of reformation that resulted in the concept of Freedom Studios.

What proved to be the final production of the Asian Theatre School had its genesis in a similar group process to the previous work, with particular inspiration coming to Younis as the dramaturg from his fascination with Caravaggio's humanity, from his awareness of a Bradford cake-maker, and from Zamurad's apparently unrelated experience of a hangout in a caravan on a vacant building plot. The cake-maker gave the play a central family business subject to the pressures and temptations of the wider economy, while the caravan provided a refuge for the frustrations of the young men and women on the margins of the business. Both these dramaturgical strategies rooted the play in Bradford and crossed generations without simply exploring generational conflict, while the interlinking of the fortunes of the family-run bakers with the ambitions of a local politician provided a thoroughly recognisable situation. Caravaggio was far more of a personal inspiration, with his painting *The Seven Works of Mercy* for Younis being a canvas which displayed the 'beauty and the value in ordinary people'.[13] As it evolved, the plot was to hinge on the death of the grandmother, whose husband had set up the business, and the intrigues of her son to expand and take over the plot on which the caravan was standing. But events took over. Younis and Zamurad went to London on 5 July 2005 to meet the designer, Leslie Travers, and on 6 July were celebrating the sucessful London bid for the Olympics. Younis was on his way to Kings Cross on the tube on the morning of 7 July when the bombs exploded on tube trains and a bus in central London, and was forced to stay in a hotel before returning to Leeds the following day. The experience and the aftermath, with the press 'descending on this region like it was a hothouse for suicide bombers in the UK' were bound to affect the work in progress, throwing the younger generation back into the suspicion and hostility that their parents had all too often experienced.[14]

Yet the resultant play, *Caravan*, remains what Younis calls a celebration of a community, although its picture is of a micro-economy being broken apart and the loss of cohesion within an extended family. There is little on the horizon for the young, who have no real means to defend their own space, and no alternative to the casual comforts of their caravan. The aim of the production throughout is recognition, registered through characters selected from a wider range developed by the group in workshops, offering at least one sympathetic figure to almost any audience member across generations, and an ironic humour to the audience at large. In *Caravan* the passion on

---

[13] Younis, quoted by Emma Clayton, 'Caravan Moves on for Madani', *Bradford Telegraph and Argus*, 29 July 2005.

[14] Madani Younis interviewed by Graham Ley, Bradford, 13 November 2007.

which all members of the group insist is one less of political indignation and more of commitment to an everyday being and belonging, however awkward or futile that might prove to be. Here the three 'rude boys' adjust to being the objects of suspicion, in company with the young woman, Saima.

SAIMA: Something happened didn't it, what did you do now?
KAMMY: Why does it always have to be our fault?
SAIMA: So what was it then? What happened Kash?
KASH (Reaches into his pocket and produces a pink slip.) Check this out. They've got my name and everything.
IMMY: Who?
KAMMY: The police you dickhead, dats who stopped us.
SAIMA: Where?
KAMMY: Walking up Manningham Lane.
IMMY: They can't just stop you cos you were walking down the street and dat.
KASH: They did.
IMMY: Why did they stop you?
KAMMY: Cos this fucker didn't shave this morning.
KASH: They said they were stopping us under the terrorism act. We were just walking down the street and these two policemen stopped us. All the Auntigees just stopped and watched, they didn't even ask if we were alright. And then this bitch started crying.
KAMMY: I didn't cry, I had cigarette in my eye.
IMMY: This has gone too far, it's crossed the line.
SAIMA: What are you going to do Ghandi?
IMMY: I'll write a letter on my laptop.
SAIMA: Do you even think before you open your mouth?
KAMMY: It's cos of what happened in London.
KASH: We didn't do it.
KAMMY: It doesn't matter to them does it?
SAIMA: Don't let it get you down, they'll eventually just get bored of doing it.
KASH: Like fuck they will.
IMMY: Who gives a shit.

(The rude boys and SAIMA all sit in silence, motionless.)

[*Caravan*: scene 23][15]

The cast for *Caravan* was formed by Manjinder Flora, Sidrah Shaikh, Mohammed Irfan, Ayeshah Arif, Duggal Ram, Sheraz Ali, Roxanne Firdos,

---

15 Script held in Asian Theatre School archive at Freedom Studios.

Lubna Shuja, Aliya Bhatti, Kashif Khan, Wakas Zamurad, Shireen Farkhoy, Imran Hamid, Zahir Daji, Prakswr Misstry and Zuleikah Miriam Saeed, and the assistant director was Zamurad. The play was produced alongside a series of short performances from arts groups (dance, poetry and visual arts) in the region called *Pay It Forward* (DVD 38–44).

As early as 2004 Asian Theatre School had been considering its future within Red Ladder, which generated the income for Younis as artistic director. For the period 2005–08 the Arts Council provided a small annual grant to facilitate a 're-branding' and the fundamental decision was for independence from Red Ladder and a firm relocation of the office from Leeds to Bradford. A further bid was put in to the ACE under Grants for the Arts during 2007, to cover the next three years as a regularly funded organisation, and this was awarded in late 2007 to start in 2008. One of the obvious objectives was to be able to combine effectively a national touring profile, responding to strong interest, with a continuing commitment to the local and regional community, and to the development of skills in that context. In late 2007, just before the award was made, Younis described the plans for Freedom Studios. Staffing would comprise himself remaining as the artistic director, a full-time general manager, and a fund-raising manager on a twelve-month contract.

> Beneath this we have six associate artists from across artistic disciplines; three out of the six will be regional artists, and the other three will be from a national platform ... It's our view that these six artists will work with the company in and amongst other professional work they are currently doing. Their time with us will be paid for through funding ... They will work with us for a period of two years, and at the end of that period these six artists and myself will go away for a period of eight to ten days and look to create a piece of work collaboratively. This piece might manifest itself in an installation, or a theatrical production, or a film.
>
> [Younis 2007]

At the core of Freedom Studios there would be a company of twenty, formed through auditions, with a weekly workshop for nine months of the year plus masterclasses and work taking place on a major production each year over a two-year period. Freedom Juniors, for children aged between five and nine, would meet once a fortnight on Saturday morning for a free workshop.

Alongside this new structure other work continued, notably a three-year project with Bradford Youth Offending Team and 'a national project looking at the work done within prisons with young, British-born Asian men and at their experiences of going through the judicial system and what happens to them'.

Asian Theatre School began as a summer-school initiative by Red Ladder to encourage participation in theatre training by young British Asians in the West Yorkshire region, looking from Leeds to Bradford. With the appointment of Younis as artistic director that initiative flourished, since it provided opportunities for direct self-expression in *Streets of Rage*, and gathered a committed group. Asian Theatre School also embraced the logistics of touring and co-production, and the proposal for independence from Red Ladder offered a balance between national artistic innovation and a continuing commitment to work and training in the region, with the centre now firmly placed in Bradford, and the professional aspiration granted regular funding as Freedom Studios.
[GL]

13

Rifco

Rifco is the acronym for the Reduced Indian Film Company, a title which reveals a great deal about the nature of its extremely popular theatre productions and its genesis. The continuity figure for Rifco has been Pravesh Kumar, who became its artistic director, and whose experience, skills and interests have had a major influence on its profile. Pravesh grew up in Slough, near London, and was as fascinated by film as he was by theatre. He broke with family expectations by auditioning for a number of drama schools, and finally decided on a three-year course at the Academy of Live and Recorded Arts, for which he received funding from Berkshire County Council. The course embraced radio, film and television in addition to live performance, and Kumar is frank about his success in the final showcases for agents:

> I immediately got bombarded with agents. Not because I was very good, it was because I was Asian. And to be really honest with you, that is the truth. I did say to myself 'What is going on here? There's people here that are great. Why am I getting all the cards?' And I got myself a really good agent, who within a week of meeting me had put me up for this job with Moti Roti.[16]

He auditioned, and got the lead part of Sonny, playing alongside Nina Wadia and Ajay Chhabra, who both became friends, in the production of *Moti Roti* that played at the Theatre Royal, Stratford East in 1993, and was revived in 1994. After that he did jobbing work, mostly on television, but also made the decision to follow his fascination with film to India. There was no acting work there, but he was able to make contacts and become acquainted with the industry and its methods in a number of visits during the 1990s, and received a break when he came forward to be an executive producer in 1998 for a television project, *Mr Grishna Gant Here* (*Is Mr Grishna Gant Home?*), a 'spoof of Indian B-grade horror films', working with Apurva Asrani as editor. He had also been involved in a film project with Gurinder

---

[16] Pravesh Kumar, interviewed by Graham Ley, West Wing, Slough, 13 March 2008.

Chadha, called *London*, in 1997, which finally came to nothing, but from which he learned a great deal about the industry.

Yet, despite this success with television in India, it was the theatre work in Britain that gradually provided a consistent line-through and the contacts and connections that led to Rifco. Kumar performed with Harvey Virdi in Border Crossings' production of Mahesh Dattani's *Bravely Fought the Queen* in 1996, in Parminder Sekhon's *Not Just an Asian Babe* at Etcetera Theatre London in 1997, and with Gurpreet Bhatti and Chhabra in *Arrange That Marriage* in 1998, a comedy revue that was part of a vibrant accent on satire and sketch-based comedy at Watermans during the 1990s, under Hardial Rai. Kumar was immensely impressed by Rai's success with British Asian audiences, and accepted an invitation from Sita Ramamurthy to explore comic ideas in a two-week workshop at Leicester. The four performers in the workshop in August 1998 were Kumar, Chhabra, Virdi and Bhatti, and the key moment came with a switch of roles and gender after hot-seating various characters, when Virdi and Bhatti had been playing baggage-loaders:

> Ajay and I just sat there one day, and we suddenly picked up these shawls, and put them on our heads, and became these old women. And that became the basis of *Airport*'s main story. It was about these two baggage-loaders who fell in love with these two dinner ladies in the canteen. ... It was four people coming together who were very close as friends, and also understood that genre as well. It was very British Asian humour. It was very broad as well.
>
> [Kumar 2008]

Their approach was to devise during the day and write it down in the evening, and they all wrote their own parts and co-wrote the developing script. It was shown a few months later to Paul Kerrison and Ramamurthy, who decided to programme it for three weeks in March 1999 at the Studio, Leicester Haymarket, bringing in the designer Libby Watson and the director Michael Buffong. The name of the company, Rifco, came from the fact that only four actors were performing all the parts,[17] and Kumar insists that there was intentionally a new note that he had not found at Watermans:

> Yes, it was very funny, but it was also very poignant. Everyone that saw it said 'Yes, we laughed, but actually we really felt for those characters'. And that was something quite new in the British Asian comedy that we had seen up until then.
>
> [Kumar 2008]

---

17 There was undoubtedly a glance sideways here to the Reduced Shakespeare Company, whose run of *The Complete Works of William Shakespeare* had started in London in 1996.

Despite its success the show was not reviewed nationally, and so Kumar got on the phone to theatres and eventually went with Chhabra to see Jon Fawcett, programming director at the Riverside Studios. The result was a two-week run in April 1999 at the Riverside, for which Leicester Haymarket let them borrow the set and the costumes, and that led in turn to an invitation from the Theatre Royal, Stratford East, and a further remount for the Millennium Festival at the Greenwich Theatre in February 2000, at which the Theatre Royal was in temporary residence (DVD 1–8). This was a formal co-production, for which Chhabra was listed as director and Kumar as choreographer in the production credits, with Watson retained as designer, and it introduced Rifco to the contractual side of production and employment substantially for the first time. The cast for the Theatre Royal co-production was Kumar, Raj Ghatak, Sunetra Sarker and Yasmin Wilde. In between the original workshop and the productions at Leicester and the Riverside, Kumar and Chhabra had performed for Tamasha in the original production of *Fourteen Songs …* from November 1998 to January 1999.

The question of a suitable second show coincided with this growing sense of structure, and a number of factors came together. Rifco needed a greater organisational presence, and working at Stratford East reminded Kumar of his link to *Moti Roti* and Keith Khan. Khan provided advice on applications for funding, on such factors as a mission statement, and introduced him to the Independent Theatre Company (ITC). But ultimately it was a contact made in India with Sony Entertainment Television that provided a grant of £15,000 and confirmed that the show would be Bollywood-based, ideal for the target audience of Sony ET's launch in the UK. For this Kumar was to provide a script, a radical step beyond his involvement in devising, but he was able to reflect on his experience of the Bollywood-orientation of the show *Moti Roti* and of Tamasha's *Fourteen Songs, Two Weddings and a Funeral* and aim more directly at the industry himself, through his own knowledge of it. The result was *Bollywood 2000*.

> This was an absolute spoof of the last three decades of Bollywood cinema all put together, with all the bigger stories. But commenting on the genre, and on the fact that the mother was very young, and you know, often in the film the mother looks younger than the hero … So I started to comment on all those things.
>
> [Kumar 2008]

Kumar acknowledges, significantly, that it was still a comedy revue rather than a play, but it had production values placed on it, since he brought in the Bollywood designer Pooja Shah for the three-week run at Riverside in October 2000, which was followed by performances in November at the Alhambra in Bradford, Derby Playhouse and the Centre in Slough

(**DVD 9–11**). In particular, he was able to explore the issue of audiences, and ran two performances on Sundays for families, as he explains:

> If you are from the Asian community, one thing that's really important is that when you go out together you're not going to be embarrassed with each other. Dad's not going to feel 'Oh my god, they're kissing!' or 'Oh my god, they're being too political!'. Family audiences don't want to be challenged in that way. They want to be entertained. And I knew that. And that's the start of Rifco's policy, I suppose, to entice that audience.
>
> We always do family tickets of five. And that's one thing we fight for every time we do a booking in the theatre ... Because that's our essential audience, we want to bring them in.
>
> [Kumar 2008]

The production was extremely successful, yet curiously Kumar went away from theatre to spend time working on films in India, largely because he felt over-stretched by the experience—'it was hard, hard graft'—and 'up against it', with the lack of institutional support. He was drawn back by an email from Tamasha notifying him of their Direct-Design training course, which he took in 2002, finding it gave him the sense of support he had been lacking. Subsequently he contacted Jon Fawcett once more at the Riverside, who was enthusiastic, and so planned a re-production of *Bollywood—Yet Another Love Story*, bringing in the designer Rachana Jadhav, whom he had met on the Tamasha course. His renewed confidence saw him through a successful application for £17,000 project funding from the Arts Council of England (ACE), and the show played at the Riverside in a four-week run from 20 March to 20 April 2003 with a cast of eight, with mid-week performances bringing in 'very diverse, very mixed audiences, and Friday, Saturday, Sunday ninety per cent British Asian' (**DVD 12–14**).

The script that is available from Rifco is of the revised version, *Bollywood—Yet Another Love Story*, from 2003. The characters are a purposefully and satirically generic assemblage of heroes and villains, with the heroic leads as flawed as the villains if not so violent, and the tone is set by the profiles assigned to each in the list of characters. So the mother, a widow, 'still wears her bloodstained shawl since her husband was killed twenty two and a half years ago', yet 'after twenty years of apparent celibacy, she needs the love of a man'. Similarly, the hero, who has all the requisite good looks and singing and dancing ability, 'has the IQ of a watering can', while the villains are caricatures and appropriately cowardly.[18] The plot includes the recognition of a lost twin brother of the hero alongside the statutory love story and a murderous finale worthy of *Hamlet*, and the

---

18 *Bollywood—Yet Another Love Story*, p. 1; script held by Rifco.

action is interlaced with live singing and dancing intercut with Bollywood film sequences and clips, with the song 'Raat Ke Humsafar' most prominent. Its strength lies not just in an adroit, theatrical sense of parody, but in a crisp management of comic dialogue, which is either briefly gratuitous or more carefully crafted to work our sense of character and parody. So, for example, there are sections that might come from any context from the British music hall forwards—

SHANTI: Wow, you've recovered quickly. And thank God you have changed. You look much better in your police uniform.
AJAY: Mother, have you seen a man?
SHANTI: I have not seen a man for twenty years.
AJAY: No, no. I mean a stranger.
SHANTI: Well, I don't mind a stranger either. But he must have a moustache ...

[*Bollywood*, scene 20]

—and others which work the relationship between characters to substantiate the Bollywood satire from a distinctly British Asian perspective, which was Kumar's objective. Here the heroine, Priya, is placed in a Bollywood flower garden with her companion Uma, who is there only because she is paid by Priya's father:

The Flower Garden. UMA is reading a book. PRIYA rushes in.

PRIYA: Oh Uma! I don't know what has happened to me. I keep skipping around the house. Every time the phone rings I run in slow motion. I keep looking in the mirror and smiling at myself ...
UMA: Shit yaar, did you take those white pills from my purse? They really aren't for beginners.
PRIYA: No Uma, don't you understand? I've fallen in love. I am happy! Can I sing another love song?
UMA: Not until I take one of those pills. Besides, you don't need me any more.
PRIYA: What? Why?
UMA: Because now you have Ajay, you can bore the crap out of him instead. Tell your pop I'm sorry, but the money's just not worth it.

[*Bollywood*, scene 9]

In fact, the dramaturgy of the parody creates rather more than a set of linked comic sketches. Despite the broad humour (as Kumar describes it), there is a consistency in the balance between recognition and debunking which stems from Kumar's own perceptions and experience.

> I was making cutting little jibes at Bollywood, because I'd probably got a bit bitter by now. I was going 'This is what it is like, you know this is what it is like.' Because I was giving my experience as a British Asian working in Bollywood. This is how women are treated ... You know you are not going to get a job, you're not going to get paid, and all these things I was putting in there, commenting on the genre and the industry.
>
> [Kumar 2008]

Yet despite the satisfactions and the success of the re-production, Kumar admits that he could see problems, and ironically increasing national recognition led him to negotiate a greater presence in his home town, Slough, through the Senior Arts Officer, Andy Lee. Lee found him a small sum to fund workshops in local schools, and Kumar began to give Bollywood workshops, showing a recording of the play. Very quickly he brought in Andy Kumar, the choreographer for all Rifco's work, to take on the workshops, and gradually these spread out from Slough across the country, with further funding from Arts and Business. It was this contact with schools and youth centres that prompted what Kumar calls 'the horrible issue of marriage', 'the huge umbrella term' of 'arranged marriage', something that he wished to avoid and battled against because everyone had been doing it for years.

> But it just wasn't going away. It was such a huge umbrella term in the British Asian community. It just wasn't disappearing. Everywhere I went I was confronted with all sorts of issues that related to this umbrella term, what we call 'arranged marriage'. So I came up with a story.
>
> And the first thing I did now, rather than me go ahead and do it on my own, was I applied for the development fund.
>
> [Kumar 2008]

The application was successful, and what Kumar did was to institute almost a mirror of the standard process followed by Tamasha, with an ACE-funded script development, workshops with actors, a great deal of research and development over a month talking to young people and to 'people in the elders' homes about wedding traditions'. The work was rehearsed in Slough, but the initial decision was made to remain independent.

> Because of the audiences we were getting, and because of the unique style of the work, I started to realise that we needed to build our own brand. And of course collaboration and support was important,

> but what I wanted to do was to develop the work first. I mean at the end of the development workshop with the actors and with the entire development team, we did do a sharing. And quite a few theatres came to see it, and we got offers straight away to book it.
>
> [Kumar 2008]

One of the results was a decision to co-produce with the Hawth in Crawley, which was mediated through Hardish Virk, who had been involved with Rifco's marketing and audience development since *Bollywood*. The Hawth was also supporting work with Man Mela at this time, and there were good reasons for taking the opportunity:

> We opened with the Hawth, Crawley. The reason that was a really good relationship was because they wanted to invest in the company, they wanted to invest in their local audiences, and they wanted to do something unique. And they also allowed me artistic freedom.
>
> [Kumar 2008]

The Deranged Marriage was from the beginning a sell-out show, and has retained that status through its two further re-productions. Its popularity rests in an inclusive attitude towards the auditorium, which makes the theatre into a shared space of community self-recognition and enhances the sense of shared time and experience with the characters in the progressive steps and stages of a wedding. The script itself works cleverly on this basis, by alternating the exposure of characters to the ritual formalities with their private angst, with the prospective bride and groom respectively hiding away under the stairs with a cigarette or moping, inconsolable, in the toilets. Kumar sums up its appeal:

> Basically the reason it was so successful is because the audience were treated like wedding guests. They were given orange juice occasionally, and a few Indian sweets. And the wedding-planner aunt would occasionally talk to them, and there would be photographs. The audience absolutely loved all that; it broke the fourth wall completely. It was like you were at the wedding, and I would hear audience members saying: 'What side are you on? Are you on the girl's side or the boy's side?' They started dressing up, coming in their best saris. It was an event, amazing. So it became a partnership with the audience.
>
> [Kumar 2008]

Kumar also believed that the play, despite its popular appeal, contained a challenge; more precisely, he suggests that he pursued a popular form because that was the way to make that challenge.

> I really want to challenge this community, to make them change a little bit. And I know that if I do something in a black box, dark, really hard-hitting, they're not going to come. By the third show it will be empty, or they'll be the theatre-going audience there—which is great, but then I'm not getting the core audience I want. So I've discovered there are certain ways I have to do it.

With *The Deranged Marriage* the challenge arises from Kumar's reaction, based on personal experience of the industry, to the aesthetics of Bollywood.

> Because I wanted to make it real, because by now I'm pissed off with Bollywood saying all this absolute crap that doesn't actually happen in real life. I'm saying let's use that genre but let's take it a bit further, let's start challenging people. That's what I work slowly, that's the journey, that's the Rifco Arts journey …

For Kumar, the challenge thematically was that the audience 'had to face a couple of demons in there, taboos', which were those of a widow remarrying and 'a gay groom being forced into a marriage'. These lost Rifco 'a couple of sponsors', and he confesses that he was 'petrified for the first few days, thinking "Oh my god, are we going to get burnt down?", because it could have gone that way': 'when a girl is dressed in red for her wedding, we dress her up as a goddess—that's what it means', and for this goddess to be seen smoking and drinking was 'out there and edgy'. But the challenging journey is also one of form, moving slowly away from the sketch-based song-and-dance entertainment of the stage shadowing Bollywood towards a drama, a narrative with characters. Kumar believes that *The Deranged Marriage* had moved some way along this route, although it remained 'a piece of entertainment' and was not yet a play.

Implicit in that description are its filmic qualities, part of that embrace of the audience that familiarises the theatre space by making it analogous to the cinema auditorium, or closes the experience down to a sense of the audio-visual watching-space at home. The script has seventy-nine scenes and is constructed like a story-board for a film, with great technical assurance in the integration of soundtrack, dancing sequences and projection. It has a classic Bollywood design, and is far less overtly and self-consciously satirical than the earlier *Bollywood—Yet Another Love Story*. The substantial portions of dialogue, reflecting Kumar's observations about a move towards drama, come with the disruption after the interval of the relentless progress of the traditional wedding, as a son stands up to his mother on behalf of his white wife, the bridegroom admits he is gay and a widow recognises her former heart-throb and remarries, replacing the prepared marriage. The whole conception dramatises and theatricalises the dialogue of British Asian experience with the fantasy of Bollywood without striving for the kind of parodic jokes that sustained *Bollywood*. In this short scene, the sympathetic uncle Bali, married to the formidable wedding-planner aunt, and his son Chaman are 'struggling with turban fabric':

BALI ties the turban on CHAMAN. It falls apart.

CHAMAN: Why we wearing turbans anyway?
BALI: It's a sign of celebration and pride. We are wearing pink, because we are on the girl's side.
CHAMAN: So what religion are we, exactly? I'm a bit confused.
BALI: You don't know? You should be ashamed. Well, your grandfather on my side was a Sikh and we went to the Gurudwara, and your grandfather on your mother's side was a Hindu and they went to the Temple, but my mother prayed to a great Fakir Baba, and she went to a mosque, while your mother's mother, well she thought she was god herself, and she went to a nutter's home. So you take your pick!
CHAMAN: And to make it easier, mum sent me to a Catholic school!
BALI: You can't say we didn't give you choices![19]

The Deranged Marriage ran through three productions from 2004 to 2006, starting at the Hawth on 1–4 September 2004, with a tour to the Nuffield in Southampton, Watermans, Warwick Arts Centre and The Drum in Birmingham, and finishing at the West Wing in Slough, during September and October 2004. It was revived for a second tour from late October into December in 2005, opening at the West Wing and going to Leicester Haymarket, Warwick Arts Centre, West Yorkshire Playhouse and Oxford Playhouse, before concluding with an extended run at the Riverside from 29 November to 24 December 2005. It was remounted during June and July 2006 at the Warwick Arts Centre, Theatre Royal Stratford East and the Theatre Royal Windsor (**DVD 15–21**). Its immediate success with audiences came at the point when Rifco was awarded the status of a Regularly Funded Organization by the ACE in 2005, a status renewed in 2008. While *The Deranged Marriage* provided income and greatly extended national awareness of the company, continuity was achieved with *Meri Christmas*, a script written by Harvey Virdi and derived indirectly from research and development on the previous production.

> With *The Deranged Marriage* we were doing a lot of work with the elders in the community, getting wedding songs, finding out why you

---

[19] *The Deranged Marriage*, scene 33, pp. 40–41; script held by Rifco.

> put henna on someone's hand. Why does the bride wear red? All those things came from the elders in the community. We ended up going to elders' residential homes, and that gave the elders a lot of value. Suddenly these people who are sitting there all day watching Zee TV were valued, and their opinion was valued. And from that came *Meri Christmas* which was set in a residential elders' home ...
>
> What we were really looking at was that those elders never had thought they were going to end up in a residential home, eating fish fingers and chips, because traditionally we look after our elders at home. Was this the downside of being British Asian? Were we starting to become too British Asian, and forgetting our roots? So that's the question that was posed, and it challenged our audience a bit too quickly after *The Deranged Marriage*.
>
> [Kumar 2008]

Meri Christmas fulfilled Kumar's ambition to move towards a play rather than an entertainment, and this was achieved by deploying a different writer, Harvey Virdi, who also acted the central role of Malkeet, a woman who waits to hear from her son and never does. Virdi had been an original member of the workshop group that had devised *Airport*, and had worked with Tamasha on *A Yearning* and *A Tainted Dawn*, itself a devised production. She had returned to be with Rifco on the revival of *The Deranged Marriage* in 2005, and in December 2005 she had shared with Janet Steel of Kali and Kumar a script she had started to write during the summer. In January 2006 she met Kumar:

> He said 'I have an idea for a play, Asian elders, maybe set in an old people's or elders' home ... There's four actors. Do you want to think about it, to write it?' And I said 'Can I write anything I like within that remit? I don't do madcap, Bhangra-comedy, and if you want that I know I'm not the right person, I can't write that stuff. It will probably be dark.' So I then spent January until March doing the research, going round Asian elders' places in East London and Kent, talking to people ... So all four stories are real, based on real people.[20]

Kumar's repeated term in describing Rifco's work is 'poignant', that element that departs from pure entertainment, providing a more sober background for those sharper challenges he wished to make, and Virdi is equally insistent on the serious moment even in comedy, the pathos of the performance. Virdi's script for *Meri Christmas* realises both poignancy and the artistic imperative of challenge, but is stripped of Rifco's previous Bollywood aesthetic. It is simply and economically naturalistic, highly

20 Harvey Virdi interviewed by Graham Ley, London, 17 December 2008.

suited to touring with a small cast of four, and the set is stable, representing the social sections of a residential home, the living room and television, the table and service kitchen, with garden doors to the rear. The whole play is haunted by absences, that of the owner whose voice is heard, and of the children who do not substantiate the lives of their deserted parents. It as if the British Asian experience has crashed down on Rifco's aesthetics, with the show's edgy stability presenting the end of escapism, which is confined to contact with a Pandit on the telephone and a malfunctioning television. Theatrically, the greatest shock comes when Amir assaults his elderly father, Rauf, as the financial pressures that lead him constantly to appear to ask for money prove too great for his veneer of concern. But the revelations in the continuing dialogue between Rauf and Malkeet are harsh, engaging the audience in a thoroughly troubling relationship between stage and auditorium. Rauf refuses to visit his son and daughter-in-law from bitter experience:

> RAUF: Amina did not know I was coming. Amir had forgotten to tell her. She opened the door and when she saw me her face fell. They were having a drinks party. She told me to sit in the living room. She said 'Don't you dare embarrass us in front of our friends'. I sat on their sofa. Not one sip of water, not one morsel of food passed my lips all day. …
> I asked my grandson to get me a glass of water. He swore at me and kicked my leg. His mother stood by and said nothing. This is not what I imagined when I held my son in my arms for the first time. He was so small. He came early, you know. His eyes were wide open. He stared straight at me. Defiant, even as a baby! I thanked God for giving us a son to look after us when we became old.[21]

Meri Christmas featured three actors who had performed in *The Deranged Marriage*, Rina Fatania, Rupi Lal and Harvey Virdi, with the addition of Rashied Karapiet. Virdi had written the role of Malkeet for an older actress, but three days before the production was due to open she was asked by Kumar in an emergency to take the part.

> So I turned up thinking 'What are the other actors going to say, how are they feeling?' But actually I came in the room and there were three faces beaming at me … I didn't know Malkeet's lines, but I knew where she was coming from. So actually it was just cramming.

21 *Meri Christmas*, scene 5, pp. 35 and 38; script held by Rifco.

> The rehearsal process is normally about finding the character. So I think I proved that to myself. You can learn lines for a play in three days, but what you don't do in three days is find the character: I was lucky because I had written the character, I knew her.
>
> [Virdi 2008]

Meri Christmas played in November and December 2006 at Watermans, Warwick Arts Centre, West Yorkshire Playhouse, Nuffield Theatre Leicester, Arts Depot in Finchley, Peepul Centre in Leicester and the West Wing in Slough; it was directed by Kumar (DVD 22–27).

Alongside *Meri Christmas*, Rifco ran a reminiscence project called 'Living History', funded by Heritage Lottery, which followed the pattern of similar projects in concentrating on the memories of first generation South Asians in Britain, and had involved schoolchildren going in to work with the elders in residential homes (DVD 28–29). *Meri Christmas* had presented the experience of the older generation in an uncompromising manner, but Kumar wished to work harder at actually drawing the first generation into the theatre itself. This affected the genesis of the following production, *There's Something about Simmy*:

> I started to feel that we're doing lots of lovely work, and the audiences are full of what I call second generation. But the first generation weren't coming in. So I started to go to a lot of language theatre, where it was predominantly first generation, asking myself 'Why are they not coming to see our shows?' And it was language, because a lot of first generation still do not have great English.
>
> So we decided to go with Punjabi, because Pakistanis speak Punjabi and Indians speak Punjabi ... And that's where *Simmy* really came from. I really wanted to do something in language, and with *Simmy* thirty per cent is in Punjabi.
>
> [Kumar 2008]

Rifco then invested in a surtitling machine, to maintain accessibility, which accompanied the production in all venues, while the script itself featured a young girl brought to Britain to be married who acquires a grasp of the English language as the play progresses. Initially, Kumar resisted a return to the entertainment mode of earlier productions, but was finally induced to include two songs, and the play maintains a feel-good factor by replacing a wayward bridegroom with a more sympathetic brother in Simmy's sincere affections. So although the drift to a naturalistic form is continued, the reintroduction of a comic style, the arranged marriage theme and the size of the cast, at ten, all reflect a enduring debt to the taste of Bollywood, with the script itself marked as being 'based on an original screenplay by Pravesh Kumar and Apurva Asrani', the editor with whom Kumar had worked in India. What Simmy is able to do is to probe the values and sense of identity of a British Asian family, working particularly on the son, who feels he is British rather than Punjabi. *Simmy* opened at the Theatre Royal Stratford East on 7 September 2007 for a four-week run before touring to Contact Manchester, Theatre Royal Windsor, West Yorkshire Playhouse, Nuffield Southampton, Arts Depot in Finchley and Warwick Arts Centre in October–November 2007 (**DVD 30–37**).

Rifco has grown out of two important strains that have affected British Asian theatre since the last decade of the twentieth century: the deep-rooted influence of Bollywood and the institutional support for audience development, notably in relation to British Asian communities. As a consequence, Kumar has sustained and developed the company by being resolutely audience-led, using his own experience of production to combine ACE funding with commercial sponsors and enviable box-office receipts. But, in its first ten years, Rifco also relied on a sense of an aesthetic journey to guide it, one which interrogated the Bollywood obsession while successfully translating it into theatre at the same time as probing British Asian audiences with challenges that an ideal fantasy would pass by. Those issues of form and reception will undoubtedly continue to dominate its future.

[GL]

14

Rasa Theatre

Rasa Theatre was founded by Rani Moorthy in 1998 and came to prominence through the multiple performances of Moorthy's one-woman shows, notably *Pooja* and *Curry Tales*. But the company has also been constituted through a range of contributory skills from others in the business of production, design, audio-visual expertise and choreography, and Moorthy has not acted in all Rasa productions. Moorthy herself is a performer, dramaturg and writer, whose background is unusual in the context of British Asian theatre, and who brought established skills with her when she came to Britain.

Rajana Ganesh Moorthy is from an educated Sri Lankan Tamil family in Malaysia. She was born in the early 1960s, and her childhood was severely affected by the political and ethnic conflicts of the region. With the rise of Malay nationalism and the inter-racial violence that erupted in 1969, the family chose to move south in 1970 from Kuala Lumpur to Johor Baharu, the border town just across from the independent state of Singapore. Ethnicity became emphasised for Moorthy in a series of developments. She and her family felt themselves to be Indian within an assertive Malay culture; then the impact of the Islamic revolution in Iran from 1979 began to mark Hindu from Muslim; and in the early 1980s the war in Jaffna and Sri Lanka sharpened her identity as a Tamil. She went to school across the border in Singapore, going out from home with a passport every day, and gained an increasing sense of being in a minority in both countries.[1]

Her father was a teacher, with left-wing views and a scholarly interest in Shakespeare, and her parents believed strongly in education and any involvement for their daughter in drama at school. Moorthy herself trained as a teacher, and she started to write plays for children as one aspect of a continuing interest in theatre that was acceptable both socially and to her parents and family, with her plays recognised by the Ministry of Education and some winning awards. But she also became involved, 'undercover' as she

---

1 This and subsequent biographical and professional information is provided by Rani Moorthy, interviewed by Sarah Dadswell and Chandrika Patel, Exeter, 1 March 2006.

puts it, from 1987 in a company in Singapore called Theatre Works, which she regards as the 'most innovative' in the region. Theatre Works catered for an elitist audience, whom Moorthy characterises as 'middle-class, very wealthy, liberal education, Oxbridge types, educated either in the UK or in America, ex-lawyers', and played in the up-market Victoria Theatre. The plays were typically adaptations of modern classics, with a centenary production of Strindberg's *Miss Julie* in which the servants were Indian and Miss Julie was Chinese, and one of O'Neill's *A Long Day's Journey into Night* in which the family was Indian. There was also a more extraordinary production that played at the World Trade Centre in Singapore, financed by American Express, and was called *Mixed Signals*, which had Moorthy as an Indian girl meeting a Chinese man. The play was quietly poking fun at social engineering and eugenics:

> Graduate women were delaying marriage and were not producing children, not propagating themselves. So we had this social development unit, which is a bit like the Orwellian Ministry of Love, where graduate men, engineers were brought together, because they were too shy, with women in the humanities who were too strong and funny. ... And they still have this, I think, social engineering and love boats and love cruises.
>
> [Moorthy 2006]

It was in Singapore that Moorthy met her husband, Arthur Smith, who came out to teach the Singapore Film Unit how to film drama. Her frustrations with the limitations of Singapore theatre, and her own socially and financially compromised position within it, led her to leave and come to the UK. She studied for an MPhil in Theatre in Education in Manchester, where Smith was based, during 1990–91, but ironically returned to Singapore in 1993 on an invitation from the government to lead a new theatre department. The paradox with this initiative was that there was to be no drama in the curriculum, and so her students could specialise only if they went on to teach in the elite schools. She returned to Manchester in June 1996, ostracised by her family for marrying Arthur Smith and without a sense that she could readily connect with the larger Asian communities of the Manchester conurbation. She spoke none of the North Indian languages, such as Urdu or Punjabi, and felt relatively isolated in being Tamil and Malaysian.

Moorthy's first show in the UK, with which Rasa Theatre came into being, was born from a cumulative anger that came with distance and a sense of painful independence. The anger grew from the refusal of her family to welcome her marriage and the limitations placed on her self-realisation as a performer and theatre practitioner. She began to articulate those feelings in a script, but the stimulus and opportunity came to her by chance. North

West Arts in Manchester had ring-fenced money for culturally diverse work, and Moorthy heard about the scheme at a party. The deadline was the following week, but she obtained the form and made an application, sending the small part of a script that she had. She was awarded £6,000, which was intended not just for script development but for production. She was also helped by incidental local contacts. The Arden School of Theatre offered her free rehearsal space and mentioned that there were students who would like to be involved, and those young men built the whole set between them. Her designer was a friend, Elaine Brett, who was an installation artist, and that prompted the decision to provide a constructed stage environment for a piece that was centred in Tamil and Hindu 'ritual', which is the meaning of *Pooja*, with what Moorthy calls 'a whole temple'. The show has been revived almost annually by Moorthy since 1999, and has toured throughout the UK and abroad, to Kuala Lumpur in January 2002 and Sri Lanka in March 2003, but after Sri Lanka the set was scaled down to the portico of a temple.[2]

The script of *Pooja* is totally designed for solo performance, with Moorthy herself playing twelve characters, the central of whom is herself at different ages from childhood to a symbolic moment of mature independence at the close of the play. She crosses gender as her uncle, with white suit and comic moustache, and ages to portray her grandmother on video. Smith took charge of the filming of the video sequences for back projection in the production, which punctuate the live performance; in one instance, Moorthy as herself converses with her performance as the recorded grandmother. In the remodelled, post-Sri Lanka touring production, which was directed by Celia Banner, a horoscope grid occupies the central floorspace, with a screen for projection behind it, the temple portico to stage right and a small table used for minimal costume changes to stage left. The soundtrack was by Jaydev Mistry and the performance was directed by Celia Banner. It opened at the Green Room in Manchester over 22–24 April 1999, subsequently playing at the Octagon, Bolton over 21–22 May 1999, and was revived for a week-long run in June 2000 at the Library Theatre in Manchester. In 2002, Moorthy took *Pooja* to Kuala Lumpur for ten days in January and to the Edinburgh Festival for three weeks in August. A tour to Sri Lanka in March 2003 was funded by the British Council, and there were performances in February in Loughborough and in October in Chester. In 2004 there was an Arts Alive rural tour of *Pooja* in Hereford and Shropshire in May, with further performances in Wolverhampton in March, Keswick, Reading and Bolton in May and Watermans in Brentford in June. There was a further short tour to Sale, Coventry, West Bromwich and Cheltenham in November 2005, and performances in Bath in January 2006 (**DVD 1 and 2**).

---

2 There is no programme available for *Pooja*.

The scale of *Pooja*, and its conception as a one-woman show might be explained by economy, but Moorthy locates its rationale firmly elsewhere, in that connection with anger and an insistence on personal identity:

> *Pooja* was about my point of view … I wanted to say 'Yes, it is my experience, and yes, I'm going to play the men in my life, too'. Because it's my voice, it strongly has to be my voice. I was just so aware that I didn't want any other voice or element in this whole show.
>
> [Moorthy 2006]

Moorthy carries the performance as a narrator and its central character, addressing the audience and keeping them amused with comic comments and character portrayals. She traces her willingness to engage with audiences to her experience as a teacher, and the performance is an exercise in removing the fourth wall. Although the set, the minimal props, the costume changes and the video projections of characters provide the apparent texture, the show actually works on the interplay between Moorthy's ebullient and comic engagement of the audience and her equally powerful indignation at the lifelong attempt to ensnare her as a woman, through the coercion of ritual. The other characters act clearly for the audience as the voices she carries in her head. The premise is that her birth time was miscalculated for the horoscope, and so her progress to maturity was charted as a kind of apology through ritual for her supposedly doomed disadvantages, culminating in a ritual marriage to a banana tree, which in the original production was constructed in full from fibre-glass, revealing its absurdly sexual characteristics (DVD 3). In the finale, Moorthy conducts her own '*pooja* of liberation', by pouring water from a pot over her face, in an imitation but also a rejection of the pouring of milk over her head at the time of her puberty (DVD 4). Yet, although there is a strong line and sense of direction in *Pooja*, some of the cameos are remarkable in themselves: one a recorded projection of her cousin contrasting her life as a Tamil Tiger, another a live portrayal of a Chinese woman recounting how her feet were bound in preparation for her to become a concubine for a rich man (DVD 5). Moorthy's anger is not confined to her own path to independence, but she admits to self-censorship in cutting the Tamil Tiger sequence when she took the show to Sri Lanka.

Manchester United and the Malay Warrior was conceived to bridge the gap between post-colonial Malaysia and the city of Manchester, with Manchester known to young Malaysians solely as the home of the football team and Malaysia evoked through its own form of 'Asian' martial arts. There were official cultural visits by North West Arts to arts organisations in Kuala Lumpur between the Commonwealth Games in Kuala Lumpur in 1998 and the next Games in Manchester in 2002. Moorthy became involved in these, and during one of the meetings Moorthy met Marion D'Cruz, an old friend from her theatre days in Singapore and Malaysia, who was artistic co-director of the Five Arts Centre in Kuala Lumpur. As a Malaysian living in Manchester, Moorthy had a germ of an idea for a fantasy quest based on a Malaysian myth. D'Cruz seemed interested, and Moorthy wrote a short outline and presented it to the Five Arts Centre on a family visit to Malaysia in July 2000. Moorthy had first worked with the director Krishen Jit in the early 1980s, and Jit was an Associate Professor of Malaysian Theatre at the University of Malaysia as well as an authority on traditional Malay arts. Moorthy wanted to introduce elements of the traditional Malaysian court theatre *bangsawan* and the martial arts form *silat* into a contemporary story set in Manchester. Rasa's production manager Ed Higginson and Moorthy made preliminary visits to the Five Arts Centre in 2001 and early 2002, and then embarked on a series of workshops leading to rehearsals in April–May 2002. Unfortunately, actors who started in the workshops and on whose abilities Moorthy based her play either dropped off or had other projects when it came to the rehearsal period. In the resultant production all the artistic staff still came from Malaysia, with the exception of the actress Romy Baskerville.

Manchester United and the Malay Warrior played at the Five Ways Centre in Kuala Lumpur in May 2002 and at the Contact Theatre in Manchester in June 2002, as part of the Cultural Festival accompanying the Commonwealth Games held in Manchester and as an international venture received funding from the British Council and sponsorship from Malaysia Airlines. The production had a lavish design by Bayu Utomo Radjikin, with broad, angular gauzes at the rear used for multiple back-projected images and video sequences throughout, recorded and compiled by Smith, with figures often in dialogue with live performers. The onstage set was simple by contrast, using white moveable seating and consoles to accommodate actors in relatively undefined, mythical locales and a recurrent setting of a cyber-café.

The core of the plot was the chance meeting of a woman pensioner, Alice (played by Baskerville), with a young Malaysian student Kamal (played by Mohamad Arifwaran) in a cyber-café in Manchester. Kamal feels he is a disappointment to his mother, and Alice is haunted by her own memories of her time in Malaya during the emergency, when she was married unhappily to a British officer who died in the fighting. But the production received its distinctive energy from an ensemble portraying the entourage of a court, led by the mythical warrior Hang Tuah, who is profoundly dissatisfied in his failure to find the missing Sultan to whom he owes binding allegiance. Hang Tuah was played by Adlin Aman Ramlie, a Malaysian screen superstar, and the ensemble was vigorously choreographed throughout by Mohamad Arifwaran, with displays and expressions of the physical prowess of the Malaysian martial art *silat*. The thread between the two storylines is inevitably rather tenuous, perhaps more obvious in elements of a conception than in production: so the Jin that has abducted the Sultan, whom we see and hear projected, taunting the live performers, is in some way connected to the idea of Manchester United as the 'red devils', their popular name. Similarly tenuous is the idea of football as a warrior-activity, while Kamal as a Malaysian United supporter seems to share frustrations about achievement and personal honour with Hang Tuah (**DVD 6**). Ultimately, the strong production values appear to triumph over the coherence of the whole, and the play becomes marooned in a set of unresolved possibilities as the mythical past emerges, perhaps as a computer game, in the modern city (**DVD 7**).

Dancing within Walls is a classically conceived three-hander, a realist and character-based drama of relationships written by Moorthy with an almost tragic touch in its conclusion. Moorthy had worked on Euripides' *Medea* in Singapore with Theatre Works, and the three actors, the brilliant conception of doubling roles applied to one of them, and the effect of the music and dancing in an evocation of a chorus are all strong elements of a Greek tragic form. So is the central theme, which is the flawed decision and attempt to reform and refine the Tamil temple dance-form of Bharata Natyam in a period just before the independence of India from British rule. All three figures in the play are tragic, if that is not understood to mean melodramatic. The root of the play came from Moorthy's strong recollections of the honour paid in Singapore to the memory of the founder of the Kalakshetra School of 'reformed' Bharata Natyam, Rukmini Devi Arundale, and the play emerged through a series of three development sessions and two readings held at the Contact Theatre in 2003, with close assistance from the dramaturg Eileen Murphy. Devi's husband was the theosophical scholar George Arundale, himself a disciple of Annie Besant, and his drive for the adequate expression of his beliefs is an aspiration that is seen to intertwine with his wife's desire to realise herself through dance. The idealistic and transcendent qualities of theosophy, rooted in core Hindu spirituality, potentially belittle the actual achievements of individuals fascinated by it, and this sense of doomed failure also haunts his wife's pursuit of a purified and idealistic but Indian dance-form. The suggestion of the play is that husband and wife are both in denial of their sensuality, if not of their sexual lives, and the contrast is with the proponent of the unreformed Bharata Natyam, Yellama, for whom sensuality and sexuality are both expressed in her role as a *devadasi*, a dancer and a temple prostitute.

The production moves through dialogue scenes between George and Rukmini, and Rukmini and her resultant *guru*, Yellama, in pursuit of what becomes Rukmini's ambition both to perform and to change the ethos of this traditional dance, on the eve of a new India. Permeating the whole is dancing, either in the form of practised steps, of training, or of dancing performed. In the second part of the play, Rukmini in turn experiences the quiet rejection of her discipline and its principles by a young trainee dancer, Ruth, who eventually leaves the school Rukmini has founded. Both Yellama and Ruth are played by Shobna Gulati, a trained dancer more familiar to the audience from acting roles in British television series, and both characters appear in the second part, adding to our sense of the confusions and doubts shaking Rukmini since the death of her supportive husband. The design of the production by Rachana Jadhav sets up a tension between the domesticity of the world of books and bookcases in George's study on one side and the presence of the temple to the other, with all that implies about tradition, religious practice and the material lives of the *devadasi* (**DVD 8 and 9**). But that tension is then complicated as the temple transforms itself, in the second part, to the façade of the School that Rukmini founds, with the implication that it is devoid of satisfaction for those now taught within it (**DVD 10**). The choreography was subtle; it was by Gitanjali Kolanad, who herself trained at Rukmini's School, Kalakshetra, and was known to Moorthy from Singapore. The Tamil music was composed by Manickam Yogeswaran and recorded, with Mohamed Assani playing sitar live onstage. Moorthy had discussed her requirements with Yogeswaran, and the music at times underscored emotions, and at times accompanied dance, serving implicitly as a beautifully skilled commentary mocking Rukmini's modernising impulse. The production was directed by Iqbal Khan and played at the Contact Theatre for ten days in December 2003, with Christopher Wright as George Arundale and Thushani Weerasekera as Rukmini Devi.

Earlier in 2003 Rasa Theatre had become a regularly funded organisation under the Arts Council of England (ACE) (North West Arts), and the association of Higginson with Moorthy from the outset as producer had seen the active scheduling of *Pooja*, funded tours to Malaysia and Sri Lanka, support from diverse sources of funding, prominence in the Cultural Festival for the Commonwealth Games in Manchester, and an impressive showcase, again for Rani and *Pooja*, at the Edinburgh Festival. *Dancing Within Walls* was a meticulous production with which to celebrate this new status, but Higginson continued to promote tours of *Pooja* during 2003 and 2004, across the period in which *Curry Tales* was being developed. There could be no doubt that the success of *Pooja* was rooted in Moorthy's charisma as a performer, her ability to entertain and engage an audience directly and openly, and that the longevity of *Pooja* was the core success of Rasa Theatre. So in pursuing the development of that direct link with her audience in a new production, the theme of curry seemed to offer an immediacy that had also been apparent to other British Asian practitioners.[3]

---

[3] Jatinder Verma had regularly used curry as an illustration of the 'Binglishing' of British culture, and Naushaba Shaheen Khan and Sudha Bhuchar had chosen it for *Balti Kings* in 1999, the first production with a British setting researched, developed and written by Tamasha.

The preparation of foodstuffs for ritual purposes was a repeated element in *Pooja*, with the colour and sensuality of the food contrasting with the containment of the sexuality of the living person. *Pooja* had used Moorthy's performing persona to present her story, but along the way it had offered a vehicle for her delight in character portrayals. These she could script with humour and pathos, but she also found them a ready vehicle for satire and for biting commentary at times, both of which clearly had a direct appeal to live audiences. This resource, of stepping in and out of given characters in a general, staged context provided by a binding theme was something that was carried over into the resultant *Curry Tales*. It was evident that a one-woman show could be toured effectively, and retained over time, and this was the way to reach the range of audiences that were not necessarily available just in the Manchester area. Besides, Moorthy liked cooking, and the name of her company not only suggested the broad aesthetic theories of the Sanskrit poetic treatise the *Natyasastra*, in which the *rasas* encompass the full range of human emotions ideally experienced by a theatre audience, but also the metaphor of the admixture of 'taste' (the literal meaning of rasa) in cooking from which the concept of *rasa* was drawn in the treatise. To make that metaphor live, to draw it out as a social ritual that crossed boundaries of ethnicity, was a simple but decisive step. Not a performance about curry, but a performance with curry, about those who were preparing it, and their feelings for those for whom they were preparing it, and so resolutely a performance about women.

The experience of five years led to another meticulous production. The designer, Jadhav, was carried forwards from *Dancing within Walls*, Smith provided the contextual back projection, some of it of the live preparation of the food, and Mistry again composed the musical score, as he had for *Pooja*.[4] The design of a kitchen with modular units was compact and adaptable, giving Moorthy a base from which to come forward, towards and into the audience, and to which to return. It located the successive characters to a degree, although much was achieved within the script, and Moorthy was completely at ease with the cooking apparatus that it contained. The script had advanced from the character sketches of *Pooja* to short one-hander scenes, with an impression of brash confidence at the start gradually undermined by successive characters and their deprivation or pain, but culminating in the affirmation of the power of the female goddess of food, Anapurna. The choice of subjects reflected Moorthy's leading experience: a Chinese Malaysian, a victim like her family of the race-riots, with a son who has married an Indian, and a Tamil beggar, who confronts the audience mildly but provocatively with her poverty and the barrier of language (**DVD 11**). Added to these were a childless and possibly infertile

---

4 Mistry had also worked within the region for Peshkar, on *The Masala Girls* and *Just before the Rain*.

British Asian woman, professional, married and oppressed by her position in two families; an ebullient Delhi coffee-house owner; and a Trinidadian cooking for revenge in a voodoo culture (**DVD 12**). The chosen format does suggest, notably with Smith's back projections of cooking, the ambience of the television cookery show recorded in front of a live audience. The preparation of the food occasionally involves members of the audience, and food is offered and shared, while the beggar creates a stir by looking into handbags. But the true audience engagement is address, an acknowledgement that runs throughout the production, and in which Moorthy clearly delights.

Curry Tales opened with a three-week run at the Edinburgh Festival in August 2004, building on the success of *Pooja* at Edinburgh in 2002, and subsequently played in September at the Library Theatre in Manchester and the Lyric Studio in Hammersmith, London (**DVD 13–16**). It was directed by Linda Marlowe and toured widely across the UK in 2005 and 2006, forming part of the Villages in Action scheme in Devon in 2006, following the Arts Alive rural tour of *Pooja* in 2004. In February 2008 it was given a five-week run at the Market Theatre in Johannesburg, going on from there to the Harare International Festival of Arts in Zimbabwe in April–May on the invitation of its director Manuel Bagorro, who had seen the show at its opening in Edinburgh in 2004.[5] Moorthy also received British Council funding for a tour to Mauritius in January 2009.

Between them, *Pooja* and *Curry Tales* launched Moorthy as a stage personality, reaching diverse audience across the UK and overseas and overtly dealing with issues of identity, ethnicity, post-colonial conflicts and diaspora. Her background and the sources of her inspiration were very different from those of the majority of British Asians, and British Asian practitioners, yet, being based in Manchester, she was in reach of significant British Asian communities, even if they were not her targeted audiences. In 2006 Rasa Theatre produced *Too Close to Home* in association with the Library Theatre and the Lyric, Hammersmith. It opened at the Lyric in November for ten days and moved to the Library Theatre for five days, then on to the Peepul Centre in Leicester and the Clocktower in Croydon, closing in three performances at the Warwick Arts Centre. The play was a realist drama, written by Moorthy, about a British Asian family in an undisclosed 'northern' town, with an elder son who has embraced Islam in the mosque, and a younger son whom all fear has followed in the footsteps of the young bombers of 7 July 2005. In many respects, the play is typical of those dramas that have explored generational conflicts within British Asian families. The males here take the limelight, around a long-suffering mother (played by

5 Moorthy wrote about this experience in 'Curry, but not for Uncle Bob', a piece published on the Sustained Theatre website run by ACE. It was published 6 October 2008: sustained theatre.org.uk/en/debate/view/169.

Moorthy herself) and the unattached sister of the father, who may have had an affair with the elder son before his marriage, which now tortures them both in different ways. What Moorthy brings to this as a scriptwriter is sympathy and understanding for all parties, and the play received strong direction again from Iqbal Khan and a striking design, once again, from Jadhav. Shiv Grewal, a regular actor for Tamasha and well-known from film, television and radio, took the role of the father, Ghulam, a teacher who is now disturbed by terrifying dreams and lost in the world of his beloved mystical poet, Rumi. Sartaj Garewal took the part of the elder son, Sayeed, and Dharmesh Patel that of the younger son, Saleem, with Stephanie Street as the father's sister, Raziya (**DVD 17–22**). Moorthy is clear that she drew on her own background in Malaysia for a sense of the impact of a radical vision of Islam on a younger generation in a colonial culture. The play's overt message is that the rucksack that is fixed in the audience's minds for much of the action is rejected in horror by the elder son, representing the mosque, as it is by the terrified and distressed parents.

Moorthy has combined distinctive skills as a script-maker of what she terms 'conventional, narrative plays' [Moorthy 2006] with a kind of performance art that engages immensely diverse audiences with fascination and amusement tempered by reflection. She has now established her reputation very much as a performer of one-woman shows, and this profile was extended in 2007 with *Shades of Brown*; but Rasa Theatre in its formation was a strange combination of two distinct approaches to theatre-making. Its success is attributable not just to Moorthy's remarkable talent but also to the skills of those regularly or repeatedly involved in production. [GL]

Conclusion

It would be unwise to draw expansive conclusions about British South Asian theatres for the simple reason that they are continuing and evolving. But from the evidence presented here it is plain that the foundation of Tara Arts marks a crucial turning point in British theatre history, introducing new terms of reference which eventually encourage the emergence of centrally funded Asian-led professional companies. In the section on the early years of Tara Arts a degree of emphasis was placed on the political and social circumstances of its foundation; but it is important to add that it is one of a number of related developments in representation through the arts that belong to the same period. Naseem Khan's report, written at that time, noted the establishment of the Bharatiya Vidya Bhavan in 1973 and the Asian Youth Festival and the Centre of Indian Arts in 1975, alongside the opening of the Mandeer restaurant and its performance space by Ramesh Patel in 1974. If Tara in its early days steered its activities away from the traditional South Asian arts, notably those of music and dance, then these too were finding a firmer basis in precisely the same period in Britain.

What was distinctive about Tara Arts was not only its decision to explore representation theatrically but the fact that its founding members implicitly brought pressure to bear on both sides of the contentious term 'British Asian'. Tara's constant concern in its opening years was with the broad question of what it meant to be 'Asian' in Britain 'now', and as a result it began to produce versions of what might be 'British Asian' theatre. This, alongside the characteristics of funding, professionalism and Asian-led initiatives in theatre, has remained a central concern, subject to an immense variety of interpretations by practitioners, either explicitly or implicitly. Tara also brought two further, linked, aspects into the frame: it was founded for and by the young, and launched itself into representation without a prior orientation in traditional training. The ambition to achieve professional status was to be a gradual influence within the development of what might with some justice be called a theatre movement.

The period of initiative following the foundation of Tara Arts sustains a resolute dramaturgical emphasis on the experience of what it meant to be Asian in Britain. The absence of this emphasis on the British Asian experience is a distinctive feature of the history of the South Asian-language theatres in Britain, for which we have provided only indicative evidence. Visiting and touring productions work alongside UK-generated productions within language communities, which themselves form part of a wider cultural context of association for the communities concerned. Theatre production is embedded, for the most part, in a different aspect of the experience of being a British Asian, which relates strongly to the diaspora notion of 'imaginary homelands', in Salman Rushdie's telling phrase. Such productions were and are performed by the community for the community, and have no intention of facing outwards. This has remained the case even in those few instances when language-theatre companies have been formed with the specific aim of dramatising the contemporary UK experience.

This general historical interpretation of British South Asian theatres could be aligned with the broad and possibly misleading notion of generations. It is commonplace to talk of the first generation and the second generation (and now beyond) within the communities, and it is hard not to conclude that the development that begins with Tara is the work of a second generation, which found 'itself' radically reorientated to the extent that it now felt the need to invent itself in cultural terms. Those who founded Tara were just past further or higher education in the UK, and their attention on what it meant to be an Asian in Britain fell firmly on the experience of youth, on which by that time they were reflecting. They were joined by younger people, and the search for appropriate means of expression, for appropriate material, became a major dramaturgical enterprise alongside an attendant search for an appropriate aesthetic. That dual quality encompasses most of the conscious achievements of the movement to the present day.

The early history of Tara's initiatives in these two strands of enquiry and activity reveals a constant dilemma of how to relate to traditional material, but one that is effectively eclipsed by a reliance on varieties of satirical or agitated naturalism. In a curious way, this pattern is matched in the theatrical work of the Hounslow Arts Cooperative, which played with the *Ramayana* and science fiction before settling on the stark, *noir* dramas of Parv Bancil. The satirical revue played a considerable part in the early years of both groups, and it carried itself through to considerable influence in the developments at Watermans in the 1990s, which broke into national profiles for a number of performers. But within a decade Tara had achieved a remarkable synthesis, by inventively selecting aspects of traditional South Asian performance that could be applied as an aesthetic otherwise unseen on the British stage. The approach was first tested on a Sanskrit classic drama, *Miti Ki Gadi*, but it went on to form the basis—with considerable variation—of Tara's numerous European adaptations in the decades that follow, and has a close relationship to the concept of 'Binglish' production advanced conceptually and polemically by Jatinder Verma. Some aspects of that development will be traced in the companion volume to this history, *Critical Essays on British South Asian Theatre*.

This synthesis depended on the application of skills from those immersed in distinctive kinds of performance, but who were sufficiently flexible to be able to provide a basic training to actors who had not had the benefit of a formal training. The early initiatives in British Asian theatre had come from people who on their own acknowledgement were utterly inexperienced. Raj Patel and Dhirendra brought training and experience together for the brief history of British Asian Theatre early in the 1980s. During 1984, Shobana Jeyasingh and Anuradha Kapur brought to the actors in Tara a primer of movement and presentation that was economical, disciplined and fluid. From that time, training began to have a considerable impact on the British Asian companies, and the impact of Harmage Singh Kalirai, who had trained with Lecoq in Paris, on the development of work across a number of companies during the 1980s and into the 1990s was extensive, as the accounts in this book incidentally reveal. Similarly, Rita Wolf, who had worked with the Royal Court Young People's Theatre, brought professional skills to two key moments in the history of British Asian theatre: the launch of Tara as a professional enterprise in the early 1980s, when she formed part of the first ensemble, and the foundation of Kali at the end of the decade as a company that united professional skills in performance with the nurturing of Asian women playwrights. Wolf had previously performed in three productions by Asian Cooperative Theatre, including the inaugural *Vigilantes*, and worked on administration with Harmage Singh Kalirai.

But British Asian theatre was its own training in this early period for most of its members, although professional actors were at times involved, or led significant initiatives, as did Madhav Sharma with Actors Unlimited. That situation changed drastically at the time of the foundation of Tamasha in the late 1980s, since both Kristine Landon-Smith and Sudha Bhuchar had by then considerable experience as actors, with Landon-Smith also developing skills as a director. Bhuchar had acted for years with Tara Arts, which had become professional for some of its productions from 1982. Professional status also meant that actors such as Naushaba Shaheen Khan and Paul Bhattacharjee would move forward to careers that had developed out of involvement in British Asian theatre, but flourished elsewhere. For many years after Tamasha's foundation, Landon-Smith and Bhuchar worked professionally in other capacities in order to sustain their consistent work with Tamasha: the path from inexperience to professional status is an integral part of the history of the movement. In the early 1990s Kali Theatre conducted theatre skills workshops as a clear objective for the company alongside their profile in script development, while the Asian Theatre School aimed to lift its members, if that was their ambition, through skills workshops to an enhanced level of performance. In the new millennium Tamasha has made a professional training programme a major part of its profile.

Curiously, writing for the theatre has not been a major part of the professional development achieved within British Asian theatre, with the notable and absolute exception of Kali, co-founded by the writer Rukhsana Ahmad with Rita Wolf and set up for the reading, development and production of work by British Asian women playwrights. Tara Arts has rarely been a significant vehicle for new writing, while Hounslow Arts Cooperative (HAC)'s almost total reliance on Bancil's trenchant plays in the 1980s and Asian Cooperative Theatre (ACT)'s realisation of Farrukh Dhondy's scripting received pitiful support from funders. Tamasha has worked rather more from adaptations than it has from original scripts, and this has seen Bhuchar in particular develop dramaturgical skills that also characterised Verma strongly in Tara's early years, and have characterised Pravesh Kumar with Rifco (the Reduced Indian Film Company) and Madani Younis with Asian Theatre School and then Freedom Studios. Man Mela moved to a high point of dramaturgical initiative in the *Cornershop* trilogy of 2000, but British Asian playwrights, of whom Tanika Gupta may be the most prominent example, have largely succeeded outside the confines of British Asian theatres. As a result, they have featured relatively little in this history of Asian-led companies, despite their considerable presence in contemporary British theatre. Amongst them are Hanif Kureishi, Meera Syal, Harwant Bains, Maya Chowdhry, Dolly Dhingra, Amber Lone, Shamshad Khan, Ash Kotak and Gurpreet Kaur Bhatti.

The prominence of dramaturg–directors in British Asian theatre may be attributed to the difficulty of establishing and developing theatre forms that were distinctive enough to attract funding to the companies, or in the harshest terms to ensure their survival at all. Kali Theatre would seem to form a notable exception, with varied input in direction and dramaturgy in the formative years. The choice of material and its alliance to a distinctive aesthetic may sound obvious prerequisites for any initiative or company, and there can be no doubt that in many cases there has been substantial input from a wide group or from significant members of it. But the history of British Asian theatres for the most part demonstrates the need to advance a distinctive aesthetic, and to maintain it, to create a profile that will attract and sustain funding. For Tamasha, this started as an open-stage naturalism, and has continued in various forms of naturalism that on many occasions offered an evocative visual setting for reflections on diaspora. Accordingly, Tamasha's designer Sue Mayes has been an instrumental figure, and significantly has remained with the company from the earliest days of its existence. A similar relationship pertains with Asian Theatre School, whose assertive naturalism has been designed by Lesley Ferris from the beginning, and Tara has had an associate designer for many years in Claudia Meyer, with Magdalen Rubalcava influential before that time. Rifco varies some key members of its production team, but the aesthetic is lavish and plainly allied to an ironic evocation of a Bollywood feel when it is not reliant on naturalism, as it was for the exceptional *Meri Christmas*, by the actor and writer Harvey Virdi.

Funding dictates the scale of operation and the possible production values, and with some few exceptions British Asian theatre has been dependent on public funding, from the tiniest of grants to the relative comforts of the status of a regularly funded organisation. The result has been the contentious confinement of Asian-led companies, even in security, to the small or middle scale. Some companies started as community projects, although the precise history differs. Peshkar was an initiative by the Oldham arts officer Aziz Zeria, whereas the Asian Theatre School was set up by Red Ladder Theatre Company from Leeds with funding from the Foundation for Sport and the Arts, although it operated in Bradford. HAC was certainly a community arts group, encompassing a wide range of arts, but it had minimal support from Hounslow Borough and was heavily dependent for its theatre work on the support of a teacher, Dave Purvis, from a local school in Cranford. The British Asian Theatre Company (BATC) was supported in its work, at least minimally, by the borough of Hackney. Tara Arts made great use of the Millan (community) Centre in Tooting, but although it was firmly located in Wandsworth it received relatively little support from the borough council in its first years. Its short-term funding for the first salaried person in British Asian theatre came initially from the Commission for Racial Equality (CRE), but had to be continued with a grant from the British Council of Churches.

Undoubtedly the greatest impact came from the radical reorientation of the priorities of the Greater London Council (GLC) in the early 1980s, under the regime led by Ken Livingstone. Its new Ethnic Arts Sub-committee with a focus on Black and Asian arts had an impressive budget, and this in itself offered an immense boost to morale and a sense of solidarity and practical possibilities. The timing was fortuitous for Tara, since the group had become established to a degree. The availability of capital sums and the positive thinking of Parminder Vir at the GLC resulted in the acquisition of a building by Tara, to date still the only building possessed by the movement as a whole, aside from office space. The possibility of an arts centre, which would house a practising theatre company, made Tara even more of a focus for the aspirations and incipient activities of others. Anti-racist initiatives and programmes and associated groupings such as the Black Theatre Forum were accompanied by plans for a major arts centre at the Roundhouse in London, which came to nothing with the termination of the GLC by Margaret Thatcher's government. The brief association of Asian theatre companies, called the South Asian Theatre Forum, came in this period, and the publication of a newsletter that had aspirations to become a journal, the *Asian Theatre Newsletter*, in four issues. At this time, contrasting tendencies were apparent in and between the groups. A cooperative principle was pronounced in some groups but was often at odds with strong or leading personalities, while an incipient professional impulse struggled with an externally imposed and internally seductive principle of a close relationship to the British Asian community.

The termination of the GLC in 1986 marks a significant watershed in the development of the British Asian movement as a whole. A number of groups ceased to exist in the mid- to later 1980s, with HAC fighting on just into the 1990s. The emphasis shifts from a community profile and patchwork trust- and borough-financing into an increasing dependence on the Arts Council and, to an extent, the regional arts councils. Tara had progressed through project funding from the Arts Council of Great Britain (ACGB) from the early 1980s, and remarkably had achieved revenue funding for its professional activity from 1987, a position that continued and provided security as a 'regularly funded organisation', in the current terminology of Arts Council of England (ACE), until the end of 2007. It was evident by the later 1980s and early 1990s that Arts Council funding was in principle more reliable and capable of sustaining a company in its artistic profile in the middle to long term. This certainty came home quickly to Landon-Smith and Bhuchar, who had originally sought private and corporate sponsorship energetically for Tamasha, but had largely drawn a blank. As a consequence, Tamasha settled into a regular process of advancing and defining projects and the evolving profile of the company in relation to the funding schemes of the AEGB and the London Arts Board (LAB) in particular, which in fact provided Tamasha with its first fixed-term funding for two years in 1995. This was later renewed, and the ACE provided revenue funding in 1998.

Kali theatre, as the unique new writing initiative in British Asian theatre, combined from the outset careful use of the funding schemes of the Arts Council and the LAB with the dedication of voluntary time and energy from its members. Grants were also obtained from trusts and there was initial collaborative support from individuals in two established organisations, the Asian Women's Writing Collective (AWWC) and Tara Arts. The LAB first provided revenue funding in 2002. Other companies and initiatives have had different histories. The intense period of activity and development at the Watermans Arts Centre in Brentford during the 1990s was run on a minimal budget by Hardial Rai, often by creating small companies that could operate from the Centre itself and beyond. Asian Theatre School's dependence on Red Ladder gave it a reliable basis in its early years, but as the group grew in strength and began to tour in the region and beyond a split was constructively considered that would allow an independent and reshaped company to bid for revenue funding from the Arts Council. This rebranding was successful and resulted in the emergence of Freedom Studios, with a dual profile of professional activity and continuing community engagement. Rifco differs again, since it is the only company which has had relative success in finding commercial project sponsorship through the industrial contacts of its director, Pravesh Kumar. But Rifco has also progressed to regular funding from the Arts Council after establishing a base within an arts centre (the West Wing) in its local area, Slough. Rasa Theatre has been unusual in its pattern of international touring associated with Rani Moorthy's solo performances, and this has meant that the British Council has featured alongside the Arts Council, North West, in providing support.

The history of funding is a massive subject, and the accounts in this book have only touched on those aspects that are embedded in the documentation of individual companies and related archives. Some would undoubtedly see the public funding structure for the arts as a straightjacket, with a repeated concern throughout the period of the last thirty years among practitioners being the immense difficulty of breaking out of a 'community' definition regularly imposed by funders into artistic emancipation. The recent experience of Tara Arts, which effectively had its professional middle-scale touring cut in 2008 by the ACE and faced firm encouragement to return to concentrating on its community activities, brings a sharp reminder that this concern is not outdated. Even more broadly, the extent to which funding policies have determined the shape of what is regularly called 'the sector' (formerly Black and Minority Ethnic), and the kind of work produced, would be the subject of a specialist study. What the histories given here can substantiate is the importance of public funding for the existence and development of the movement, which is arguably unique in contemporary diasporic world theatre for its diversity of activity and longevity, certainly among movements sustained by any nation-state artistic policy.

One of the enduring characteristics of the full pattern and history of funding is the emphasis that has fallen on touring. British Asian theatre has no dedicated performance space of its own, although the Tara studio at Earlsfield has had a significant role in small-scale work and rehearsal, and as a host venue for readings. From the beginning, Tara members were on the road at weekends, taking their shows to venues in London and hacking further afield in a battered green Ford Cortina. Any British Asian theatre company has its catalogue of venues, with some proving to be regular slots, relied upon over an extended period of operation. Touring obviously has exacting economies of scale, and these also apply when the venues are of the middle to large scale. Touring for some companies may be combined with a pronounced reliance on collaborative theatres in the immediate locality: this has been true of Peshkar and of the Asian Theatre School, and was also true for a time of Man Mela and the local council-owned theatre in Lewisham, London. Some venues have played a very significant role over many years merely as hosts—the Riverside and Watermans in west London are two obvious examples—but others have featured strongly as co-producers. The Lyric in Hammersmith, again in West London, the Theatre Royal in Stratford in East London, Contact Theatre in Manchester and the

Birmingham Rep have performed this function at important moments, and Tara's arc of success and prominence in the 1990s took it into successive co-productions with the National Theatre: *Tartuffe* in 1990 went on tour, while *Cyrano* in 1995 did not. Collaboration and co-production has offered financial and institutional support, but has also brought frustrations and a telling awareness of dependency.

Whether acting as host venues or in co-production, theatres have often been influenced by the issue of widening audiences, with British Asian companies seen as an instrument of an artistic policy that was to a degree driven by funding policies for those theatres, or by a developing sense of the role of a theatre within its own community. The Birmingham Rep is a good example of a theatre that has plainly intended to reach out more effectively to its potential South Asian audiences, and both Tamasha and more recently Kali have been regularly invited to perform. In an earlier period, from the later 1980s into the 1990s, the Theatre Royal Stratford East pursued a number of initiatives to this same end. As a touring company without a local community base, Tamasha quickly saw the merits of a conscious strategy of audience development, led by Suman Bhuchar, which was consolidated in the mid-1990s in the Birmingham venue.[1] Kali's work has continued that presence, combining it with another element of policy, an accent on new writing. The Hawth in Crawley, a far smaller venue, has been dedicated to audience development since its inception, employing the skills of Hardish Virk; he and Suman Bhuchar have professional profiles in this field that stretch beyond British Asian companies to other ventures. Rifco has consciously targeted the South Asian communities through its productions, with a clear intention to bring families into the theatre on a regular basis, but not exclusively within a local area. In this respect, Kumar's commitment is surprisingly similar to Hardial Rai's approach at Watermans in the 1990s, although Rai was necessarily intent on bringing British Asian audiences into the one venue: the policy Rai had was to provide Asian-led work primarily for Asian audiences, and to provide a programme that embraced the different generations. In recent years some mainstream companies have taken independent steps to attract British South Asian audiences, most notably in the programming and activity of the National Theatre under Nicholas Hytner. It remains an open question whether the involvement of British Asian theatre companies in the audience-development policies of other theatres and venues will be as significant as it plainly was in the 1990s.

---

1 Suman Bhuchar addresses this aspect of her work in her essay 'The Marketing of Commercial and Subsidized Theatre to British Asian Audiences: Tamasha's *Fourteen Songs, Two Weddings and a Funeral* (1998 and 2001) and *Bombay Dreams* (2002)', in *Critical Essays on British South Asian Theatre* eds Graham Ley and Sarah Dadswell (Exeter: University of Exeter Press, 2012).

The question of the audiences for British Asian theatre is an easy and possibly obvious one to ask, but it is extremely difficult to answer in a holistic or unitary way. There can be no doubt that having British Asian performers on stage was both exciting and fascinating for members of the British Asian community in the 1970s and throughout the 1980s. At that time, many young British Asians were drawn in to working with the emergent groups in London, just as, later, those in both Oldham and Bradford and the surrounding region many have been drawn in a similar way to working with Peshkar and the Asian Theatre School. Audiences could, however, be pitiful in numbers in that period, and were by no means confined to British Asians for early Tara productions. When work was performed in community centres they would be British Asian, and would embrace those who actively (and violently, on some occasions) disapproved of what was on offer. What Hardial Rai wanted at Watermans was essentially an Asian arts centre for west London; Dominic Rai, with Man Mela, was almost certainly as much concerned with providing for the Asian community in south-east London, with an accent on poetry as well as social drama; Kali's remit in the early period was explicitly to provide good-quality plays for Asian audiences; and Pravesh Kumar pitched some 30% of *There's Something about Simmy*, his production about a Punjabi girl-bride learning English in the UK, in the Punjabi language as a new element in a continuing policy to reach out to the first generation of South Asians.

But British Asian theatre has also, from the beginning, been equally defined by its desire to acknowledge both parts of the term 'British Asian' with work that might be viewed and heard from any sense of identity, and Moorthy's *Curry Tales* explicitly presented a set of identities for herself as a woman performer, ranging well outside the British Asian and purposefully not settling on any one. If British Asian theatre has had as a major concern the expression of the experience of what it means to be a British South Asian, then it follows that this is open to be viewed from any angle, as indeed the multiplicity of the experiences may be presented from any angle. What Rajni Shah offers with her performances is a long way from Tara's migration narrative in *Journey to the West*, and the riots of the *Streets of Rage* from Asian Theatre School or of *Just Before the Rain* from Peshkar are geographically located a long way from the traumas of Partition or the Indian emergency, respectively in Tamasha's *A Tainted Dawn* and *A Fine Balance*—but all these reflective expressions may be taken to be different parts of the possible experience of being a British South Asian. It would be naive to ignore the role that Asian audiences have played in the minds and motives of British Asian theatre practitioners. But, at the same time, it is evident that many if not most productions have been consciously opened to those who might be interested or entertained, but who do not belong to those communities. Neither *There's Something About Simmy* nor Tamasha's *Strictly Dandia*, with its accent firmly on the Gujurati and

Muslim communities, were seen exclusively by Punjabis and Gujuratis or exclusively by British Asians, and neither the directors nor the casts, nor the collaborating venues, would be remotely surprised about that. Indeed, established touring venues that host British Asian theatre companies have repeatedly shown great confidence in the broad appeal of the shows to their audiences.

Implicit in the consideration of audiences is the issue of language and languages in performance, and once again it is hard to find a consolidated conclusion rather than pointing to the materials available for a separate and complex study. From the beginning, Tara was determined that the language for its own expression of contemporary British Asian experience was to be English. This was a calculated contradiction of what its members saw as the outdated example of the language theatres, which they criticised for looking away from the lived reality in Britain. This point of view has been shared by many, strongly by playwrights for a variety of reasons, and both Bancil and the plays produced by Kali consistently reveal this conviction. Yet Tara, under Verma's influence, gradually moved to a position where the integration of elements of the South Asian languages into scripts and performances was seen to be a constituent element of a production style and aesthetic that he called 'Binglish', one that in his view more naturally reflected the status of a British Asian art. Companies such as the Asian Theatre School have historically been determined to emphasise that they too, despite attempts to marginalise their region and the communities within it, are to be recognised without qualification as being as English (in terms of rights) as the language their youth members use. For them, this is an assertive political point, while a performer such as Moorthy uses English to draw attention to that which is not English, to draw in audiences comfortingly and warmly to a point of the acknowledgement and acceptance of difference. Peshkar's approach has been multilingual, with English featuring alongside Bengali, Bangla, Urdu, Hindi and Punjabi, and Man Mela has retained an emphasis on Punjabi and Urdu in much of its work, although its largest dramaturgical production, *The Cornershop*, was firmly in English.

The designs of the earliest productions of British Asian theatre were of necessity bare, with everyday clothing, limited properties and an emphasis on dialogue drama to make a point. It was not long before Tara introduced snatches of popular song and dance. Verma was at pains to create workshops for the group members that would introduce them to elements of a traditional South Asian culture, notably music and dance. Later in Tara's development Verma chose to place an emphasis repeatedly on the popular theatre-form *bhavai* from the Gujarat region, selecting this gradually from the more composite 'folk theatre' techniques introduced to the company by Anuradha Kapur. In Oldham, Peshkar from the beginning offered both dance (the north-Indian *kathak*, taught by Minoo Lord) and music workshops as an attraction, with music embracing Bhangra and choreographed Bangla folk music, and the dance group the Masala Girls, directed by Shobna Gulati, contributed an important strand to Peshkar's productions. One of Pehskar's early production successes, *A Beautiful Violin*, was cast in the *jathra* form of Bengal and Bangladesh, with two musicians interweaving both contemporary and folk music. Tamasha introduced songs based on the sounds and sentiments of those sung by Rajasthani women workers without truly departing from naturalism in *Women of the Dust*, and there was a similar principle at work in *Strictly Dandia*, in which the Gujarati dances were the central occasion of the play's narrative. But probably the greatest general influence has been that of Bollywood, which has exercised a fascination for a number of theatre-makers because of its immense potential—as a major element of a shared, diasporic culture—to draw British South Asian audiences. Tamasha struck gold with its stage version of the highly successful film *Hum Aapke Hain Koun* (*Who Am I to You?*), while the title for their own production *Fourteen Songs, Two Weddings and a Funeral* echoed the successful Brit-film *Four Weddings and a Funeral*. Dance sequences and songs may derive from specific films or be a pastiche or parody, and, like Bhangra, they provide for the theatre an immediate connection with the successful impact of another industry and medium. Bollywood has been an almost constant point of reference for Rifco, and it was even bizarrely present as the germ of an idea for a different kind of theatre at Tara that resulted in *Miti Ki Gadi*. Yet, despite the attractions of a Bollywood-strain, many productions have retained a firm footing in the conventions of realist drama in conception, and in the practices of direction.

The interaction between the activities of the Asian-led companies documented in this volume and other theatre production in Britain in the same period is a vast and complex subject. It is most pronounced in the involvement of actors, who have either brought their established skills into the Asian-led companies—figures such as Madhav Sharma, Jamila Massey and Shelley King are prominent examples—or who have taken skills developed in British Asian theatre into work on radio, film and television, or for other theatre companies. Of the playwrights, Parv Bancil, Ayub Khan Din (with *East Is East*) and Meera Syal provide the obvious examples of those whose careers have been launched in Asian-led companies, but who have worked extensively outside that environment, and there are many writers who have forged careers outside British Asian theatre. Contrastingly, the directors of Asian-led companies have rarely been invited to operate independently of the companies with which they are most associated, which is a continuing source of dissatisfaction to prominent figures among them. The direction of Gurpreet Kaur Bhatti's *Behzti* for the Birmingham Rep in 2004 by Janet Steel, the director of Kali Theatre, is one prominent exception. It may be that this general phenomenon should be linked to the increasing number of non-Asian-led productions that have attempted to draw British South Asian audiences, in both the subsidised and commercial sectors. Since

Brook's *Mahabharata*, it has been clear that there is much that may be appropriated, either in terms of dramaturgical material or of performance skills and production values, from South Asian culture, and this may force limitations on what is expected of British Asian theatres. Evidence gathered in the first section of this book on the early history of performances might suggest that this recent phenomenon could be connected to a longer history of an orientalising tendency in British culture.

The broader context, which undoubtedly contains radio, film and television as well as other theatre and multi-media, must also include companies that are not Asian-led but which have consistently worked towards British South Asian audiences and involvement with a variety of material. Two examples here would be Chol Theatre, founded by Adam Strickson (also author of Peshkar's *The Beautiful Violin*) and Border Crossings, directed by Michael Walling. M6 Theatre Company in Rochdale has placed a strong accent on diversity, and the long-established company Red Ladder had a history of work with British Asian practitioners and audiences which led to its initiative in founding the Asian Theatre School. There are also important practitioners whose work eludes the relatively narrow and historical scope determined for this volume. In Scotland, Annie George has worked consistently in film and theatre as a director and performer, and has more recently founded Wave Theatre, which places an explicit emphasis on Black and Asian experience. Vayu Naidu advanced and developed her own art of story-telling over many years and fused that with more ambitious and fully theatrical values in the Vayu Naidu Company from 2003. Hardial Rai has followed his experience with HAC and at Watermans by establishing Zeroculture, a production company that embraces multiple artforms, including theatre. Other companies to be noted in this context would include Khayaal, Naatch Theatre, Ankur Productions, Duende, Theatre Insaan and Conspirators' Kitchen. **moti**roti and the subsequent emergence of British Asian live artists and performance poets in relatively recent years provide a shifting emphasis on varieties of the concept of performance, in contrast to the more stable view of theatre embraced by most of the British Asian practitioners featured in this book.[2]

There are significant features to which the accounts given here have alluded, but which they have not traced. Of these, perhaps the most important is the cultural setting in which the theatrical initiatives have occurred. With a number of companies, the full range of activity puts theatre among music and dance, poetry recital, comic sketches, art installations, small-scale publication and fine art practices. HAC was a broad grouping of

---

2 For Vayu Naidu's work, see the essay by Chris Banfield 'Directing Storytelling Performance and Storytelling Theatre', in *Critical Essays*, eds Ley and Dadswell (n. 1 above); Stephen Hodge provides an account of motiroti in his essay 'British Asian Live Art: motoroti' in the same volume.

this sort, and the programming at Watermans with Hardial Rai in the 1990s repeated this kind of diversity, with the addition of live and performance art. In a different way, the Tara Arts Centre in Earlsfield opened up an era for Tara in which theatre was only one of a number of activities, albeit the most dominant, and the history of the Tara Centre and related developments needs to be written. Peshkar to an extent ran itself as an Asian arts grouping, and recent developments such as Freedom Studios and Zeroculture have wide-reaching interpretations of artistic development and production. Man Mela, to an extent that the account in this book has barely represented, has been involved over many years with poetry recitals, *mehfils*, with an accent on Urdu and Punjabi recital, and this strand has had a great influence on Dominic Rai's sense of performance possibilities, as reflected in the recent performance poem *A Lifetime on Tiptoes*, from 2007 forwards. In a similar way, Kali's emphasis on theatre writing was born out of the broader terms of the AWWC, and Rukhsana Ahmad, for many years its leading figure, has remained active in genres other than playwriting, including the translation of poetry, performed with Man Mela as *We Sinful Women*. A more holistic account might lend a different interpretation to these acts of theatre and underline the distinction from those theatrical initiatives such as Tamasha and Rifco that have not noticeably emerged from, or been part of, a larger Asian arts context.

But even with its limiting accent on live theatre, this history is provisional: the accounts of Tara, Tamasha, Kali and Man Mela all stop short of their full scope. The extension of these company histories would radically alter the impression given here of the larger history of the movement as a whole, and the resource represented by this book will hopefully be a stimulus to continued research into the diverse phenomena it has mapped, with an understanding of what that map should contain developing over time.

Index

Please note that the minimum specifications for running the DVD-ROM are as follows:

For PCs: Windows XP SP2 +
Pentium 4, 2.8 Ghz
Media Player

For Macs: Mac OSX 10.4 (Tiger) +
Quicktime 7+ Player

Graphics card minimum 32 Mb
Sound card
512 Mb RAM
4xDVD-ROM
Minimum screen resolution 1024 x 768

Please close down other applications while running this DVD-ROM.